The Evolution of Morality

Life and Mind: Philosophical Issues in Biology and Psychology
Kim Sterelny and Robert A. Wilson, editors

Cycles of Contingency: Developmental Systems and Evolution, ed. Susan Oyama, Paul E. Griffiths, and Russell D. Gray, 2000

Coherence in Thought and Action, Paul Thagard, 2000

Evolution and Learning: The Baldwin Effect Reconsidered, Bruce H. Weber and David J. Depew, 2003

Seeing and Visualizing: It's Not What You Think, Zenon Pylyshyn, 2003

Organisms and Artifacts: Design in Nature and Elsewhere, Tim Lewens, 2004

Molecular Models of Life: Philosophical Papers on Molecular Biology, Sahotra Sarkar, 2004

Evolution in Four Dimensions, Eva Jablonka and Marion J. Lamb, 2005

The Evolution of Morality, Richard Joyce, 2006

The Evolution of Morality

Richard Joyce

A Bradford Book
The MIT Press
Cambridge, Massachusetts
London, England

MIT Press books may be purchased at special quantity discounts for business or sales promotional use. For information, please email special_sales@mitpress.mit.edu or write to Special Sales Department, The MIT Press, 55 Hayward Street, Cambridge, MA 02142.

Set in Stone Sans and Stone Serif by The MIT Press. Printed and bound in the United States of America.

Library of Congress Cataloging-in-Publication Data

Joyce, Richard, 1966–
The evolution of morality / Richard Joyce.
    p. cm. — (Life and mind)
"A Bradford book."
Includes bibliographical references (p.) and index.
ISBN 0-262-10112-2 (alk. paper)
1. Ethics, Evolutionary. I. Title. II. Series.
BJ1311.J69   2006
171'.7—dc22   2005049649

10 9 8 7 6 5 4 3 2 1

for my mother, in gratitude for letting me think for myself

Contents

Acknowledgements   ix

Introduction: Human Nature   1

1 | **The Natural Selection of Helping   13**

2 | **The Nature of Morality   45**

3 | **Moral Language and Moral Emotions   75**

4 | **The Moral Sense   107**

5 | **The Evolutionary Vindication of Morality   143**

6 | **The Evolutionary Debunking of Morality   179**

Conclusion: Living with an Adapted Mind   221

Notes   231
Bibliography   247
Index   269

Acknowledgements

Initial research on this project was supported by a much-appreciated grant from the UK Arts and Humanities Research Board and by a sabbatical leave from the University of Sheffield's Department of Philosophy. During this time I was aided by the diligent efforts of my occasional research assistant, Ali Fanaei. By the time the sabbatical was over I had a new job at the Australian National University (Research School of the Social Sciences), allowing me to devote a large portion of my energy to completing the book, and for which I am forever grateful to Michael Smith. I thank the Leslie Humanities Center at Dartmouth College for inviting me for a semester in 2004, and Walter Sinnott-Armstrong most especially for making this possible. I am appreciative for all the feedback and stimulating exchanges I had with those involved in our weekly reading groups at Dartmouth, and in particular Owen Flanagan, Don Loeb, and Chandra Sripada. Back at the RSSS, I benefited enormously from weekly meetings with a group of graduate students working through my penultimate manuscript, and I thank all concerned.

I owe a great debt to those who read all or portions of the manuscript, but must single out for praise Kim Sterelny, for suffering through an early and much flawed draft (and wearing out several red pens on marginal expletives in the process). Others who gave invaluable feedback include George Botterill, Brett Calcott, William Casebeer, Oliver Curry, Tyler Doggett, Ragnar Francén, Ben Fraser, Daniel Friedrich, Peter Godfrey-Smith, Gil Harman, Marc Hauser, Shaun Nichols, and Walter Sinnott-Armstrong.

In the course of my traveling sabbatical several people in one way or another helped me find quiet (and often beautiful) spaces to think and write: Pierre and Mary Boulle, Patricia Robinson, Jackie and Frick Atkins, and Jim and Kayo Nolan. Thanks also to Michael Whitehead for unearthing a copy of Frances Cobbe's *Darwinism in Morals* in Canberra (of all places). Finally, I am deeply thankful for the constant love and support of my wife, Wendy, and for the mere existence of Max—who, arriving halfway through chapter 5, made finishing the book a great deal harder but a lot more fun.

The Evolution of Morality

Introduction: Human Nature

Whoever came into the world without an innate idea of good and evil, beauty and ugliness, becoming and unbecoming, happiness and misery, proper and improper, what ought to be done and what ought not to be done? Hence we all make use of these names, and endeavor to apply our preconceptions to particular cases. "So-and-so has acted well, not well; right, not right; is unhappy, happy; is just, is unjust." Who among refrains from using these names? Who postpones the use of them till he has learnt them . . . ? The reason for this is that we come instructed in some degree by nature upon these subjects, but from this beginning we go on to add self-conceit. "Why," you ask, "should I not know what fair and base is? Have I not an idea of it?"— You have. "Do I not apply this idea to particulars?"—You do. "Do I not apply it correctly, then?"—Here lies the whole question; and here arises the self-conceit. . . . Now, since you think you make a suitable application of your preconceptions to particular cases, tell me whence you derive this.

Because it seems so to me.

But does it not *seem so* to another, and does not he too form a conceit that he makes a correct application?

He does.

Is it possible, then, that each of you should apply your preconceptions correctly, on the very subjects about which you have contradictory opinions?

It is not.

So do you have anything to show us for this application, preferable to its *seeming so* to you? And does a madman act any otherwise than it seems to him right? Is this, then, a sufficient criterion for him too?

It is not.

Come, therefore, to something preferable to what *seems*.

   —Epictetus, "What the beginning of philosophy is," in *Discourses*

This book attempts to accomplish two tasks. The first is to address the question "Is human morality innate?" (chapters 1–4). To begin with, we will need to understand what the question is asking; after several chapters, we will arrive at a positive answer. This result will be provisional and to a degree speculative, since the present evidence does not warrant answering the question in either a positive or a negative way with any confidence. The second task of the book is to ask "So what?"—in a philosophical tone of voice, of course (chapters 5 and 6). If we suppose that morality is innate (under some specification of the hypothesis), does this in some manner *vindicate* morality, staving off the threat of moral skepticism, and perhaps even undergirding some version of moral realism? Or, if morality is ultimately just something that helped our ancestors make babies, might the correct implication instead be that the authority of morality is *undermined*—that, in the words of Michael Ruse (1986: 253), "morality is a collective illusion foisted upon us by our genes"?

These are big questions for a small book. I don't pretend to settle anything here; I will be content to sketch a philosophical viewpoint and make a modest contribution to an ongoing research program. My goals are synthetic and interdisciplinary, and I am aware of the dangers that such aspirations invariably bring. Nevertheless, there are pressing and important questions that simply cannot be profitably addressed from within the bounds of a single academic discipline, and this book is about one of them. These questions certainly deserve a weighty tome, and it was just such a book that I originally set out to write, but a number of considerations persuaded me that a relatively concise and agile work would serve my purposes better, despite the fact that such an approach inevitably leaves numerous discussions incomplete. Ralph Waldo Emerson once observed that "in skating over thin ice our safety is in our speed"; but speed has other virtues too, and I trust that no one will think that my ambition to cover a lot of material in few pages is a reflection of the unreliable quality of the ground underfoot.

Before we can assess the truth of a hypothesis we need to understand its content. What might it mean to assert that human morality is innate? First, there are issues concerning what is meant by "innate." Some have argued that the notion is so confused that it should be eliminated from serious debate (Bateson 1991; Griffiths 2002). I think such pessimism is unwarranted, but I agree that anyone who uses "innate" in critical discussion should state what he or she has in mind. I suggest that what people generally mean when they debate the "innateness of morality" is whether morality (under some specification) can be given an adaptive explanation in genetic terms: whether the present-day existence of the trait is to be explained by reference to a genotype having granted ancestors reproductive advantage.[1] It doesn't follow that an innate trait will develop irrespective of the environment (for that isn't true of any phenotypic trait), or even that it is highly canalized. It does not follow that there is a "gene for morality." Nor do this conception of innateness and the references to "human nature" that routinely come with it imply any dubious metaphysics regarding a human essence. Asserting that bipedalism is innate and part of human nature doesn't imply that it is a necessary condition for being human (paraplegics will be relieved to hear).

The hypothesis that human morality is innate is also bedeviled by obscurity concerning what might be meant by "morality." A step toward clarity is achieved if we make an important disambiguation. On the one hand, the claim that humans are naturally moral animals might mean that we naturally act in ways that are morally laudable—that the process of evolution has designed us to be social, friendly, benevolent, fair, and so on. No one who has paused to glance around herself will ever claim that humans *always* manifest such virtuous behaviors, for it is obvious that we can also be violent, selfish, lying, insensitive, unspeakably nasty creatures (to quote Machiavelli: "ungrateful, fickle, dissembling, anxious to flee danger, and covetous of gain"). By saying that humans naturally act in morally laudable ways, we might mean that these morally unpleasant aspects of human behavior are "unnatural," or that both aspects are innate but that the morally praiseworthy elements are predominant, or simply that there exist some morally laudable aspects among what has been given by nature, irrespective of what darker elements may also be present.

Alternatively, the hypothesis that humans are by nature moral animals may be understood in a different way: as meaning that the process of evolution has designed us to think in moral terms, that biological natural selection has conferred upon us the tendency to employ moral concepts. According to the former reading, the term "moral animal" means *an animal that is morally praiseworthy*; according to the second, it means *an animal that morally judges*. Like the former interpretation, the latter admits of variation: Saying that we naturally make moral judgments may mean that we are designed to have particular moral attitudes toward particular kinds of things (for example, finding incest and patricide morally offensive), or it may mean that we have a proclivity to find something-or-other morally offensive (morally praiseworthy, etc.), where the content is determined by contingent environmental and cultural factors. These possibilities represent ends of a continuum; thus, many intermediate positions are tenable.

These two hypotheses might be logically related: It has often been argued that only beings who are motivated by moral thoughts properly deserve moral appraisal. The traditional criterion of insanity in a criminal court—

i.e., the criterion of whether the defendant could be considered morally blameworthy—was whether he or she "knew the difference between right and wrong" (and in many places this remains a criterion). If this relation is correct, then humans cannot be naturally morally laudable unless we are also naturally able to employ moral judgments; thus establishing the truth of the first hypothesis would suffice to establish the truth of the second. However, this strategy is not a promising one, because the connection mentioned—roughly, that moral appraisal of an individual implies that the individual is morally motivated—is too contentious to rest arguments upon with any confidence. (In fact, as I will mention later, I doubt that it is true.)

It is the second hypothesis with which I am concerned in this book, and I will be investigating it directly, not by establishing the first hypothesis. With it thus made explicit that our target hypothesis concerns whether the human capacity to make moral judgments innate, it ought to be clear that arguments and data concerning the innateness of human prosociality do not necessarily entail any conclusions about an innate morality. Bees are marvelously prosocial, but they hardly make moral judgments. But what *is* a moral judgment? This question cannot be shirked or treated flippantly, for we cannot profitably discuss the evolution of X unless we have a firm grasp of what X is. Chapter 2 will be devoted to this.

Before I get down to business, though, a number of preliminaries must be discussed to ward off misunderstanding. The kind of account that is under review—that some aspect of human behavior or thinking is innate—has in recent decades proven to be so incendiary in some quarters that it is with a degree of trepidation that one even broaches the topic. My actual views will, I am sure, prove quite disconcerting to many readers, and I am quite prepared to have them criticized, but it would be tiresome to be also accused of holding stupid or pernicious views that I don't hold at all. In an attempt to dodge the latter risk, let me first carefully and clearly position myself with respect to certain theoretical commitments and research programs.

"Sociobiology" is the name of a research program, which took shape in the 1970s, that seeks to explain social behavior by reference to biology, coupled with the assumption that the biology in question is innate. Insofar as it is to biology that we all turn for explanations of the social behavior of bees, ants, or naked mole rats, the program is broadly vindicated and successful. (A contemporary sociobiology journal contains such un-scandalous titles as "On the social structure of offspring rearing in the burrower bug" and "Apparent sibling rivalry in the freshwater fingernail clam.") It is only when it is applied to humans that the debate turns sour.[2] At some point, the remit of sociobiology expanded, such that to explain any human behavior by reference to biological natural selection was considered to be offering a "sociobiological explanation." In the 1980s sociobiology reinvented itself as evolutionary psychology, but this involved much more than just a change of name. Sociobiology focuses on innate behavior, whereas evolutionary psychology focuses on the psychological mechanisms underlying that behavior. The important difference is that psychological mechanisms productive of adaptive behavior in a prehistoric past may, when operating in creatures no longer living in such an environment, result in different, surprising, and/or maladaptive behavior. Three implications are worth noting immediately:

(i) Evolutionary psychology does not claim that observable human behavior is adaptive, but rather that it is produced by psychological mechanisms that are adaptations. The output of an adaptation need not be adaptive.

(ii) Nor does evolutionary psychology imply that an adaptation must result in cross-cultural universals in human behavior. The evolved mechanisms may be designed to be environmentally sensitive, may operate unexpectedly in unanticipated environments, or may not develop at all if not properly triggered. It is only in the absence of such defeaters that cross-culturality might be expected. This noted, cross-culturality can be offered as evidence of innateness in the absence of any better hypothesis indicating a universally present exogenous explanans.

(iii) Though preserving the word "innate" primarily for psychological mechanisms, there seems nothing to prevent evolutionary psychologists from speaking also of "innate behaviors"—where this does not mean *any behavior produced by an innate mechanism*, but rather is a claim about the past: roughly, that the behavior in question is generated by an innate mechanism in accordance with the mechanism's design (i.e., the mechanism is "supposed" to produce this behavior in these conditions), in the sense that the existence of the mechanism is to be explained in part by reference to our ancestors having engaged in this type of behavior in these environmental conditions.

Broadly speaking, no sensible person can object to evolutionary psychology. Why do we have emotions at all? Why is the human memory better than that of a goldfish, and why are we better at remembering faces than sequences of numbers? Why are we generally interested in sex and food? Why is it that we have good eyesight but cannot see ultraviolet light and have no capacity for echolocation? It is incontrovertible that for answers we should look to the conditions of life of our ancestors. This being so, one might well wonder why there is so much hostility toward evolutionary

psychology. The reason is that the title "evolutionary psychology" is typically reserved for a claim that goes beyond the view that the basic faculties
of the human mind are due to evolutionary pressures, extending to the
claim that *a great deal* of the human mind is to be so explained: that the
mind consists of many (perhaps hundreds of) innate domain-specific psychological mechanisms, each geared to respond to some discrete ancestral
threat or opportunity. But this is terribly vague. How much of the human
mind does one have to think can be thus explained, how many domain-
specific mechanisms must one countenance, before earning the title (or, in
some circles, meriting the denunciation) "evolutionary psychologist"?
There doesn't seem to be any clear demarcation between the sensible and
incontrovertible view expressed above and the controversial and divisive
view that seeks to explain "a lot" of human mentality by reference to biological natural selection. No doubt this vagueness contributes to the confusion and misapprehension surrounding the discipline.

Though evolutionary psychology allows that a great deal of observable
human behavior may be evolutionarily "accidental" (in the sense that it is
the result of innate mechanisms thrown into a novel environment), it also
allows that humans are "supposed" to be behaviorally malleable in many
respects—that the very plasticity of many psychological mechanisms is
an adaptation. That, after all, is what a brain is for: to produce variable
responses to environmental variation. Thus, it is reasonable to suppose that
the extraordinary human brain is an organ designed to deal with environmental variation par excellence, and that open-ended plasticity is a human
forte. (See Godfrey-Smith 1996.) It is widely assumed that biological natural
selection has granted us a wonderful all-purpose faculty of rationality, with
which we can work out how best to respond to an infinite range of environmental stimuli. This seems to be what sets us apart from the rest of the
animal kingdom: our capacity to work out how to do things "on our own,"
to operate successfully in living conditions that bear little resemblance to
the environments within we were designed to operate. I don't think anyone
can seriously doubt that humans enjoy an extraordinary plasticity of this
sort, unlike any other known creature (though whether we should put it
down to a faculty called "rationality" is another matter). Just think of surf-
ing (either on waves or on the web), of collecting baseball cards, of contemplating Shakespeare, or of negotiating day-to-day life in Manhattan. The
enormous range of behaviors we can perform in response to an enormous
range of stimuli cannot all be "programmed," even by conditional instructions, for no version of the ancestral environment contained such stimuli,
and in any case the human genome isn't large enough to contain the

instructions that would be needed to cover all such contingencies. It is possible that all this wonderful variation is "accidental" (in the sense specified above), but it is vastly more likely that across a range of domains this malleability is a design feature. Regarding a wide array of types of stimuli, it is reasonable to suppose that what one of our ancestors encountered in his or her lifetime (including what could be gleaned from watching others) provided a far more reliable basis for practical decision making than what his or her ancestors had encountered in past generations.

On the other hand, the idea that the human mind is *nothing but* all-purpose flexibility is obviously wrong. In reality, the thesis of the human tabula rasa (blank slate) has never been held in pure form by any serious thinker. The word "tabula" has to be a metaphor for something that at the very least has innate abilities pertaining to acquisition, manipulation, and storage of beliefs—for one cannot gain the capacity to learn through learning—so the very capacity to acquire beliefs from the environment demands a complex array of inbuilt mental mechanisms. Even John Locke, the father of the idea of the tabula rasa, credited humans with an extensive range of inborn mental faculties: memory, emotion, perception, deliberation, will, understanding, etc. The important thing for Locke was that no beliefs were inscribed on the human slate, but it was clear even to him that it is rich with innate capacities and constraints. When Locke writes that "of all the men we meet with, nine parts of ten are what they are, good or evil, useful or not, by their education" ((1693) 1989: 83), if he means to imply that 10 percent of character is innate, one might think that more than enough to qualify him as an evolutionary psychologist!

An important question that Locke was in no position to answer is "Why *these* faculties as opposed to a bunch of others?" Why, for example, do we have emotions at all, and why *these* emotions—fear, happiness, jealousy, guilt, etc.—instead of other unimaginable ones? It can now be claimed with assurance that the answers lie in our past. Having emotions, and having *these* emotions, provided our ancestors with benefits, and thus these traits were selected for, and thus we have them. Of course, there is flexibility even in the stability. All but brain-damaged humans reliably have the capacity for fear, but *what* to fear (leopards, Lyme Disease, a stock market crash, or God's wrath) is something we learn from our environment—which includes, importantly, what we learn from other humans. It is easy to see why the emotion of fear would be both fixed and flexible in this way. In any ancestral environment there was always something worth being afraid of, but precisely which things warranted the response might vary for different versions of that environment, for different individuals, and at different times of an individual's life. An intriguing possibility is that there may be certain types of fear-warranting things that cropped up in the ancestral environment with such reliable frequency that natural selection found it efficient to give humans a fixed fear with a certain content.[3] It has been argued, for example, that humans are more prepared to find snakes and spiders frightening than guns and power sockets (Öhman et al. 2001; Öhman and Mineka 2001). Although there is conflicting evidence regarding this particular example, there is certainly no a priori reason why a targeted fear response might not be thus fixed. The main general considerations against such fixed fine-grainedness, some have claimed, are the limited size of the human genome and the possibility that the trait cannot be selected for in isolation (that is, without selecting other deleterious traits along with it). But there can be little doubt that we are fixed to respond to certain broad, reliable and important environmental threats and opportunities with markedly determined responses. All humans are disposed to be interested in food and sex, for example. When food or sex is scarce, we become even more interested in them. (When food *and* sex are scarce, food wins out: People starving to death on a lifeboat aren't eyeing each other's fleshy limbs with amorous thoughts.)

The early opponents of sociobiology were so eager to discredit the program that they kept chanting "genetic determinism!" until this accusation lodged in the popular consciousness. But in fact no sensible person is a genetic determinist, and certainly none of the prominent sociobiologists were. Nor, as the above comments should testify, am I. The nature/nurture dichotomy is so dead and buried that it is wearisome even to mention that it is dead and buried. By claiming that human morality is genetically "programmed," one doesn't deny the centrality of cultural influence, or even imply that *any* manifestation of morality is inevitable. With how much ease environmental factors may affect or even prevent the development of any genetically encoded trait is an empirical question. Phenylketonuria (PKU), for example, is a genetic metabolic disorder that can cause terrible mental retardation but can be easily avoided with a restricted diet; Down's Syndrome, by comparison, is a genetic disorder about which nothing can at present be done to avoid the expression of its characteristics.[4] There is no general relationship between genotype and phenotypic expression. So I think Stephen Jay Gould was dead wrong when he wrote: "If we are programmed to be what we are, then these traits are ineluctable. We may, at best, channel them, but we cannot change them either by will, education, or culture" (1977: 238). Unless by "programmed" Gould just *means* something that cannot be changed by will, education, or culture (in which case his claim would be trivial), there is no reason to think that it is generally true. PKU is just one clear counterexample of a trait that is genetically "programmed" in some individuals but straightforwardly preventable.

It is also conceivable that the tendency to make moral judgments is the output of an innate conditional strategy, in which case even the existence of societies with nothing recognizable as a moral system would not be inconsistent with morality being part of human nature, for such societies may not satisfy the antecedent of the conditional.[5] Indeed, if our living conditions are sufficiently dissimilar from those of our ancestors, then in principle there might have been *no* modern society with a moral system—not a single moral human in the whole wide modern world—and yet the claim that morality is innate might remain defensible. These possibilities are highlighted just to emphasize the point that something being part of our nature by no means makes its manifestation inevitable. But of course we know that in fact modern human societies do have moral systems; indeed, apparently all of them do. (See Roberts 1979; Brown 1991; Rozin et al. 1999a.) We see something of a collapse of morality across a community only when something is going badly and obviously wrong for that community. In trying to think of some historical examples of a total breakdown of morality in a community, I initially considered the appalling impact upon northern Europe of the Thirty Years' War, during which (among other horrors) human flesh was on sale in the streets of Nuremberg. But then I realized that the very fact that it was *for sale* indicated that some kind of moral framework remained in place even there. Even in the most dire situation, morality clings on—or rather, humans cling on to morality. This is a striking phenomenon that cries out for explanation.

Since moral beliefs are unlikely to be inevitable even if they have an innate basis, any worries that an evolutionary account of morality would in some sense deprive us of our freedom are countered. Patricia Williams (1993) has argued that if morality were innate then our moral judgments would be coerced from within, but that, since in order to be ethical beings we must be free, it is incoherent to appeal to evolution in order to explain our ethical nature; therefore morality cannot be innate. I have very little to say on the matter of human free will, and I consider it something of a red herring in this debate. According to many philosophers, freedom does not involve the capacity to alter the course of neural causation by an act of pure mental determination; it simply means acting on your desires. Thus an evolutionary explanation of an action may actually amount to a clarification of the nature of the action's freedom, since it may well be an explanation of where the relevant desires came from. Human desires, after all, don't come from nowhere—all desires have a history, and some of them have an evolutionary history. Everyday thinking allows that beliefs and desires are frequently caused by environment factors without thereby counting as "coerced," and I fail to see why things would stand differently if some beliefs and desires are caused by genetic factors.

Nor need the hypothesis that morality is innate be undermined by observation of the great variation in moral codes across human communities, for the claim need not be interpreted as holding that morality with some particular content is fixed in human nature. The analogous claim that humans have innate language-learning mechanisms does not imply that Japanese, Italian, or Swahili is innate. We are prepared to learn some language or other, and the social environment determines which one. Though there is no doubt that the content and the contours of any morality are highly influenced by culture, it may be that the fact that a community has a morality *at all* is to be explained by reference to dedicated psychological mechanisms forged by biological natural selection. That said, it is perfectly possible that natural selection has taken *some* interest in the content of morality, perhaps favoring broad and general universals. (Later, I will discuss some evidence indicating that there are a number of recurrent themes among all moral systems.) This "fixed" content would pertain to actions and judgments that enhance fitness despite the variability of ancestral environments. Flexibility is good if the environment varies; but if in some respect the environment is very stable—for example, it is hard to imagine an ongoing situation where fitness will be enhanced by eating one's children—then moral attitudes with fixed content may be more efficient. After all, speaking generally, phenotypic plasticity can be costly: Learning introduces the dangers of trial-and-error experimentation, and it takes a potentially costly amount of time. (Consider the nastiness of getting a sunburn before your skin tans in response to an increase in sun exposure, or the dangers of suffering a disease before your immune system kicks in to combat it.)

There is one traditional complaint against sociobiology and evolutionary psychology that has, thankfully, receded in recent years: that the program would, if pursued, lead to unpleasant political ends. It shouldn't be forgotten that much of the tone-setting early invective against these research programs was politically motivated. In their withering and influential attack on sociobiology, *Not in Our Genes*, Richard Lewontin, Steven Rose, and Leon Kamin are, if nothing else, refreshingly honest about this, admitting that they share a commitment to socialism, and that they regard their "critical science as an integral part of the struggle to create that society" (1984: ix).

Elsewhere, Lewontin and Richard Levins proudly made this declaration: ". . . we have been attempting with some success to guide our research by a conscious application of Marxist philosophy" (Levins and Lewontin 1985: 165). It is not these disturbing confessions of political motivation that I mean to highlight here—intellectually repugnant though they are (and should be even to Marxists)—but rather the bizarre presupposition that a Darwinian approach to human psychology and behavior should have any obvious political ramifications. Unlike some, I do not deny the very possibility that Darwinian psychology might have political implications (for political decisions can be affected in principle by any type of factual input). But if it does have such implications, then demonstrating the fact will require a careful and complex argument of an order that no one has yet provided. Certainly the political fears that lay behind earlier diatribe—that sociobiology would exonerate racism, sexism, classism, etc.—were naive and ill-founded. The persistent worry was that if one were to be provided with an evolutionary explanation for some morally obnoxious behavior, this would in some manner validate the behavior, or would supply an excuse for its unpleasant perpetrators, or would show that attempts to correct the behavior are futile. But we have already seen that the claim that evolutionary psychology reveals behaviors to be "inevitable" or "determined by the genes" or "not free" is (and always has been) a straw-man argument. Suppose that evolutionary psychology were to reveal that the human mind is adapted to living in an extended family group. This alone would not justify this behavior, would not show that it is unavoidable, and would not even show that such a living arrangement is likely to make us happy. (Who says that natural selection prefers happy organisms?) And even if evolutionary psychology *were* to turn out to have specific political implications, so be it! The policy of letting political preferences determine our acceptance of scientific theories, of denying a theory irrespective of its empirical support simply because of uneasiness about its practical implications, has never, so far as I know, deserved a place among the virtues of intellectual inquiry.

On the question of how much human psychology is to be explained by reference to discrete innate faculties (as opposed to resulting largely from learning and all-purpose flexibility), let us keep our indecision proportional to the available evidence. As to the question of whether any such findings may have practical or moral implications, let us assume that they do not until we see a plausible argument clearly laid out to that shows that they do. It is hard to imagine that anyone would find such principles objectionable. Despite all that I have just said against some misguided opposition to

Darwinian psychology, I appreciate the need for caution, and I am aware that not all opponents are so naive.[6] In this book I am not committed to the view that a great many aspects of the human mind are open to direct evolutionary explanation—I am not pushing for a "massively modular" view of the human mind to the exclusion of general organizing mechanisms—and so I am not sure whether the ideas that will be looked upon sympathetically in coming pages should even count as favoring evolutionary psychology in the more controversial sense of the label. When it comes to the question of an innate moral faculty, neither hypothesis should be rejected in advance of examining the evidence. It is perfectly plausible that biological natural selection should have developed dedicated mechanisms designed to produce such judgments. It is just as plausible that it did nothing of the sort, and that moral judgment is a culturally generated capacity flowing from more general psychological faculties. Most of this book—the first four chapters—is devoted to this puzzle.

1 | The Natural Selection of Helping

1.1 Altruism and Selfishness

What is the value of moral thinking? What benefits do we get from engaging in this way of judging ourselves and each other? It is reasonable to assume that the answer has something to do with helpfulness and cooperation. In some vague manner we expect that a person who thinks of human interactions in terms of "virtue," "obligation," or "justice" is more likely to be a useful member of society than someone for whom these concepts are entirely alien. This natural thought will be examined in detail in chapter 4; I mention it now because one might suppose that it represents an immediate barrier to the hypothesis that morality is innate. Surely, one might think, natural selection is a competitive race where the laurels go to the untamed individualist? The main goal of this first chapter is to show that this doubt is misguided. I will outline several means by which helpful, cooperative traits may evolve. But before embarking on that task we should get our thinking straight on a misleading piece of terminology. Much of the literature on the topic of how helpful behaviors might naturally emerge professes to concern the evolution of *altruism*, but this is a word that has, over the years, been muddied and fudged in discussions about evolution, leading to persistent confusion and erroneous conclusions in some quarters. In the context of this book it is important to be exact about what we mean in this respect, and so I will begin with a three-way distinction.

Helping Behaving in a way that benefits another individual. Contrast: harmful behavior. (I am happy also to call this "cooperation" or "prosocial behavior.")

Fitness sacrificing Behaving in a way that advances another individual's reproductive fitness, at the expense of one's own reproductive fitness. (This is often called "evolutionary altruism.") Contrast: fitness advancing.

Altruism   Acting with the intention of benefiting another individual, where this is motivated by a non-instrumental concern for his or her welfare. Contrast: selfishness.

In restricting "altruism" in this way I take myself to be respecting ordinary English. In English, an action is altruistic only if done with a certain other-oriented deliberative *motivation*, in the sense that the welfare of another was the agent's ultimate reason for acting. Suppose Amy acts in a way that benefits Bert, but what motivates the action is Amy's belief that she will benefit herself in the long run. Then it is not an altruistic act but a selfish act. Suppose Amy's belief turns out to be false, so that she never receives the payoff and the only person who gains from her action is Bert. Does this cause us to retract the judgment that Amy's action was selfish? No. Whether an action is selfish or altruistic depends on the deliberative motivating reasons for which it was done—the considerations in light of which it was performed[1]—not on who ends up benefiting from its performance. Some people doubt whether *any* human actions are altruistic in this respect; they think that all actions are done from the ultimate motive of self-gain. As we will see later, these people (psychological egoists) are almost certainly wrong. Many human actions are done from a genuine regard for others, and are not motivated by considerations of self-gain.

There are few non-human animals, if any, that can be spoken of uncontentiously as having motivating reasons—in the sense of having considerations that figure in their deliberations—and certainly there are few non-human animals that have the concept of *self* necessary to have a selfish motivation. Therefore there are few non-human animals, if any, that can be spoken of uncontentiously as being altruistic or selfish. I am not going to define with any precision what a motive or intention is, nor am I going to attempt to gauge where to draw the line between creatures that have them and those that don't. It is enough to point out that, say, plants do not have the requisite sort of motives and intentions, and so, although plants may behave in ways helpful to others, and perhaps they may behave in fitness-sacrificing ways, I judge it best to eschew describing a plant's behavior as "altruistic" or "selfish."

Quite obviously organisms help each other, though there are some difficulties that would have to be straightened out before we could be satisfied that we had nailed down the notion fully.[2] Presumably "benefiting X" can be treated as synonymous with "advancing X's interests," but worries arise concerning what it takes to "have an interest." (Even when we are dealing with humans, who clearly have interests if anything does, things are far from straightforward.) If one squashes a cockroach on the kitchen floor, there would be nothing unusual in claiming that doing so "frustrated its interests" (and in saying this we need not be indulging in any dubious anthropomorphism according to which the cockroach has conscious desires, motives, or experiences pain), but it proves difficult to say what a cockroach's interests amount to. Perhaps in the end the notion cannot be explicated, and such appeals are confused. What is important is that we don't unthinkingly equate a creature's interests with its reproductive fitness. A creature's interests *might* coincide with its reproductive fitness—this might be how we end up explicating cockroach interests—but it certainly doesn't need to. When I buy a birthday present for my friend, this is a kind of helping behavior (even if it is only pleasure I'm trying to bring). But it is *her* interests that I am seeking to advance—the individual who is born, lives, and dies—not those of her genes. Talking of "the interests of genes" is even more shaky than talking about the interests of a cockroach. Genes don't really have an interest in replicating, any more than a river has an interest in not being dammed. But that a gene has the characteristics that it does have is explained by the contribution those characteristics have made to its successful replication and endurance; thus we can speak—in a quasi-metaphorical way—of a gene being "designed" to replicate, of replication being its "purpose." And if we allow ourselves to talk this way, then speaking of a gene having "an interest" in replicating is hard to resist.

If we give in to this temptation, and allow ourselves to talk of my friend's genes having interests as well as of *her* having interests (or, if you prefer, of her "genetic interests" versus her "individual interests"), it is clear with whose interests I, as a friend, am concerned when I choose a birthday present. It may be a year's supply of contraceptives that I give her for her birthday, thus preventing the replication of her genes, but it is no less helpful for that. Conversely, it is *possible* that I might be concerned with the interests of her genes (though that would be pretty strange), in which case I might perform the action of secretly sabotaging her supply of contraceptives. But in advancing my friend's genetic interests in this way I would hardly be acting helpfully to *her*. Similarly, an act of patricide or matricide may advance the genetic interests of the perpetrator, and thus also those of the murdered parent, but it is no less harmful to the victim for that! And there is nothing incoherent in the idea of a person's interests being ruined by her being forced to have a large family. In short, to confuse a person with her genes is as silly as confusing her with her lungs or her lymph nodes, but as soon as the distinction is enforced, so too must be the distinction between a person's interests and the "interests" of her genes.

I admitted that when we get down to organisms that cannot experience anxiety or pain it *may* be permissible to identify the organism's interests with the advancement of its reproductive fitness. A useful thought experiment is to ask ourselves whether our view about harming an individual organism would change if we were to find out that it is sterile and not in a position to give aid to any kin in their reproduction. In such circumstances we can do no harm to the organism's reproductive fitness; thus, if we still feel comfortable saying that squashing or killing the organism "harms it" (as, I submit, we usually do), we must be employing a different notion of "harm" or "interest": one that pertains to the harming of *the individual*.[3] (Likewise with helping the organism.)

There can be little doubt that "fitness-sacrificing" behavior occurs. People sometimes give up on their plans of raising a family in order to devote themselves to charity work in distant countries. There are cases of people in times of war committing suicide in order to save the lives of their comrades. If their comrades were family members, then such acts of heroic sacrifice might still count as "fitness-advancing" behavior; but in many cases the beneficiaries of the sacrifice are unrelated. What *is* controversial about fitness-sacrificing behavior is not whether it occurs, but whether it might be selected for by the forces of natural selection. Some people argue that fitness-sacrificing behavior cannot be favored by natural selection. Richard Alexander (1987: 3), for example, asserts that there is "not a shred of evidence" that such behavior is a "normal part of the functioning of every human individual." A corollary of this might be the claim that non-accidental fitness-sacrificing behavior cannot be found outside the human species.

We will see later in this chapter that, on the contrary, fitness-sacrificing behavior might well be produced by biological natural selection. The key is that the population upon which natural selection works is structured in a certain grouped manner. But in fact this is not a dispute that matters here; relative to the aims of this book, what matters is that certain kinds of *helpful* behavior have been selected for in humans. Whether these helpful behaviors are also fitness sacrificing, or whether they are really a form of fitness advancement, is something I am content to leave open. The question in which I am interested is "What proximate mechanisms might be favored by natural selection in order to regulate this helpful behavior?" One possible answer, which I think is correct, is "Altruism." In other words, in order to make an organism successfully helpful, natural selection may favor the trait of acting from altruistic motives (assuming the organism has the cognitive sophistication to have motives at all). Another possible answer, which I also think is correct, is "Morality." In order to make an organism successfully helpful, natural selection may favor the trait of making moral judgments. Exploring this second answer is the main task of this book.

The goal of the rest of this chapter is to identify the principal evolutionary processes that may lead to helpful organisms. This will put us in a good position then to ask whether a moral sense may have developed in humans as a means of governing helpfulness. But first a further cautionary word. Suppose that the above approach leads to a positive outcome, and we decide that human moral thinking is governed by dedicated mechanisms that evolved through the process of Darwinian selection. The conclusion that would be absolutely incorrect to draw is that what these arguments show is that all human action, even what is helpful and what is deemed morally virtuous, is "really selfish." Drawing the distinctions above should be sufficient to show what is wrong with this conclusion; but the tendency to leap to this assumption appears to be so persistent, and is so pernicious, that it pays to underline the error. Richard Dawkins (1981: 3) concludes, on the basis of his "selfish gene" view, that "we are born selfish." Alexander (1987: 3) writes that we will not understand human conduct until we grasp that societies are "collections of individuals seeking their own self-interest." And Michael Ghiselin (1974: 247) memorably tells us "Scratch an altruist, and watch a hypocrite bleed." But such attitudes, posing as hard-nosed realism, erroneously conflate distinct explanatory levels. (See Tinbergen 1963.) In particular, they commit the basic blunder of confusing the cause of a mental state with its content. If a person's nervousness about a pending job interview is partially caused by the fact that he just drank four cups of strong coffee (had he not drunk the coffee, he wouldn't now be nervous), it would be crazy to conclude that really he is nervous *of the coffee*! Yet people who think that evolutionary explanations reveal the "true" content of all our motivations, reasons, and interests fall foul of exactly this piece of mistaken reasoning. Suppose Fred is looking after his sick wife. When asked why he does so, he reports sincerely that he wishes to alleviate her suffering for her sake, because he loves her. An evolutionary psychologist might then tell us that it is to Fred's reproductive advantage to look after his spouse, for then he will have help in raising his offspring, adding that the love that Fred feels for his wife is the output of a proximate mechanism by which natural selection ensures that a person helps his mate when she needs it. Thus, an evolutionary explanation has been provided for a cognitive/emotional/behavioral phenomenon: Fred's love for his wife. But this explanation reveals nothing about the content of Fred's motivations, and doesn't show that he "really" cares about his reproductive fitness and only derivatively cares about his wife's welfare.

One might object that there is a disanalogy here. In the case of an evolutionary psychological explanation, it might be thought, the explanans that is appealed to is something that (unlike a cup of coffee) itself has interests: genes. But we have already seen that talk of genes literally having interests is shaky stuff. (I think the metaphor causes more confusion than it's worth—exactly the kind of confusion an author has to waste time combating in the first chapter of a book on the evolution of morality.) But even if we were to earn the right to that kind of talk at a literal level, the argument would still be unsound. It would require the endorsement of the following "principle of interest transferal":

If X has interests *a*, *b*, *c*, etc., and X having those interests is explained by the fact that Y has interests *p*, *q*, *r*, etc., then X's interests are "subservient" to Y's, and in fact X's "real" or "ultimate" interests are *p*, *q*, *r*, etc.

But there is no reason to believe in this principle, and good reason to reject it. It continues to confuse *explaining the origin* of a mental state (or interests) with *providing the content* of that state (or interests). The source of this common confusion may be an ambiguity in the notion of "a reason." *Fred's* reason why he cares for his wife is her suffering. This is what motivates him and figures in his deliberations. *The* reason why her suffering motivates him (or, better, *a* reason) may be that caring for one's partner advances one's fitness, and thus has been selected for in humans, and Fred is a human. When we explain a person's behavior and mental states by appealing to the fact that his genes have replication-advancing characteristics, we are giving reasons for his having these mental states and behaving in this way. But to conclude that these are therefore *his* reasons—the considerations in light of which he acts—is a gross mistake. In exactly the same way, we can wonder about the reason that an avalanche occurred, but in doing so we are hardly wondering about what malicious motives the melting snow harbored.[4] I am not claiming that a person's reasons must always be obvious and apparent to her; all I am saying is that they are not all "ultimately" concerned with genetic replication.

The three categories of action that have been identified in this section can be conjoined in any combination. Ignoring for a while those cynics who deny the existence of altruistic behavior, we can come up with examples satisfying all of the following conditions[5]:

- behavior that is helpful, fitness sacrificing, and altruistic
- behavior that is helpful and fitness sacrificing, but selfish
- behavior that is helpful, fitness advancing, and altruistic
- behavior that is helpful, but fitness advancing and selfish

- behavior that is unhelpful, but fitness sacrificing and altruistic
- behavior that is unhelpful, fitness sacrificing, and selfish
- behavior that is unhelpful and fitness advancing, but altruistic
- behavior that is unhelpful, fitness advancing, and selfish.

With these distinctions made and some potential confusions nipped in the bud, we can turn to the first step of the argument. Note that our focus is not on altruism—either in the vernacular psychological sense or in the evolutionary sense (which I have been calling "fitness-sacrificing behavior"). Altruism is not an important issue in this book. Nor is our focus, in the first instance, on "moral" behavior. Rather, our initial task—the task of the rest of this chapter—is to outline the evolutionary processes that may lead to the development of *helping behavior*. In due course we will ask the question of whether moral thinking may be a mechanism that in humans regulates helping behavior—but noting this is to look downstream. Issues pertaining to morality are what we are working toward, but they will not surface in our discussion for a while.

Just as there are many evolutionary reasons for organisms having the capacity for locomotion, say, there may be many evolutionary reasons for organisms having the capacity to help each other. My objective, then, is not to alight upon *the* way in which helping behavior is selected for, but to sketch some of the broad evolutionary forces: kin selection, mutualism, reciprocity, and group selection. Lastly I will discuss how culture may have affected helping traits in the special case of humans.

1.2   The Evolution of Helping: Kin Selection

Always the first to be mentioned is what is usually called *kin selection*, the locus classicus of which is William Hamilton's 1964 paper "The Genetical Evolution of Social Behaviour" (though it was a selective force vaguely appreciated by Darwin[6]). It helps if we think, as Richard Dawkins has famously urged us to, of organisms as vehicles by which genes succeed in reproducing themselves. An organism that is kind and helpful to its family members—that is, to those that are guaranteed to share its genes—may be a useful sort of vehicle for a gene to inhabit. As far as the gene is concerned, if its "vehicle" sacrifices its life to save three offspring, or three siblings, or nine cousins, then that's a good deal. Talking of life sacrifices is a bit dramatic; we're just as much concerned with more modest sacrifices: sharing food with your siblings, looking after your young nieces and nephews, educating your own children. That a creature should care for its own offspring is so engrained in our minds that it takes some effort to attain the critical distance needed to realize that it requires some explanation in evolutionary terms. Many creatures don't care for their offspring, preferring to opt for quantity over quality. But most mammals go for quality offspring, and this requires the provision of a degree of caring, feeding, and nurturing. A human infant is remarkably dependent on the help of others, and remains so for many years. Therefore we should expect that the trait of caring for one's children has been strongly selected for in humans. A gene inhabiting a human vehicle that wasn't inclined to care for its children—that left them to fend for themselves upon birth—would quickly become history.

Consider the Hymenoptera class of social insects: ants, bees, and wasps. We can point out three interesting features of such insects. First, they are paragons of social success. If any group of individuals can be said to count as a "super-organism," it is an ants' nest or a beehive. Second, they manifest an unusual amount of helpful behavior. Bees have their suicidal sting, which they use in defense of the hive. There are castes of ants in the nest that are born sterile, and spend their days tending the offspring of others. Evolutionary theory needs to explain these peculiarities. How could the trait of sterility or a suicidal tendency possibly evolve by biological natural selection? Wouldn't natural selection favor the bee that *doesn't* sting? Indeed, Darwin recognized that the social insects raised a problem "which at first appeared to me insuperable, and actually fatal to my whole theory" ((1859) 1998: 352). Hamilton was able to provide an answer unavailable to Darwin, by drawing attention to the third peculiarity of these insects: their genetic interrelatedness. In a nest of ants, bees, or wasps, many of the individuals are much more closely related in genetic terms than in a group of, say, monkeys, groundhogs, or humans. The mammals that we are familiar with share, at most, 50 percent of their genetic material with their immediate family members (identical twins notwithstanding).[7] But things are different with the Hymenoptera, due to their unusual chromosomal arrangement: The male bee has half the number of chromosomes as the female bee, and the female "sisters" of the nest (by far the majority of nest members) share 75 percent of their genetic material with each other.[8] Hamilton's Rule states that a trait of helping others at some cost to the individual can be expected to be favored by natural selection if

$$rB > C,$$

where r is the degree of genetic relatedness to the individual, B is the benefit to the recipient, and C is the cost to the individual. In the Hymenoptera, r is often higher than it is with mammalian conspecifics, allowing C to be proportionally higher. Given this unusual circumstance, we would predict a greater amount of sacrificial helping behavior in bees than in, say, mice—and this is precisely what we do observe.[9]

So we have a perfectly plausible and highly confirmed theory about why and how biological natural selection produces organisms who help out family members at some cost to themselves. Yet it seems that this could hardly explain human *morality*, in which (at least in the Western tradition) the tendency to favor one's own family members is a vice to which we have given the name "nepotism." Moreover, kin selection seems unable to explain the evolution of helping behavior toward non-kin, which, clearly, is an important element of human morality. If two creatures are unrelated, then r in Hamilton's Rule will be zero, and thus so will be rB, and thus kin selection will be unable to explain any helpful behavior for which $C > 0$—that is, helpful behavior that is in any way costly to perform.

Yet kin selection may still be an important factor in explanations of helping offered to non-kin. First, it should be borne in mind that the trait of helping kin must involve proximate mechanisms that allow organisms to recognize kin, and these mechanisms may be sufficiently fallible—especially in novel environments—that they prompt helping behavior towards non-kin. In many species kin recognition is achieved via scent; for example, nurturing behaviors in the parent may be triggered by the odor of the newborn activating hormonal responses (Yamakazi et al. 2000). But kin-identifying mechanisms may be much coarser than this. If the population is structured in small family groups such that the conspecifics with which an individual most frequently interacts are very likely to be kin, then natural selection could plump for a simple solution: "Provide help to those conspecifics with whom you interact frequently." A good example of nature using such coarse-grained mechanisms is how hatchling chicks "imprint" on the first object they see moving, be it a human or a rotating red cube. (See Lorenz 1937; Bateson 1966.) In the natural environment the mechanism works well enough, since the first moving object seen is nearly always the mother. We can find evidence of this sort of phenomenon in humans too. Studying people raised on kibbutzim, the anthropologist Joseph Shepher (1971, 1983) found that there is a strong tendency not to be sexually attracted to any individual with whom one was raised, irrespective of whether he or she is genetically related. The hypothesis (which had been put forward by Edward Westermarck in the nineteenth century) is that this is a mechanism for incest avoidance. Natural selection does not make humans avoid sibling incest by developing a "sibling detector"; it prefers the simpler "familiar-from-childhood detector." In the ancestral environment, the two mechanisms would pick out pretty much the same extension of individuals, and the latter has lower running costs. (For modern confirmation, see Lieberman et al. 2003.) If, then, human helping towards kin (or certain classes of kin) is regulated by a "provide-help-to-those-conspecifics-with-whom-you-interact-frequently" mechanism, and humans now live in societies in which we interact with far more conspecifics than natural selection ever dreamed of (including the "virtual interactions" supplied by TV, newspapers, and so forth), then one would expect to observe, ceteris paribus, a great deal of helping behavior towards non-kin, despite the fact that kin selection is the only explanatory process in play.

A second reason why kin selection may be important regarding helping behavior toward non-kin is that in it we at least have an explanation for how and why certain creatures will have in place the mechanisms that regulate helpful behavior. Biological natural selection is a conservative process, bending old structures into new, pressing into service available material for novel purposes. For example, the hormone that in mammals seems to govern maternal nurturing behavior is oxytocin—an ancient hormone, found even in mollusks, that was co-opted for the job more than 200 million years ago (Allman 2000: 97, 199). We now know that oxytocin is also centrally involved in pair-bonding behavior, suggesting that natural selection has tweaked its role over millions of years in order to encourage more extensive helpfulness beyond the mother-offspring bond. (See Gimpl and Fahrenholz 2001; Uvnäs-Moberg 2003.) If kin selection gave our distant ancestors the psychological and physiological structures needed for regulating helpful behavior toward family members, then those structures became available for use in new tasks—most obviously, helpful behavior toward individuals outside one's family—if the pressures of natural selection pushed in that direction. And there are several ways in which they may have pushed in that direction.

1.3   The Evolution of Helping: Mutualism

Sometimes there are ends that would benefit a creature but which it cannot achieve alone. A lion might want a piece of elephant for dinner—or there may be nothing else available—but one lion will not be able to accomplish this by itself. If a group of lions find themselves in this situation, they will do well by cooperating in the bringing down of an elephant. If they don't cooperate, all of them will go hungry; maybe if they don't cooperate, all of them will die. Even if it's not an elephant that is on the menu but something that a lone lion might stand a chance of capturing, by hunting together the lions vastly improve the probability of success and lower the risks. Clearly, such lions do not need to be genetically related in order for natural selection to push in favor of traits that encourage this kind of cooperative behavior. This kind of helping is sometimes called *mutualism* and sometimes *cooperation*. However, in ordinary contexts the word "cooperation" can be applied to many other kinds of mutually beneficial arrangements as well (such as reciprocal exchanges, which are to be discussed next), and so employing it in a restricted sense is apt to lead to confusion. "Mutualism" is sufficiently unfamiliar outside its theoretical context that it is the preferable word.[10]

Helping behavior that is explained by reference to mutualism is not fitness-sacrificing behavior. A lioness who doesn't cooperate threatens to spoil the whole hunt (for herself as well as the other lions), and thus lowers her own reproductive fitness. There may be circumstances where the participation of *all* the lions is not needed to bring about the desirable end, and in those circumstances there will be a selective pressure upon lions to hang back and let others do the work. But given that, as a general rule, the more lions are involved in the hunt, the higher the probability of a successful kill (and the lower the probability of any hunter getting hurt), often joining in the hunt will be a better means of advancing reproductive fitness than not doing so.

One feature of mutualism to which it is important to draw attention—in order to contrast it with the next process of helping—is that it does not require ongoing relationships among the participants. For example, when a group of small birds "mob" a large threatening animal in order to drive it off (another example of mutualistic helping), they have each advanced their fitness right then and there, and this fact wouldn't alter if all the birds then dispersed and never interacted again. So mutualism is not a reciprocal relation. The simple difference can be brought out using a nice example from David Hume, who imagines two oarsmen pulling together in order to row to a destination each desires. No promises are exchanged between the two, for none are needed: If either stops rowing, the boat will go in circles; it is a situation in which the desired end will be reached only "if all perform their part, but loses all advantage if only one perform" ((1751) 1983: 95). We can imagine a comparative case involving the kind of rowboat that can be propelled by a single oarsman. If one person promises to take the other to her destination if she agrees to row him to his destination later in the day, then this is a different kind of arrangement, involving a kind of contract (though perhaps a tacit one). The former case is an example of mutualism, the latter of reciprocity. Let us now turn to reciprocity directly.

1.4 The Evolution of Helping: Direct Reciprocity

It is a simple fact that one is often in a position to help another such that the value of the help received exceeds the cost incurred by the helper. If a type of monkey is susceptible to infestation by some kind of external parasite, then it is worth a great deal to have those parasites removed—it may even be a matter of life or death—whereas it is the work of only half an hour for the groomer. Kin selection can be used to explain why a monkey might spend the afternoon grooming family members; it runs into trouble when it tries to explain why monkeys in their natural setting would bother grooming non-kin. In grooming non-kin, the benefit given by an individual monkey might give a great deal more benefit than cost incurred, but still the groomer incurs *some* cost: That half-hour could profitably be used foraging for food or arranging sexual intercourse. So what possible advantage could there be in sacrificing *anything* for unrelated conspecifics? The obvious answer is that if those unrelated individuals would then groom *her* when she has finished grooming them, or at some later date, then that would be an all-around useful arrangement. If all the monkeys entered into this cooperative venture, in total more benefit than costs would be distributed among them. The first person to see this process clearly was Robert Trivers (1971), who dubbed it *reciprocal altruism*.

One of Trivers's primary examples of these values working out in favor of helping exchanges is the "cleaning stations" on a coral reef. Small "cleaner fish" (or shrimp) indicate their willingness to remove from a large fish its external parasites by approaching the host with a distinctive swimming pattern. The large fish, if it wants cleaning, responds by opening its mouth and gill plates in order to allow the cleaners to go to work. When the host has had enough, it gives a distinctive signal to this effect, and the cleaners depart. The host fish could, on any given occasion, get a cleaning *and* an easy meal at the end of it. If the undersea world were teeming with willing cleaner fish, then perhaps it should do just that. But given that the reef will support only so many groups of cleaners, it is to the large fish's fitness advantage to keep this exchange going. It then knows where to go for a good cleaning, it knows that these are reliable cleaners, and that's worth something. It's worth more than a free meal. If the big fish gives up a free meal for long-term benefit, what do the cleaner fish give up? By approaching the large fish—entering its mouth even—they take a risk; so they give up safety. It's actually impossible for the cleaner fish to gain their benefit (eating ectoparasites) without paying this price. However, they could still "cheat" by taking small mouthfuls out of the unsuspecting large fish's fins (as certain species of "cleaner mimics" do), thus increasing their immediate net gain at the other's expense. But this would be a myopic choice. Just as it is hard to find a good cleaner, so is it hard to find a loyal customer.[11]

A relationship whose cost-benefit structure is that of reciprocal altruism could exist between plants: organisms with no capacity to cheat, thus prompting no selective pressure in favor of a capacity to detect cheats. Even with creatures who have the cognitive plasticity to cheat on occasions, reciprocal relations need not be vulnerable to exploitation. If the cost of cheating is the forfeiture of a highly beneficial exchange relation, then any pressure in favor of cheating is easily outweighed by a competing pressure against cheating, and if this is reliably so for both partners in an ongoing program of exchange, then natural selection doesn't have to bother giving either interactant the temptation to cheat, or a heuristic for responding to cheats. But since reciprocal exchanges will develop only if the costs and benefits are balanced along several scales, and since values are rarely stable in the real world, there is often the possibility that a reciprocal relation will collapse if environmental factors shift. If one partner, A, indicates that he will help others no matter what, then it may no longer be to B's advantage to help A back. If the value of cheating were to rise (say, if B could possibly *eat* A, and there's suddenly a serious food shortage), then it may no longer be to B's advantage to help A back. If the cost of seeking out new partners who would offer help (albeit only until they also are cheated) were negligible, then it may no longer be to B's advantage to help A back. For natural selection to favor the development of an ongoing exchange relation, these values must remain stable and symmetrical for both interactants.[12] What is interesting about many reciprocal arrangements is that there is a genuine possibility that one partner can cheat on the deal (once she has received her benefit) and get away with it. Therefore there will often be a selective pressure in favor of developing a capacity for distinguishing between cheating that leads to long-term forfeiture and cheating that promises to pay off. This in turn creates a new pressure for a sensitivity to cheats and a capacity to respond to them. An exchange between creatures bearing such capacities is a *calculated* reciprocal relationship; the individual interactants have the capacity to tailor their responses to perceived shifts in the cost-benefit structure of the exchange (de Waal and Luttrell 1988).

The cost-benefit structure of a reciprocal relation can be stabilized if the price of non-reciprocation is increased beyond the loss of an ongoing exchange relationship. One possibility would be if individuals actively punished anyone they have helped but who has not offered help in return.

Another way would be to punish (or refuse to help[13]) any individual in whom you have observed a "non-reciprocating" trait, even if you haven't personally been exploited. One might go even further, punishing anyone who refuses to punish such non-helpers. The development of such punishing traits may be hindered by the possibility of "higher-order defection," since the individual who reciprocates but doesn't take the trouble to punish non-reciprocators will apparently have a higher fitness than reciprocators who also administer the punishments. Robert Boyd and Peter Richerson (1992) have shown that this is not a problem so long as the group is small enough that the negative consequences of letting non-reciprocators go unpunished will be sufficiently felt by all group members. They argue, however, that we must appeal to cultural group selection in order to explain punishing traits in larger groups. (More on this in section 1.7.)

Two important things need to be noted. First, these "reciprocal altruists" are not *altruists* in the sense that I have defined it. The example, after all, is of types of fish, which do not satisfy the psychological prerequisites for performing actions that are either altruistic or selfish in the vernacular sense of these words; they may not satisfy the prerequisites for performing *actions* at all. Second, and perhaps less obvious, these helping organisms are not exhibiting fitness-sacrificing behavior either (therefore they are not "evolutionarily altruistic"—see Sober 1988). In a reciprocal exchange neither party forfeits fitness for the sake of another. As Trivers defined it, "altruistic behavior" (by which he means *helpful* behavior) is that which is "apparently detrimental to the organism performing the behavior" (1971: 35)—but obviously an *apparent* fitness sacrifice is not an actual fitness sacrifice, any more than an apparent Rolex is an actual Rolex. Others have defined "reciprocal altruism" as fitness sacrificing *in the short term*. But again, forgoing a short-term value in the expectation of greater long-term gains is no more an instance of a genuine fitness sacrifice than is, say, a monkey taking the effort to climb a tree in the hope of finding fruit at the top. So despite claims that reciprocal altruism and kin selection together solve the so-called paradox of evolutionary altruism, if (i) by "altruism" we mean *fitness sacrificing* (not *apparent* nor *short-term* fitness sacrificing), and (ii) by "fitness" we mean inclusive fitness, and (iii) by "*solving* the paradox of evolutionary altruism" we mean showing how such altruism is possible, then I see no reason at all for thinking that this frequently repeated claim is true. It is possible, however, that reciprocity is an important process by which traits regulating *helpful behaviors* evolve. For these reasons, what Trivers called instances of "reciprocal altruism" I prefer to call *reciprocal exchanges* or just *reciprocity*.[14]

Trivers thought that one way of modeling the reciprocal exchanges observed in nature is via the prisoner's dilemma—long the fascination of game theorists. The prisoner's dilemma (PD) involves two individuals who are deciding how to interact: They can both cooperate, or they can both defect, or one may offer cooperation while the other defects. But they have to make a decision simultaneously, and then compare results. Each possible outcome is associated with a "payoff" for the players (figure 1.1). In the conventional labeling, 8 is R (for *reward for cooperation*), 10 is T (for *temptation*), 1 is S (for *sucker's payoff*) and 3 is P (for *punishment for joint defection*). A prisoner's dilemma requires that T > R > P > S, and that 2R > T + S.[15]

If you are allowed to play this game just once, with one other player, it is difficult to know what to do. You might feel that mutual cooperation would be a good outcome, but to choose "cooperation" as your choice immediately opens you to exploitation. Can you trust your opponent not to leave you with 1? Better, perhaps, to be on the safe side and choose "defect," since at least getting 3 is better than 1. Of course, if the opponent reasons in the same manner, you'll both end up defecting. Things are different in an *iterated* game, when you're going to play a whole series of games with the same person, though you don't know how many games. There you need to develop a strategy which may be sensitive to what the player did on previous rounds. You may decide to defect for a while, and then try to "apologize" by offering cooperation. Or you may simply decide to always defect regardless of what your opponent does. The strategy made famous by Robert Axelrod (though it was designed by Anatol Rapoport) is known as "tit for tat" (TFT) (Axelrod 1984). TFT is terribly simple: Offer cooperation on the first round, and from then on just imitate your opponent's previous move. This amounts to cooperating so long as the opponent is cooperating,

Player A

	cooperates	defects
cooperates	8 8	10 1
Player B		
defects	1 10	3 3

Figure 1.1

never defecting first, responding to any defection with your own prompt defection, and, if involved in mutual defecting, waiting patiently for the opponent to "apologize" (for she must have started it). TFT is "friendly," not open to serious exploitation, and not exploitative.

Think again of our free-riding, non-grooming monkey. Suppose she offers herself for grooming for the first time to a non-kin individual (call him "A") who promptly grooms her. Later, A offers himself to the free rider and gets nothing. Since A is "playing TFT," he will not groom her again, unless she decides at a later date to groom him. So far the free rider is up on the deal, since she got one free groom whereas A spent half an hour doing something for nothing. But if we give consideration to all the other grooming interactions going on, then she is not winning at all. She got one free groom from A, and let's say she manages to get one free groom from every other member of the group (each of whom is also playing TFT). After that, she is out of luck; no one will touch her (except kin, and we'll assume, in order to make the point, that the attentions of kin alone are insufficient to fend off parasite infestation). The others, meanwhile, are happily grooming each other for as long as they keep interacting. The non-groomer dies of parasite infestation. So much for free riding!

A common misconception is that TFT wins always, or nearly always. On the contrary, TFT never wins. The only way of ever getting more points than an opponent in a round is to defect while she offers cooperation—and by definition TFT will do this only when it has already been on the receiving end of the same treatment in an earlier round. The best TFT can do against any opponent is draw. However, TFT can win if by "winning" we mean something different. If there are a whole bunch of strategies playing off against each other (and perhaps versions of themselves), and winning consists of having the most points at the end of the whole tournament (and it is not a "knock-out" tournament), then TFT can prosper. Although with any given opponent it only draws at best, if all its opponents encounter fluctuating fortunes when playing with each other, then TFT can end up winning. Depending on the design of the tournament, it usually does remarkably well.

But in fact things are considerably more complicated than this. The triumph of TFT is entirely the result of the way the game has been set up, and there are a number of reasons for thinking that the rules of the game fail to model many aspects of real-world reciprocal exchanges. (For further discussion, see Hirshleifer and Martinez Coll 1988.) Here are half a dozen.

1. The whole point of a PD game is that players make their choices simultaneously, whereas Trivers emphasizes the time lag that characterizes recip-

rocal exchanges. Suggestion for improvement of model: Introduce the *alternating* prisoner's dilemma game, in which players know their opponent's move before they make a decision.

2. Creatures in the real world are not infallible; mistakes are likely to occur in communicating to each other. This is disastrous for two TFT players happily cooperating: If one thinks that the other has defected, it will immediately defect, leading to ongoing mutual defecting. Suggestion for improvement of model: Introduce "noise" into the game, whereby there is some probability of miscommunications and accidents.

3. In evolutionary terms, some strategies are going to be more costly to play than others. Someone playing TFT has to deploy skills of discrimination that someone playing "always cooperate" (ALL C) or "always defect" (ALL D) does not. Thus in a population of only TFT-ers and ALL C-ers—all busily cooperating with each other—those playing ALL C will have a fitness advantage, and thus will take over. Suggestion for improvement of model: Introduce a "complexity tax" on strategies.

4. We are often in a position to observe others interacting before we need to interact with them. In other words, before we sit down and make the first move with our opponent, we might have good grounds for believing what kind of a strategy she pursues. This might well affect what kind of strategy we offer her, how forgiving we are of her occasional "defect," etc. Suggestion for improvement of model: Allow players to develop a "reputation," and to alter their strategy according to the reputation of the co-player. (This may involve offering players a "scrutiny deal," such that they can gather varying degrees of information on their potential co-players at a proportional cost.)

5. In a standard PD tournament one is locked into playing with a partner regardless of how unpleasant a strategy he is employing, but in real life one can often simply choose to abandon an interaction. Combined with 4, one might choose not to interact with someone at all on the basis of his reputation. Suggestion for improvement of model: Allow *refusal to play (any more)* to be an option in the game.

6. Though TFT is said to "punish" those opponents who defect, it's really not much of a punishment. It's not even necessarily "an eye for an eye," since the only way to give the cheating opponent exactly the treatment she dealt (the "sucker's payoff") would be to *force her* to cooperate while you defect. Trivers talked of reciprocal exchanges in humans as being characterized by "moralistic aggression." This is more than just TFT's response of "Well, I'll defect with you from now on, until you mend your ways"; rather, it's a positive *penalty* of disapproval, ostracization, or possibly violence

leveled at a defector. Suggestion for improvement of model: Allow players to punish others (at a price) beyond merely defecting on them.

Most of the above features have been tried in PD tournaments (though with some of them one wonders whether it still counts as a prisoner's dilemma at all), and the conclusion is that TFT does not come out on top. First consider the introduction of "noise" into the interacting environment. As noted, this spells a disaster for the stable evolution of TFT. An alternative strategy—one that deserves its 15 minutes of fame—is called "PAVLOV." PAVLOV (whose abilities were discovered by Martin Nowak and Karl Sigmund (1993)) follows a "win-stay, lose-shift" strategy, where *winning* means receiving the R or the T payoff and *losing* means receiving the S or the P payoff. PAVLOV is far more forgiving of accidents than TFT. Suppose two PAVLOV players, Ernie and Bert, are busily engaged in mutual cooperation, when Ernie accidentally hits the *defect* button. Bert lost that round, so immediately switches to "defect" for the next round. Ernie, meanwhile, stays playing *defect*, since he won with it on the previous round. Having, then, both defected, both players immediately flip back to joint cooperation. (An exclamation mark indicates noise interference.)

Ernie: . . . C C D! D C C . . .
Bert: . . . C C C D C C . . .

Nice recovery. But see what happens when PAVLOV accidentally reveals an undiscriminating cooperator. In the first pair of rows, noise disrupts PAVLOV; in the second pair, it disrupts ALL C.

PAVLOV: . . . C   C D! D D D . . .
ALL C: . . . C   C C C C C . . .

PAVLOV: . . . C   C C D D D . . .
ALL C: . . . C   C D! C C C . . .

Ruthless exploitation, until noise interferes again. Some commentators, vaguely aware that TFT is not the end of the story in PD tournaments, nevertheless endorse the indistinct claim that "TFT-like" strategies will win the day. But if we think that TFT's "non-exploitative" characteristic is important, it is clear that PAVLOV does not count as "TFT-like." It is merciless toward the foolishly friendly, and this contributes a great deal to its success.[16]

Though organisms probably pursue something like a "win-stay, lose-shift" strategy against the environment (in making foraging decisions, for example), it would be a mistake to expect it to be an evolved strategy that dominates intelligent creatures' social interactions. Why? An important source of PAVLOV's superiority is the fact that it uses noise to weed out the

ALL C players, and then profitably exploits them to death. However, if there is a crucial advantage to be had from uncovering the undiscriminating players and exploiting them, it is not plausible that biological natural selection would plump for the inefficient mechanism: "Wait until you accidentally defect, then see what happens." If such a value is to be had from uncovering the undiscriminating, then natural selection is likely to prefer a somewhat more direct means of flushing them out. One might instead try *purposely* defecting to see what happens. But such an experimental defection might meet with a severe penalty. (If you're wondering whether a country's laws uphold the death penalty for treason, an especially poor way of satisfying your curiosity would be to travel to that country, commit treason, and see what happens.) If identifying suckers and defectors is important, then probably the best way to do it is to observe other players interacting. Needless to say, gathering information may cost something (in fitness terms), but the rewards of having advance warning about what kind of strategy your partner is likely to deploy may be considerable. There have been several attempts to model this element in PD playoffs (e.g., Sugden 1986; Pollock and Dugatkin 1992; Nowak and Sigmund 1998; Panchanathan and Boyd 2003, 2004). Usually, however, the notion of reputation that is employed reflects only whether one has given unprompted defections in the past. But the success of PAVLOV suggests that reputations should also reflect whether one is an unconditional cooperator.

1.5 The Evolution of Helping: Indirect Reciprocity

"The purest treasure mortal times afford," Shakespeare tells us, "is spotless reputation." In his less flamboyant manner, Darwin agreed: ". . . love of praise and the strong feeling of glory, and the still stronger horror of scorn and infamy" are together a "powerful stimulus to the development of the social virtues" ((1879) 2004: 133, 156). By introducing reputation into our understanding, we move away from standard reciprocal exchanges to what has been called "indirect reciprocity." This lies at the heart of Alexander's account (1987) of the evolution of moral systems, and I agree that it is of central importance. In indirect reciprocal exchanges, an organism benefits from helping another by being paid back a benefit of greater value than the cost of her initial helping, but not necessarily by the recipient of the help. We can see that reputations involve indirect reciprocity by considering the following: Suppose A acts generously toward several conspecifics, and this is observed or heard about by C. Meanwhile, C also learns of B acting disreputably toward others. On the basis of these observations—on the basis, that is, of A's and B's reputations—C chooses A over B as a partner in a mutually beneficial exchange relationship. A's costly helpfulness has thus been rewarded with concrete benefits, but not by those individuals to whom he was helpful. Alexander lists three major forms of indirect reciprocity:

(1) the beneficent individual may later be engaged in profitable reciprocal interactions by individuals who have observed his behavior in directly reciprocal relations and judged him to be a potentially rewarding interactant (his "reputation" or "status" is enhanced, to his ultimate benefit); (2) the beneficent individual may be rewarded with direct compensation from all or part of the group (such as with money or a medal or social elevation as a hero) which, in turn, increases his likelihood of (and that of his relatives) receiving additional perquisites; or (3) the beneficent individual may be rewarded by simply having the success of the group within which he behaved beneficently contribute to the success of his own descendants and collateral relatives. (1987: 94)

One possible example of indirect reciprocity is the behavior of Arabian babblers, as studied by Amotz Zahavi over many years (Zahavi and Zahavi 1997). Babblers are social birds that act in helpful ways toward each other: feeding others, acting as sentinels, etc. What struck Zahavi was not this helpful behavior per se, but the fact that certain babblers seem positively eager to help: jostling to act as sentinel, thrusting food upon unwilling recipients. The "Handicap Principle" that Zahavi developed states that such individuals are attempting to raise their own prestige within the group: signaling "Look at me; I'm so strong and confident that I can afford such extravagant sacrifices!" Such displays of robust health are likely to attract the attention of potential mates while deterring rivals, and thus such behavior is, appearances notwithstanding, squarely in the fitness-advancing camp.

Consider the enormous and cumbersome affair that is the peacock's tail. Its existence poses a prima facie threat to the theory of natural selection—so much so that Charles Darwin once admitted that the sight of a feather from a peacock's tail made him "sick!" (F. Darwin 1887: 296). Yet Darwin also largely solved the problem by realizing that the primary selective force involved in the development of the peacock's tail is the peahen's choosiness in picking a mate.[17] If peahens prefer mates with big fan-shaped tails, then eventually peacocks will have big fan-shaped tails; if peahens prefer mates with triple-crested, spiraling, red, white, and blue tails, then (ceteris paribus) eventually peacocks will sport just such tails. Sexual selection is a process whereby the choosiness of mates or the competition among rivals can produce traits that would otherwise be detrimental to their bearer.[18] I am not categorizing sexual selection in general as reciprocity, only those examples that involve the favoring of traits of costly helpfulness. If a male is helpful to a female (bringing her food, etc.) and as a result she confers on him the proportionally greater benefit of reproduction, this is an example of direct reciprocity. If a male is helpful to his fellows in general, and as a result an observant female confers on him the proportionally greater benefit of reproduction (thus producing sons who are generally helpful and daughters who have a preference for helpful males), this is an example of indirect reciprocity.[19] Just as sexual selection can produce extremely cumbersome physical traits, like the peacock's tail, so too can it produce extremely costly helping behaviors. We can say the same of reputation in general if the benefits of a good reputation are great enough. If a good reputation means sharing food indiscriminately with the group, then an indiscriminate food-sharing trait will develop; if a good reputation means wearing a pumpkin on your head, then a pumpkin-wearing trait will develop. The same, moreover, can be said of punishment, which is, after all, the flip side of being rewarded for a good reputation. If a type of self-advancing behavior (or any type of behavior at all) is sufficiently punished, it will no longer be self-advancing at all. (See Boyd and Richerson 1992.)

Once we see that indirect reciprocity encompasses systems involving reputation and punishment, and that these pressures can lead to the development of just about any trait—extremely costly indiscriminate helpfulness included—then we recognize what a potentially important explanatory framework it is. As a way of reminding ourselves of how important reciprocity can be, we should recall Aristotle's shrewd observation in *Politics* that for creatures who trade there is nothing that has only one function: A spear is good for hunting but may also be swapped; a pot is handy for carrying water but may also be used to bargain with; the skill of gathering foodstuffs contributes to satisfying nutritional needs but may also be exchanged for other favors; and so on. That the advantages of doubling the functionality of one's resources are considerable is obvious.

1.6 The Evolution of Helping: Group Selection

Skills of discrimination lie at the heart of both direct and indirect reciprocal exchanges. In the former, one helps only those who will help one back; in the latter, one favors or punishes others depending on their past performance. But there are other models to which we can appeal that need involve no such powers of discrimination on the part of the helpers. These helpers need not be reciprocal helpers at all; they will help anyone at all in their group, irrespective of the treatment they receive in return. It seems hardly credible that natural selection could favor such behavior. One way of putting this incredulity is to note that such helpers would appear to be genuine *fitness sacrificers*. But how could natural selection possibly favor a fitness-sacrificing creature over a fitness-advancing creature?

In their defense of group (or multi-level) selection, Elliott Sober and David Sloan Wilson (1998) have shown how it can work. First let's give a model in which helping *doesn't* take off. Suppose we have a population of 200 individuals. It doesn't matter whether they're humans, frogs, lions, plants, or computer programs. The important point is that they reproduce at a certain rate. Let's put the base-line rate at 1.1. By "base-line rate" we mean the rate at which an individual reproduces without any interference: without receiving any help, without making any sacrifices. So if there were nothing special going on in the population—no sharing or sacrificing—then it would grow by 10 percent each generation. (To make things simpler, we're assuming that reproduction is asexual and that the old generation immediately disappears upon the arrival of the new.) But let's put into the midst of this population a few helpful individuals. In performing helpful behaviors toward non-kin, helpers lower their own reproductive capacity. Let's say that they sacrifice 9 percent of their reproductive capacity in order to help 10 of their comrades get a boost of 0.4—that distribution of benefits being uniform and undiscriminating of whether the recipient is helper or non-helper. If we put 10 such characters into the mix, then 100 individuals will get their capacity boosted by 0.4. And since the distribution is uniform, five of those 100 will be helpers. We end up with the following spread of reproductive capacities in our population: five helpers with a reproductive rate of 1.4, five with a rate of 1.0, 95 unhelpful individuals with a rate of 1.5, and 95 on the base line with 1.1. This results in the following for generation 2:

population = 259 (12 helpers, 247 non-helpers).

First note the enormous impact that the helpers have had. Instead of the base-line growth of 10 percent, the total population has grown by almost 30 percent. But note secondly the percentage of helpers in the new population: It has dropped from 5 percent to 4.6 percent. After another round, things look as follows for generation 3:

population = 330 (14 helpers, 316 non-helpers).

The percentage of helpful individuals has dropped further, to 4.2. And if we carry on we'll see it continue to drop. If there's any environmental pressure restricting population growth—as there must be—then helpfulness, for all the benefits it has brought to the group, goes extinct. Not only does helpfulness have trouble getting established in a population, but it's vulnerable to overthrow. If we run a similar test, but this time starting with 199 helpers and just one non-helper, then despite the fact that the group will grow explosively with the values assigned, gradually, steadily, the percentage of unhelpful individuals in the population will increase, and the helping trait is doomed.

Now let's turn to group selection. Start again with 200 individuals, 10 of whom are helpers, just as we did above, with the same values holding. But this time the population is split into two groups of 100 each, which are, for a time at least, isolated. One of the groups—group A—has only unhelpful individuals therein, so will grow at a rate of 1.1, increasing to 110 individuals in the second generation. Group B has the 10 helpers, who give out the same benefit as above (a boost of 0.4 to 10 fellows, spread evenly and indiscriminately). In the second generation, group B will have 149 individuals, 14 of whom are helpers. The interesting thing is that the percentage of helpers relative to the size of group B has fallen from 10 percent to 9.4, whereas relative to the global population (A + B) their percentage has risen from 5 to 5.4. (This is an instance of Simpson's Paradox; see Simpson 1951.) After another round, things look as follows for generation 3:

Group A   Group B
population = 121   population = 218
(all non-helpers)   (19 helpers, 199 non-helpers).

The percentage of helpers relative to group B has dropped further (to 8.7), while rising further relative to the global population (to 5.6). If we just went on like this, nothing interesting would have been shown; assuming a limit on population growth, we would observe the trait of helping run to extinction just as we did before. But suppose that before this occurs the population is shaken up in some special way. Imagine that the total population—both groups A and B, now standing at 339—is mixed together and proportionally cut back to its original size of 200, again in two groups. Since the percentage of helpers will have grown in the interim, they will enjoy a larger representation in the new starting lineup than they began with. And here's the important part: Suppose we allow members to express some preference regarding with whom they associate in these new groups (such that no one is able to force unwanted association upon another). This preference might be nothing more than selecting individuals from whom one is likely to gain. Anyone stands to gain most from getting into a group with helpers, and this includes helpers themselves. The consequence will be a tendency for the helpers to "clump" together when the two new groups form.[20] In the third generation the percentage of helpers had reached 5.6, which out of 200 amounts to 11. Suppose all these helpers clump together in one of the groups of the new starting lineup.

So now we start again, with two new groups: A and B. Everything is the same as before, except that now group B begins with 11 helpers instead of 10. If we run it again to the third generation before shaking things up, then the percentage of helpers, relative to the total population, is over 6. If we cut back again to two groups of 100, assuming again that the helpers end up clumping, then this time there will be 12 helpers in group B's starting lineup. If we run it to the third generation one more time, then helpers reach over 7 percent of the global population, putting even more into the new starting lineup. Things are starting slowly, but if we were to go on running this growth program we would see a curve favoring the takeover of the helping trait. I purposely haven't made things easy for the helpers. If we allowed them the option of sacrificing a further 0.1 of their reproductive capacity in order to help another 10 individuals each get a bonus of 0.4, then their numbers would take off much faster. By comparison, in the "single-group model" that we considered above—where all 200 individuals were lumped into one undifferentiated group—this further sacrifice on the part of the helpers would just have led to their swifter demise.

We saw how, in the single-group model, a population of non-discriminating helpers was terribly vulnerable to takeover by non-helping individuals. What happens in this multi-group model when non-helpers turn up in a population of helpers? Let's run a similar model to the previous one, but starting out with 10 non-helpers in group B (not forgetting that just *one* was enough to take over in the single-group model). Both groups A and B are otherwise populated entirely by helpers. Here's how things go.

Generation 2:

Group A	Group B
population = 500	population = 461
(all helpers)	(414 helpers, 47 non-helpers)

Generation 3:

Group A	Group B
population = 2,500	population = 2,125
(all helpers)	(1,904 helpers, 221 non-helpers)

Helping, as we saw above, can potentially allow for remarkable growth. At a glance, the trait of unhelpfulness appears to be doing well: Its numbers have jumped from 10 to 47 to 221. Indeed, it is slowly taking over group B.

But notice what has happened to the percentage of non-helpers in the global population. It has dropped from 5 to 4.9 to 4.8. Suppose we were then, as before, to pare the whole lot back to two groups of 100 each (preserving the ratio of helpers and non-helpers when we do so), allowing individuals to choose with whom they associate. There will be fewer non-helpers to go into the mix. Again, everyone—both non-helpers and other helpers—wants to be with helpers, and so non-helpers get consigned to a group by themselves. If we run it out again to the third generation the percentage of non-helpers will have dropped even further, putting even fewer offspring into the next starting lineup. And so on, till unhelpfulness goes extinct.

One might complain that this is all just fiddling with numbers to get the desired result. There is a hint of truth in that. But remember that the objective is to show how helping behavior *could* develop through the forces of biological natural selection. Natural selection could spend millions of years throwing up a whole range of characters who help too much, or not enough, or in the wrong way, and on all such occasions the trait falls flat. But if among the myriad of values that won't work there is one that strikes the right balance and allows helping behavior to take off, then we might expect it to be eventually hit upon. Nature is nothing if not patient.

Nor should this business of allowing things to run for three generations and then shaking them up be taken literally. Waiting for three generations is just a useful illustrative means of showing how the frequency of traits can grow or fall relative to different domains. It is not being suggested that any actual population follows this "three generations, followed by regrouping" pattern. The important point is the tendency of the helpers to associate together, which follows directly from the dictum "Everyone loves a helper." Groups containing helpers will outperform groups containing fewer or no helpers. And thus the helping trait—that is, indiscriminate, non-reciprocating helping—can develop. It is pedagogically useful to think of the multi-group model as involving, say, tribes in neighboring valleys, or mice living in separate haystacks, all of whom periodically come together to mate and form new groups, but it is just that: a useful picture. It can work just as easily in a population that to all appearances is one big group, so long as we allow that within that group the helpers are tending to associate together.

Are the helpers being described here really sacrificing their fitness? That would be the equivalent of genuinely "altruistic genes"—to stand in contrast to Richard Dawkins's famous metaphor. We saw that in the case of direct reciprocal helping the fitness sacrifice was only apparent. The big fish of the coral reef sacrifices a free meal, but only because it gets a valuable long-term payback (ongoing freedom from parasites). The helpers we are now considering really do seem to be giving up some reproductive fitness: They have a trait of advancing the reproductive interests of others at the expense of their own fitness. In the original group B (90 non-helpers with a fitness of 1.1, plus 10 helpers with a fitness of 1.0), who has the higher starting fitness? The non-helpers. Now let's take the benefits that those 10 helpers have to offer and distribute them among the group. On average, the helpers' fitness will rise to 1.4, while the non-helpers' will rise to 1.5. It still pays to be unhelpful.

The only way to calculate the numbers such that being a helper actually turns out to *increase* the individual's fitness is to include group A in our figuring. When we look at the fitness of the average helper across *both* groups, then we see that it is 1.4 compared to the non-helpers' average fitness of 1.28. But this, it has been argued, is not the pertinent calculation. Sober and Wilson refer to this as an instance of "the averaging fallacy." Their main concern is that focusing on the global calculation in order to determine fitness obscures the dynamics of the processes that are really at the heart of selection. If we ignore the fact that there are two groups growing at different rates, and instead just said there is one big group of 200 individuals, 10 of whom have a fitness of 1.4 and 190 of whom have a fitness of 1.28, we have lost sight of what *explains* these figures. What explains them is that the former 10 individuals are distributing a benefit that is available to 90 of the latter individuals (plus themselves) and unavailable to the other 100.

It seems that the only judicious conclusions are (1) that in one sense these helpers are genuinely fitness sacrificing but in another sense they aren't and (2) that there is an argument is favor of the greater explanatory productiveness of the former perspective. I am willing to end with this somewhat uncommitted view on the matter, since the existence of genuinely fitness-sacrificing traits is not necessary to this project. What is important is that *helping* behaviors have been selected for, and the multi-group approach provides a further model for how that might occur.

We have now seen how this multi-group model might allow non-discriminating helpfulness to develop. Clearly, if we were to run the same multi-group model with *discriminating* helpfulness, then helpful behavior would develop all the more easily. The values assigned to helpfulness can be such that the dynamics of a group-structured population alone will be insufficient for its development, whereas if we make the helpfulness a little discriminating (e.g., such individuals are reluctant to help the unhelpful) then the trait will evolve. In other words, there exist circumstances in which group selection and reciprocity together may lead to a degree of helpfulness that either process alone could not produce. We need not see them as exclusive alternatives.

There is a stronger sense in which reciprocity and group selection might not be alternatives: namely, if reciprocity just *is* a form of group selection. Sober and Wilson would object, I think, to the way I have structured the preceding few sections, since they would argue that kin selection, mutualism, and reciprocity should all be subsumed under group selection. Before moving on, I should briefly say something to defend my taxonomy on this score.

Consider direct reciprocal altruism. Sober and Wilson argue that the relevant notion of a group constituting a vehicle of selection is a *trait group*—a population of n individuals (where $n > 1$) "that influence each other's fitness with respect to a certain trait but not the fitness of those outside the group" (1998: 92ff.). On this basis, they conclude that reciprocal altruism is really just a special form of group selection, involving a group of two. But Kim Sterelny (1996) has argued plausibly that there is a difference *in kind* between groups that satisfy the above criterion (including partners in reciprocal exchanges) and the "superorganisms" often used as paradigmatic examples of group selection (including especially colonies of social insects). Examples of the latter category exhibit an extreme degree of cohesion and integration, their members share a common fate, and such groups possess adaptations that cannot be equivalently re-described at the individual level (e.g., the tendency of newly hatched queens to kill their sisters). Such groups have as respectable a claim to being robustly objective vehicles of selection as do organisms. Concerning examples of the former category, by contrast, the decision to describe selection as occurring at the level of the group is a purely optional one, for this group-level description is equivalent to an individual-level description. Regarding this category, Sterelny (following Dugatkin and Reeve 1994) advocates a pluralistic approach, where the only difference between preferring individuals or trait groups as the vehicle of selection—that is, of regarding the process as one of individual selection or group selection—is a heuristic one, depending "on our explanatory and predictive interests" (1996: 572).

Going along with Sterelny, I am willing to concede that, on a certain liberal understanding of what it takes to be a group, reciprocal relations may count as group selected, or they can be equivalently described in terms of individual selection. Any debate on the matter, says John Maynard Smith, is not "about what the world is like . . . [but] is largely semantic, and could not be settled by observation" (1998: 639). But it is clear that there is a kind of group selective process which they are *not* an example of: what Sterelny calls "superorganism selection" (1996: 577). One could argue that human cooperative faculties (e.g., morality) are the product of superorganism selection, or one might instead argue that they may be explained by invoking only, say, reciprocity. These are quite distinct hypotheses, and it cannot be reasonably denied that if we were unable to distinguish between them due to a methodological decision to lump reciprocity (along with kin selection) under the umbrella term of "group selection" this would be an unacceptable loss of explanatory detail in the service of theoretic unification.

1.7 The Evolution of Human Ultra-Sociality

I have reviewed four processes whereby traits of helpfulness can develop by the forces of biological natural selection: kin selection, mutualism, reciprocal exchanges (both direct and indirect), and group selection. The biologist Lee Dugatkin (1999) has called these "the four paths to cooperation"; they are almost certainly the most important processes by which traits of helpfulness evolve in the animal world, though we should be open to the possibility of others (e.g., Connor 1995; see also Sachs et al. 2004). However, it is not at all clear that these processes alone can account for the ultra-sociality that is characteristic of human life. It is not unreasonable to view human social complexity as having more in common with the cooperative life of social insects than with the small-scale groupishness of our closest primate cousins. Yet unlike the Hymenoptera, whose traits of extreme helpfulness appear to be due to unusual genetic relations, an important part of the explanation of human ultra-sociality is surely our unique capacity to transmit masses of adaptive cultural information in a cumulative way. Though the kinds of reciprocity I have discussed almost certainly have played a major role in human ancestry, and have left their marks on the human mind, available models (Boyd and Richerson 1988, 1989, 1992) suggest that they will work only for relatively small groups: something along the lines of a chimpanzee troop. This is not a problem for the hypothesis of this book, for it is quite possible that morality evolved when our ancestors were still in relatively small bands. However, insofar as this chapter has the more general aim of outlining processes that can lead to helpfulness, any discussion is incomplete to the extent that it fails to explain human ultra-sociality.

The apparent fact that reciprocity alone cannot explain large-scale helpfulness isn't altered even if we factor in the possibility of punishing non-reciprocators, since doing so leaves us with the question of why those administering the punishments don't lose out in the evolutionary struggle to "easy-going reciprocators": those who reciprocate but aren't willing to expend energy on punishing others. Sober and Wilson appeal to group selection to explain how punishing traits evolve: A group of punishers may outperform a group of easy-going reciprocators. One might wonder why their model need invoke punishment at all. Couldn't group selection just directly produce reciprocal helpfulness? Answer: It *could*, but it is much more likely that group selection will produce helpfulness via punishing traits than that it will produce them directly. The reason for this is that, although administering punishment generally costs the administrator something, typically it doesn't cost her much (proportional to the group benefit provided). Suppose you own a small business and someone comes in one day and asks you to give him 20 percent of your monthly earnings. That's quite a sacrifice. But if the penalty of forfeiture is death, then handing over the 20 percent is the prudent thing to do. Now compare your sacrifice with how much it costs the racketeer to create a credible threat of penalty. Perhaps all he need do is occasionally drive slowly past your house in a menacing manner.

When a fitness-sacrificing trait evolves by group selection, it is always as a result of winning a competition: The forces of individual fitness advancement tug in one direction, the forces of group-benefiting fitness sacrifice in the other. A major contribution of Sober and Wilson's work is to show how the former forces need not always win. But obviously the fitness-sacrificing forces are more likely to win when the fitness-advancing forces are smaller; in other words, behaviors that benefit the group but cost the individual a great deal are less likely to evolve than comparable traits that cost the individual less. And if the punishment is the withdrawal of social esteem (McAdams 1997), which can be distributed or denied like a magical substance, or exclusion from ongoing beneficial exchanges (Panchanathan and Boyd 2004), then punishment can often be meted out at no cost.

However, though no one believes that genetic group selection is impossible, it is questionable how large a role it played in human ancestry. The main hindrance is the degree to which group membership affects mating choices. Two tribes of humans may be in intense competition, but any allowance of intermarriage or migration between the tribes will count against the likelihood that group selection is taking place at the genetic level. Even if the two tribes participate in all-out warfare, so long as the result of victory is the taking of the women of the conquered tribe, or the assimilation of the survivors, then genetic selection is militated against.

But group selection need not occur at the genetic level. Bear in mind that natural selection is not concerned essentially with genes at all. Darwin articulated the theory beautifully while remaining utterly ignorant of genetics. So long as there is trait variation, heritability, and trait-dependent differential reproduction, then there is selection. (See Lewontin 1970.) (If this selection is guided by purposeful design, it is artificial selection; otherwise it is natural selection.) There is nothing in the theory that says that the traits in question must be genetically encoded, or that the reproducing entities must be individual organisms. Learned cultural practices may result in trait variation among groups, may be transmitted between groups, and may affect the persistence and proliferation of groups; thus *cultural* group selection may occur in circumstances that are not conducive to genetic group selection.[21]

In order for group selection to occur, there must be a degree of uniformity within groups and a degree of variability between groups. Though it is not impossible that these criteria may be satisfied at the genetic level, such widespread phenomena as migration and intermarriage present obstacles to their actual satisfaction. These criteria seem much more plausibly satisfied at the cultural level. The anthropologists Joe Henrich and Robert Boyd (1998) show how having a tendency to conform one's behavior to that of the majority of one's group can be adaptive in a variable environment, since it allows reliable and efficient access to those behaviors that are likely to be successful in the immediate environment. (See also Boyd and Richerson 1985.) Copying the successful, or (what will tend to amount to the same thing) copying the majority, can allow individuals to "short-cut the costs of individual learning and experimentation, and leapfrog directly to adaptive behaviors" (Henrich and Boyd 2001: 80). Thus, Henrich and Boyd hypothesize that genetic evolution has produced in humans psychological mechanisms that support conformist transmission, and, further, that this trait lies at the heart of humans' unique cumulative culture. Especially when coupled with traits pertaining to the employment of punishment strategies, conformist transmission explains how within-group cultural variation may be suppressed while intergroup variation is enhanced. The thing about punishment, as we saw earlier, is that it can in principle fix just about any behavior in a group, even weird and seemingly maladaptive behaviors. But this is where cultural group selection may play an important role: Once there exists a meta-population of culturally distinct groups, there is selective pressure in favor of the persistence and proliferation of those cultural traits that are broadly "prosocial." A group whose cultural value system revolved around wearing a pumpkin on one's head would, on the whole and in the long run, lose out to a group that valued intragroup peacefulness and a degree of self-sacrifice for the welfare of one's fellows. This, then, is another theory explaining the evolution of helpfulness.

An important addition to this story of cultural group selection is that in creating cultures our ancestors enormously influenced the environmental niche within which they lived. There is no reason to doubt that as cultural group selection occurs genetic individual selection may be ongoing, and if this has been the case then the course of the latter process will have been highly influenced by the outcome of the former process. For instance, a cultural activity such as dairy farming may affect the genetic makeup of the population by favoring the trait of lactose tolerance. In West Africa the cultivation of yams led to the clearing of the rain forest, which resulted in more standing water, which allowed more mosquitoes to breed, and the consequent multiplication of the malarial risk magnifies the pressure in favor of the sickle-cell allele, which in its heterozygotic form gives protection against malaria (Durham 1991). It has even been hypothesized that the ancient cultural invention of cooking meant that less energy had to be expended on the human digestive system, making possible the explosive growth of the energy-hungry hominid brain (Aiello and Wheeler 1995). If this is correct, then it is not only true that our big brains made possible culture; it is also true that that culture made possible big brains.

In much the same way, if we allow that cultural group selection can produce a climate within which non-reciprocation will be punished, and perhaps also where a reluctance to punish non-reciprocators will be punished, and perhaps also where non-conformity to the majority will be punished, then we must allow that individuals within this environment may have new selective pressures upon them—pressures that did not exist before cultural evolution. Thus individual selection occurring at the genetic level could now produce psychological traits designed to enhance one's success in this environment where prosociality is so heavily rewarded. (See Henrich and Boyd 2001.) Individual genetic evolution and cultural group evolution may then engage in a positive feedback loop, producing not only highly social creatures but creatures whose ultra-sociality is to a significant extent genetically encoded.[22] Since humans are the only known organisms for whom significant cultural evolution occurs, this process of cultural-genetic coevolution is a special case among the explanations of animal helpfulness.

1.8 Conclusion and Preview

A great deal more could be said about all these evolutionary processes that favor the development of helpfulness, but a more detailed taxonomy is not my concern here. The question to which I now turn concerns natural selection's *means* of achieving helpfulness. Suppose that in a population of ancestral bees there is pressure in favor of additional helpfulness, and the explanation of this pressure is kin selection. Knowing that this is the source of the pressure doesn't tell us anything about *how* the additional helpfulness might be achieved. One thing we know is that natural selection can't achieve the result of a more helpful bee by magic; it must go to work on whatever mechanisms are already in place governing the organism's behavior, tweaking them or transforming them so as to encourage new or stronger helpful behaviors. For this reason, there is no general answer to the question of what means Mother Nature employs in order to achieve helpfulness, any more than there is one concerning the means by which organisms achieve locomotion. The mechanisms in place that determine the helping behaviors of bees are unlikely to bear much resemblance to those that ensure the helping behaviors of chimpanzees. The evolutionary *processes* that explain such helpful behaviors may be broadly the same (it may be kin selection in both cases, for example), but the *means* by which those processes achieve results are going to differ remarkably.

The thesis to be examined in the next three chapters is that among the means favored by natural selection in order to get humans helping each other is a "moral sense," by which I mean a faculty for making moral judgments. It is possible that such a mechanism may be the result of any of the processes outlined above, or any combination of them. My own judgment is that if there is such an innate faculty the process that most probably lies behind its emergence is indirect reciprocity, but it is not an objective of this book to advocate this hypothesis with any conviction. (I do, however, discuss the matter further in section 4.6. See also Joyce forthcoming c.) We have a prior and more pressing task to attend to, which will require us temporarily to put aside issues pertaining to evolution. Any attempt to understand how our ability to make moral judgments evolved will not get far if we lack a secure understanding of what a moral judgment is. (To neglect this would be like writing a book called *The Origins of Virtue* without any substantial discussion of what virtue is.) This is the purpose of the next chapter—though, for reasons that will unfold, the chapter will start out discussing kin selection and love.

2 | The Nature of Morality

2.1 Love in the Pleistocene

Though we remain ignorant of many of the details of the social life of our ancestors, there is one thing of which we can be certain: Even tens of millions of years ago, each was cared for as an infant. In the hominid line, the helplessness of infants is exacerbated by the combination of bipedalism and an enlarged brain. (In modern humans, two-thirds of neural growth has to occur post-natally, since there's only so much brain that will fit through a human pelvis.) And because our hominid ancestors were mammals, the infants were suckled. These obvious observations mean that we know that at least one kin member had to be intensely involved in the task of helping a newborn: the mother. To what extent fathers were also involved is something that might be argued over. If we assume that chimpanzees display a fair likeness to our very distant (5–7 million years ago) ancestors, we must conclude that at one time mothers bore the brunt of child raising, with fathers very much in the background. If we add the assumption that modern hunter-gatherer societies reflect the living arrangements of our more recent (say, 100,000 years ago) ancestors, we must conclude that at some point things changed so that "high male parental investment" became the better arrangement for maximizing fitness. (See Wright 1994.) This change probably had something to do with the move from an arboreal to a savannah-type habitat.

Thus, the unquestionable importance of the mother-child relation is sufficient for us to conclude without going to much trouble that kin selection was an important force in our heritage. That a partiality to kin is an element of human nature has been recognized by numerous thinkers. Hume writes:

Nature has given all animals a like prejudice in favour of their offspring. As soon as the helpless infant sees the light, though in every other eye it appears a despicable and miserable creature, it is regarded by its fond parent with the utmost affection, and is preferred to every other object, however perfect and accomplished. The passion alone, arising from the original structure of human nature, bestows a value on the most insignificant object. ((1742) 1987: 162–163)

And centuries earlier, the Stoics recognized an additional important point: that further affections can flow from this bond between parent and offspring. Cicero writes:

The Stoics consider it important to realize that parents' love for their children arises naturally. From this starting point we trace the development of all human society. . . . It would hardly be consistent for nature to wish us to procreate yet be indifferent as to whether we love our offspring. . . . Thus our impulse to love what we have generated is given by nature as manifestly as our aversion to pain. . . . This is also the source of the mutual and natural sympathy between humans. . . . Hence we are fitted by nature to form associations, assemblies and states. ((45 BC) 2001: 84–85)

A Darwinian might put this as follows: Since the neural mechanisms for regulating the mother-offspring bond were already present in the mammalian brain when our ancestors were still scurrying around on four legs, biological natural selection had something to tinker with in order to get us engaging further helping relationships. The theory of kin selection predicts that those further helping relationships will concern family members, and many studies suggest that the modern human brain does have in place more extensive proclivities for helping other family members.

Gift giving, for example, is found in all human societies. If kin selection and reciprocity were important explanatory processes, we would expect to find that gifts tend to be given to non-kin only in expectation of reciprocation, whereas those given to kin tend not to be. Marshall Sahlins's (1965) extensive review of the anthropological data revealed precisely this: a decisive relationship between the degree of relatedness of the recipient and the expectation of return for the gift. Susan Essock-Vitale and Michael McGuire (1980) surveyed a broad range of anthropological field studies (from the 1950s through the 1970s) with an eye to assessing their support for the following predictions: that kin will be given more unreciprocated help than non-kin, that kin will be given more help than non-kin (and close kin the most), that friendships will be reciprocal, that large and/or long-term gifts are more likely to come from kin, and that individuals needing extensive unreciprocated help will eventually be abandoned, first by non-kin, then by distant kin, and finally by kin. With few exceptions, the predictions were borne out. In a famous study, Martin Daly and Margo Wilson (1988) discovered a persistent difference, across many cultures, between murder rates among consanguineous family members and among affinal family members. Napoleon Chagnon and Paul Bugos (1979) showed that knowledge of the genetic relatedness of the participants would greatly improve one's chances of predicting who would take sides with whom in a complex Yanomamö physical conflict. It has even been shown that monozygotic twins are significantly more likely to enter into cooperative exchanges with each other (when playing prisoner's dilemma games) than dizygotic twins (Segal and Hershberger 1999). It would not be challenging to carry on presenting evidence in support of the hypothesis that humans have a strong, hard-wired "nepotistic" streak. (For further discussion, see chapter 3 of Barrett et al. 2002.)

If human reproductive fitness was enhanced by a proclivity for helping family members (the degree of help being roughly proportional to the degree of relatedness), what might the process of natural selection have done to our brains in order to accomplish this? An important part of the answer, I think, is clear, simple, and rather agreeable: love. Mothers and fathers love their children, siblings love their siblings, uncles and aunts love their nieces and nephews, and so on. We could argue endlessly over what species of thing love really is, but let's just plump for the natural answer and say that it is (perhaps among other things) an emotion.

One thing must be made clear here: Although the love that is explained by kin selection may be highly choosy, it does not follow that it need be anything other than sincere, non-instrumental, and genuinely other-regarding. As an illustration, just compare it with sexual love. If Amy is an uncomplicated heterosexual, then there is a certain kind of love that she will have only for men; women just don't do it for her. Despite this conditionality, there is no reason to assume that Amy's love for her boyfriend suffers from the vice of really being self-oriented (i.e., psychologically selfish). At the risk of being repetitive, I'll also reiterate a point I made earlier: The possibility that love (say, a father's love for his child) might be given an evolutionary explanation of the kind just provided does not imply that the father's love is "really selfish" on the grounds that it is motivated by an unconscious desire to optimize his own inclusive fitness. Human fathers do not typically have unconscious motivations concerning their inclusive fitness any more than mollusk fathers do. To be ignorant of an element of the explanation of why you are feeling love—to be ignorant of the evolutionary ancestry of the emotion, for example—is not to be mistaken about the true object of your emotion, and is not in any sense to be self-deceived.

Not only is it *possible* that discriminating love be psychologically altruistic, but there is good reason to think that this would be much the better scheme upon which natural selection would alight, at least as far as kin selection goes. A non-altruistic love (if that isn't an oxymoron) would consist of a person caring about the interests of the beloved only derivatively, because the other's welfare contributes to her own well-being, which is what ultimately motivates her. (An economist might say that the welfare of the beloved is a term in the utility function of the lover.) One of the most interesting features of kin selection, however, is that it can favor helping behaviors where the interests of the individual are compromised or sacrificed for the sake of the welfare of her kin, with a zero probability of reciprocation. A love that was ultimately centered on the self simply couldn't support such sacrifice. A love that *could* work in this respect would be one that was ultimately centered on one's genes—imagine that humans had been designed to have deliberations that really did concern their inclusive fitness, and were blessed with a faculty that calculated according to Hamilton's Rule and activated motivations accordingly. But no one seriously believes this; the proposal that we have the concept *gene* hard-wired into us is clearly absurd. How would such a wonderful thing evolve? If natural selection wants to get people acting for the sake of their genes, and employs the emotion of love as a proximate mechanism to achieve this, then gene-directed love is not feasible, and self-directed love (though no doubt important) is not going to generate the kinds of self-sacrificing behavior that the maximization of inclusive fitness may call for. When some of the genes that matter reside in other individuals (one's kin, in particular), the natural solution is to create a (discriminating and conditional) non-derivative, other-directed love. (See Kitcher 1998, 2005.)

All the empirical evidence shows that humans are often motivated by genuine regard for others, and not ultimately by selfish motives (Pilliavin and Charng 1990; Batson 1991, 2000; Ray 1998). Perhaps surprisingly, some of this evidence comes from observations of how humans are willing to punish transgressors even at material cost to themselves—and even when they are unaffected observers of the transgression (Fehr and Fischbacher 2004; Knutson 2004; Carpenter et al. 2004). The opposing view seems to me (if an ad hominem comment may be excused) to be generally motivated by a certain cynical attitude about human behavior, and is not based on any real empirical foundation. Yes, of course humans are frequently conniving, self-centered, self-deceived and despicable creatures—we can all agree to that—but it would be a mistake to express that sentiment by seriously advocating the universal psychological thesis that *all* human actions are guided by an internal profit-hungry homunculus. There is no a priori reason for preferring the claim and there is no empirical evidence in its favor; quite the contrary.

Once the neurological mechanisms are in place for such altruistic emotions and motivations, biological natural selection may fiddle with them in order to press them into new service. For example, the capacity for loving one's kin might be exploited to create a capacity for loving certain classes of non-kin. Romantic love may be the result of this, bonding parents and (to take what is perhaps a more cynical view) motivating an adaptive spot of adultery (Griffiths 1997: 119). It used to be fashionable to claim that romantic love was an invention of medieval Europe; a nineteenth-century art critic, Henry Finck (1887), even dated its advent to May 1, 1274, when the young Dante fell head over heels for Beatrice. Though a noteworthy cultural elaboration of love certainly took place in medieval Europe, romantic love in a more general sense has probably been around for tens of thousands of years, contra La Rochefoucauld's mischievous claim that hardly anyone would fall in love if they hadn't first read about it. The most comprehensive cross-cultural study to date found romantic love in 89 percent of societies, with the researchers concluding that the remainder probably experienced it but didn't talk about it sufficiently to gain the anthropologist's notice (Jankowiak and Fisher 1992; see also Jankowiak 1995). It is likely that in creating the capacity for romantic love natural selection exploited neural mechanisms that were already in place for other prosocial motivations. (I have already commented on the role of oxytocin; see section 1.2.)

Why am I discussing kin selection and love? I want to establish—and I take it that the above discussion has sufficed for this—that in kin selection we have a quick and easy, empirically supported, evolutionary explanation for why humans might have "prosocial emotions" (e.g., love) toward certain others: emotions that provide the motivation for helping behaviors. But what I really want to emphasize here is how far this answer falls short of explaining *morality*. It is not just the nepotistic choosiness of kin-selected helping that is the problem, for, as was mentioned, the process of kin selection can explain altruistic helpfulness toward non-kin. Forget about the kin/non-kin aspect of the question for a moment; that's not the issue. Suppose that we additionally appeal to mutualism or group selection and as a result can provide a cogent evolutionary explanation for a range of human prosocial emotions (love, sympathy, altruism) that extend generally, perhaps even universally, to our fellows. Many theorists seem willing to conclude that we would thereby have found the origin of human morality, that we could on such grounds declare that morality is part of human nature. I am keen to emphasize how mistaken this would be.

2.2 Inhibitions vs. Prohibitions

A few days ago I visited a friend's home for lunch. He served a rather large meal, and as I was nearing the end he said "Don't feel obliged to finish it all." I replied (tucking in) "No, I don't; I really *want* to." This simplest of familiar exchanges underlines an important point that, despite being obvious, is often overlooked: To do something because you *want* to do it is very different from doing it because you judge that you *ought* to do it.[1] We can easily imagine a community of people all of whom have the same desires: They all want to live in peace and harmony, and violence is unheard of. Everywhere you look there are friendly, loving people, oozing prosocial emotions. However, there is no reason to think that there is a moral judgment in sight. These imaginary beings have *inhibitions* against killing, stealing, etc. They wouldn't dream of doing such things; they just don't want to do them. But we need not credit them with a conception of a *prohibition*: the idea that one shouldn't kill or steal because to do so is wrong. And moral judgments require, among other things, the capacity to understand prohibitions.

This point must not be confused with one famously endorsed by Immanuel Kant: that actions motivated by prosocial emotions cannot be considered morally admirable (Kant (1783) 2002: 199–200). I am more than happy to side with common sense against Kant on this point. We often morally praise people whose actions are motivated by love, sympathy, and altruism. In fact, I am willing to endorse the view that on occasions a person whose motivations derive from explicit moral calculation rather than direct sympathy is manifesting a kind of moral vice. So it is not being denied that the imaginary beings described above deserve our moral praise, or even that they are, in some sense of the word, morally virtuous. My point is the far less controversial one that someone who acts solely from the motive of love or altruism *does not thereby make a moral judgment* (assuming, as seems safe, that these emotions do not necessarily involve such judgments). If, then, our object is to investigate whether it is part of human nature to make moral judgments—to think about each other and the world in moral terms—we must conclude that an explanation of how natural selection might end up making human beings with altruistic, sympathetic, loving tendencies toward each other—how, that is, it might produce *nice* humans (or, if you prefer, *virtuous* humans)—misses the target. Claiming that humans "by nature have a moral sense" but then giving evidence only that our ancestors acted in ways that may be considered (by us) morally laudable, is like claiming that humans by nature have a native arithmetical ability and then giving as evidence the fact that our ancestors grew ten fingers.

In drawing attention to this fact I do not mean to imply that sympathy and other social emotions are not important to our moral lives; indeed, as we shall see in due course, emotions are of central significance to human morality. Moreover, I have no particular objection to using the label "moral sentiments" for the prosocial emotions of love, sympathy and altruism, or to using the label "moral virtues" for the prosocial behaviors that might flow from such emotions (though in the philosophical tradition a moral virtue is a lot more than this); but this concession must include the caveat that the capacity for moral judgment is not necessary for such moral sentiments or such moral virtues. Of course, these moral sentiments are very often accompanied by moral judgments: When you love someone, typically you judge that it would be morally wrong for you to hurt that person. But the judgment is not a necessary part of the emotion, for we can easily imagine an individual who satisfies the criteria for loving another (and simply doesn't want to cause harm) but lacks any sense of obligation to refrain from causing harm. The nature of emotions will be discussed in much more detail in the next chapter. Here, all that is being emphasized is that an explanation of how humans came to have prosocial inclinations and aversions—whether grounded in love and sympathy or anger and disgust—is not an explanation of how humans came to judge things morally right and wrong, and to this extent is no explanation of an innate moral faculty. At best it is the start of an explanation.

2.3 What Is a Moral Judgment?

I have made much of the fact that "merely wanting" to help your fellows (or "merely wanting" to see those who fail to help your fellows suffer harm) in and of itself involves no moral judgment. So now we must face the question squarely: What is a moral judgment? What is it for one's resolve to refrain from doing something to be guided by a judgment that it is prohibited, as opposed to having a non-moralized inhibition against it? We don't need a complete *conceptual* account of a moral judgment (we don't need to be able to pick out moral judgments on any possible world), for it is enough for the project of this book that we know the behavioral consequences of moral thinking. But nevertheless we do need to do some work in order to identify our quarry, or else we will suffer from the ignorance (described by

Socrates in Plato's *Meno*) of being incapable of discussing the matter in any useful way because we have no stable handle on our subject matter:

Meno: Can you tell me, Socrates, whether virtue is acquired by teaching or by practice; or if neither by teaching nor practice, then whether it comes to man by nature, or in what other way?

Socrates: . . . You have far too good an opinion of me if you think that I can answer your question. For I literally do not know what virtue is, and much less whether it is acquired by teaching or not.

Socrates' avowals of ignorance are not always ingenuous, and we may feel the same is true here; surely we all know what a moral judgment is? But I submit that the matter is extremely complex, and I know from experience that almost anything specific one says on the subject will meet with howls of complaint. There are numerous cases—both real and imaginary—where ordinary people and philosophers alike are uncertain whether a moral judgment has even occurred (if, for example, a psychopath assents to "Stealing is wrong" but has no motivation whatsoever to comply). Philosophers cannot even agree on what *kind* of thing a moral judgment is. Some will insist that it is a type of mental event, others that it is a species of linguistic utterance. Perhaps on this point it is safest to go with the vernacular and allow that it can be either. But even when we focus on moral judgments as utterances, disagreement reigns. What kind of utterance is a moral judgment? Some philosophers say that moral judgments express commands; some say that they are ways in which we evince our feelings. Others claim that moral judgments report facts. But what kind of facts? Some answer that moral judgments report facts about the speaker, or facts that concern the speaker's culture, or facts that concern God's commands; others—moral realists—hold that moral judgments report mind-independent objective facts. And what kind of mind-independent facts? There are many options. The field of metaethics—which undertakes the unenviable task of trying to decide among these competing views—can be bewildering.

Obviously it is not necessary to settle all such disputes here—a good thing, since attempting to do so would fill up a book that has many other concerns. But there are certain theoretical options that I wish to exclude—"pure non-cognitivism" being the prominent one—and there are features of moral judgments that I consider it important to underscore at some length so that we don't confuse them with other sorts of evaluative judgments. These tasks will occupy the remainder of the present chapter. I will discuss moral emotions in chapter 3, after which I will return to issues concerning evolution.

When we think of moral judgments as a kind of public utterance, the question upon which the above metaethical views diverge is "What kind of mental state do moral judgments express?" We must take some care to understand what is meant by "express" in this question. We are not asking what kind of mental state *causes* a moral utterance. It is true that sometimes, regarding other matters, we mean "express" in this way. If we say that by kicking over her brother's sand castle Emily expressed her anger, we may mean that anger caused her action or that it is an important element in an adequate explanation of the action. If it turns out that Emily in fact isn't angry at all, we will have to reject this explanation. But often "express" is used differently. When Emily later apologizes for kicking over the sand castle, she expresses regret. Suppose, though, that Emily's apology is insincere, in the sense that she has not a glimmer of regret for what she did. This doesn't change the fact that she apologized. An insincere apology still succeeds in being an apology (just as an insincere promise is still a promise, and an insincere assertion is still an assertion). Nor does insincerity change the fact that Emily thereby expressed regret, for an apology *is* an expression of regret. Here "express" does not denote an explanatory or causal relation holding between Emily and her mental states; rather, it indicates a much more complex relation holding between Emily, her brother, and a range of linguistic conventions according to which when a person utters "I'm sorry" in the appropriate circumstances then she has (among other things) *expressed regret*.[2] Thus it is perfectly possible that one can express regret over something when in fact one has no regret at all. This shows that the expression relation cannot be a causal or explanatory one, but is, rather, a matter of linguistic convention.

Pure non-cognitivism is the view that moral judgments (as utterances) do not express beliefs but rather perform some other kind of speech act. When presented as a semantic thesis, non-cognitivism states that the evaluative predicates (". . . is wrong," ". . . is good," etc.) are predicates only in the grammatical sense; below the surface—when we get to the "real meaning" of a moral judgment—the predicate disappears. The non-cognitivist A. J. Ayer famously claimed in the 1930s that the judgment "Stealing money is wrong" does not express a proposition that can be true or false, but rather it is as if one were to say "Stealing money!!" with the tone of voice (or exclamation marks, if it is written) indicating that a special feeling of disapproval is being expressed (Ayer (1936) 1971: 110). My own view is that there is something right about non-cognitivism, but that when presented in its pure form it is far too extreme. Compare, for example, what it means to describe someone as "a kraut" as opposed to describing someone as "a

German." To say "Hans is a German" is to describe Hans as having a certain nationality. To say "Hans is a kraut" is both to describe Hans as having that nationality and to express a derogatory attitude. The contemptuous attitude of someone who uses the word "kraut" is not merely an expectation that interlocutors will have formed on the basis of past observation; it is, rather, a firmly entrenched convention surrounding the word—someone who didn't know that it was a contempt-expressing term could reasonably be said not to understand the term properly at all, even if able competently to apply it to all and only German people. Now, it is clear that asserting "Hans is a kraut" is not equivalent merely to saying "Hans!!" in a scoffing, scornful tone making clear one's contemptuous attitude toward him, for (i) one is also expressing the belief that Hans is German and (ii) one is expressing scorn not just for Hans but for a national group. An Ayer-type interpretation of the predicate ". . . is a kraut" is therefore not at all plausible, which leads one to wonder whether it might be implausible for moral predicates for exactly the same reason. Perhaps when we say "Stealing money is wrong" we are *both* asserting something about stealing money *and* expressing a conative acceptance of a standard that condemns the activity. (In choosing this way of articulating the conative element I am looking to Gibbard (1990).) This is the view that I support, having been persuaded by a simple argument.

On the understanding we now have of the expression relation, it is clear that if a type of sentence S, uttered in circumstances C, functions to express mental state M, we would expect that someone in C who utters a token of S should prompt confusion in her audience if she immediately added "but I don't have M."[3] If, then, we observe such confusion for some particular instantiations of S, C, and M, and no other obvious explanation of this confusion is forthcoming, we should take it as evidence that S functions to express M in C. Consider somebody saying the following in circumstances where "Sorry" alone would constitute a successful act of apology:

(1)   Sorry. But I don't regret it for a moment.

This would certainly prompt perplexity; it is, in the words of J. L. Austin, "a statement that fails to get by" (1971: 18). The addressee would not think that an apology had been properly given. It is not just that (1) "sounds odd," for so does the sentence pair "Sorry; but I have no intention to comb the goat" (uttered in circumstances where the relevance of goats is unapparent); all sorts of sentences "sound odd." But (1) is baffling in a very special way. The first sentence expresses a mental state and the second sentence reports a mental state—and the oddity arises because the expression and the report disagree. The second sentence seems to nullify the speech act that the first, uttered alone, would otherwise perform. G. E. Moore introduced us to the peculiarity of statements like "The cat is on the mat; but I don't believe it"—a phenomenon that has become known as *Moore's paradox*. It's called a paradox because although such sentence pairs contain no contradiction (it is perfectly possible that the cat be on the mat while I don't believe it), to *state* the whole is to void the speech act of the first part, leaving the listener confused as to what should be assumed about the speaker's attitude toward the cat being on the mat. It makes "a peculiar kind of nonsense" (Austin (1970) 1990: 112). The following are, I think, instances of the same phenomenon:

(2) Hans is a kraut. But I have no contempt toward Hans or the people of his nation.

(3) Thank you. But I have no gratitude to you.

We might be tempted to read "But I have no . . ." as retrospectively implementing a fictional context. If we heard someone utter one of these sentence pairs, we might, after a moment's hesitation, say "So you were only kidding when you called Hans a kraut?" (". . . when you thanked me?" etc.). This, though somewhat rough, strikes me as a useful observation. If "But I do not have mental state M" is sufficient to undermine the seriousness of what precedes it (that is, could sensibly be interpreted as proclaiming a fictional or joking context for what precedes it), then it seems reasonable to assume that what precedes it must function to express M. Let's try this for a couple of moral judgments.

(4) The Elgin Marbles ought to be returned to Greece. But I don't believe that they ought to be returned to Greece.

(5) Hitler was despicably evil. But I don't believe that he was despicably evil.

Someone who uttered either of these sentence pairs, in circumstances wherein had they not added the second comment they would have been naturally interpreted as having made a moral judgment, would, I think, prompt much the same response as someone who uttered (1), (2), or (3). Accordingly, the first sentence in either of (4) and (5) should, if uttered in circumstances wherein they would naturally be counted as moral judgments (i.e., not in a sarcastic tone of voice, not as part of a play, etc.), be considered an expression of belief—that is, as an assertion. This amounts to evidence against pure non-cognitivism. But now consider the following two sentence pairs:

(6) The Elgin Marbles morally ought to be returned to Greece. But I subscribe to no moral standard that commends their return to Greece.

(7) Hitler was despicably evil. But I subscribe to no moral standard that condemns his character or actions.

These sentence pairs certainly are odd and would be challenged if uttered, so in some sense they "fail to get by." I am cautiously tempted to diagnose their oddity as further instances of Moore's paradox, leading to the conclusion that moral judgments are assertions *but not merely assertions*, that they express both beliefs *and* conative states (e.g., subscription).

That we might be able to imagine circumstances in which a person intelligibly asserts (6) or (7) is irrelevant if we remain in doubt as to whether she made a moral judgment. We need to ask ourselves whether any such imaginative act involves us thinking of aberrant subgroups, or people speaking in a joking, playful manner, or the speaker using a sarcastic or ironic tone of voice, or using a moral term in a non-moral manner, or introducing a new convention by example, or a world with slightly different linguistic conventions than we actually do have. If the imaginative act involves any such feature, it is no counterexample to my claim. (The matter is more complicated than we should pursue here. For further discussion, see Copp 2001 and Joyce forthcoming a.) For example, there is little doubt that "slut" functions as a pejorative in English. Yet by introducing the overarching convention of joking—which may be achieved in an instant with a shift in tone or a twitch of an eyebrow—one might in a playful manner say to a close female friend "Oh, you're such a slut" with all offensiveness nullified. Yet this observation doesn't undermine the claim that there is a linguistic convention according to which "slut" expresses contempt. Even when used jokingly, "slut" continues to be a contempt-expressing term, for that, after all, is what makes the joking comment funny.

The view to which I subscribe, then, holds that moral judgments (as speech acts) express both beliefs and conative non-belief states. By insisting on the first conjunct, I am rejecting pure non-cognitivism, such as that espoused by Ayer. (Some further considerations in favor of this decision are given in the next section.) By insisting on the second conjunct, I am rejecting a pure form of cognitivism, according to which to say that someone is evil is simply to ascribe to him a property—like *being tall*, or *being Norwegian*—without thereby announcing how one feels about the person. I reject this option willingly, since it strikes me as clearly inadequate. To say that Mary is *morally bad* is not like making a neutral statement, such as "She took the book from the book shop without paying for it." In this latter statement one's attitude toward Mary is left uncommitted; it is possible that the speaker is an anarchist who heartily approves of shoplifting. But if the sentence "Mary is morally bad" is seriously put forward (not jokingly, not using "bad" in an aberrant way, etc.), then this option is closed off; we would know that the speaker disapproves of Mary.

Were we thinking of the expression relation as *causal*, this might seem an unattractive conclusion, since on this view any such "joint judgment" would have to flow from a kind of mental state with both belief-like and desire-like aspects—a "besire," to use a term coined by J. E. J. Altham (1986)—and an aversion to this psychology might lead one to reject the premise. But the realization that the relevant expression relation is non-causal allows us to see that no such conclusion follows. The fact that a kind of utterance may express belief *and* attitude implies nothing about the modal relations holding between the speaker's belief states and attitude states. This worry deflected, there seems nothing philosophically troubling in the idea of a linguistic convention that decrees that when S is uttered in C the speaker thereby expresses *two* mental states.[4]

This is a noteworthy conclusion, and the rejection of pure non-cognitivism in particular will reappear as a premise in later arguments. But it must not be thought that these observations succeed in cornering what is distinctive about moral judgments. Just how modest are the conclusions so far reached can be seen by pointing out that all that has been said about judging Hitler to be "evil" also holds for judging an old horse to be "a nag." Calling a horse "a nag" is an evaluation; there is a linguistic convention in English according to which it is a way of expressing an attitude of mild disdain toward the animal in question. But there is surely more to the practicality of moral judgments than just a linguistic arrangement whereby the choice of one predicate over another will allow us to express our attitudes as well as communicating what we believe. The apparent practical clout of morality must be more than a little linguistic trick.

2.4   The Practical Clout of Moral Judgments

We are still addressing the question "What is a moral judgment?" One important feature of moral judgments that must be underscored and discussed is the degree of *practical clout* that they often purport to have in our deliberations and interactions: Calling an action "morally correct" or "virtuous" or "wrong" or "just" is (putatively) to draw attention to a deliberative consideration that cannot be legitimately ignored or evaded.

But merely to "express one's feelings" about something, to communicate that one has an attitude, is not to put forward a *deliberative consideration* at all, as becomes apparent if we reflect on the fact that an expression of a feeling (e.g. "Yum!") can always be replaced by an assertive report that one has the feeling in question ("I am enjoying this food"). *Expressing* one's feelings and *reporting* one's feelings are different linguistic activities—on a roller coaster, screaming is not the same as stating calmly "I am feeling very excited now"—yet both provide one's audience with pretty much the same information about one's inner states. But simply to report the presence of a feeling is never, in itself, to provide one's audience with a practical consideration. Suppose that Roger is a vehement anti-hunting activist. As a group of fox hunters trot by, Roger asserts to them "Your activities arouse a feeling of disapproval in me." We could hardly fault the fox hunters if they responded with a perplexed "Yes, but so what?" But then much the same response would be reasonable if Roger, instead of reporting the presence of disapproval, *expressed* his disapproval by yelling "Boo to fox hunting!" If the former report didn't provide (or purport to provide) the hunters with a reason to stop hunting, neither will the latter expression, and it would be odd if Roger thought that it might. If moral judgments were nothing more than expressions of the speaker's conative attitudes, then they too would be equally irrelevant to others' deliberations (unless those others happened to care about the speaker's inner states). Yet—and this is the crux of the argument—we most certainly do *not* think of moral matters as practically irrelevant unless one happens to care about others. If Roger calls out "Fox hunting is morally wrong! Your actions are evil!" then he has purported to say something that demands consideration irrespective of the hunters' attitudes toward Roger. Needless to say, the fox hunters will probably trot on as unresponsively as before, because they think that Roger has said something false, but even if they disagree with Roger they will acknowledge that in articulating a moral judgment Roger is *purporting* to put forward a practical consideration of importance.[5] This is another mark against pure non-cognitivism.

So where does the practical clout of morality come from? It proves a lot easier to identify where it *doesn't* come from. For example, the applicability of a moral prescription does not typically depend on the punishment that may ensue if the action prescribed is not performed. Later in this chapter we will see that the concept of punishment has a very important role to play in a moral judgment, in that we generally think that a person who morally errs *deserves* to be punished. However, holding that moral misdemeanors deserve punishment is not to be confused with the thesis that the applicability of a moral judgment *depends on* the unpleasantness of punishment, or on the pleasantness of reward. To hold that the applicability of a moral judgment depends on potential punishment would be to hold that moral imperatives are pieces of advice, depending for their validity on an undesired consequence of not being heeded. The important feature of such practical advice is that if it turns out that the recipient of the advice wants to suffer the punishment, or has some special way of avoiding the usual punishment, then the "ought" statement must be retracted. Moral judgments do not appear to be like this. This isn't to deny that if we are trying to explain to someone why he shouldn't (say) break promises then the negative consequences that will befall him are likely to be among the first things we mention. We may even have a deeply entrenched and institutionalized cultural tradition of appealing to the punishments of an all-powerful divine entity in order to back up our moral judgments. But the fact that something may be morally contemptible *and* a bad idea on prudential grounds mustn't blind us to the real and important distinction here. When we say that it is morally wrong to break promises, we include people who don't care about suffering the consequences of such actions, we include people who broke promises and went to their graves unpunished (discounting for the moment the possibility of post-mortem punishment), we include people who might somehow stand a good chance of avoiding the usual penalties, and we include people who don't give a fig for morality. The "we" here is intended to be a pan-cultural, human "we." I would be astounded to hear of a culture whose members' practices revealed that they generally conceive of transgressions as wrong because they are punished, rather than punishable because they are wrong.

It will be widely agreed that moral judgments do not derive their applicability from external sanction, but there is a long-standing school of academic thought that holds that their applicability derives from internal sanction. According to such thinking, one who morally trespasses in some manner harms *himself*, and thus a moral judgment might be like a piece of advice on how to avoid such self-harm. There are a number of reasons for finding this view inadequate. For a start, despite thousands of years of trying, no convincing theory has ever been put forward regarding exactly what form this self-harm takes. One can simply state "One who practices vice thereby damages his soul," but without details and supporting evidence this amounts to nothing. To my mind, this tradition owes a great deal to the views of academic philosophers, and little to the moral practices of ordinary persons employing moral judgments in everyday life. Consider a case of a wrongdoer, Jack, who commits some kind of clear and obvious wrong—brutally harming people he has no business harming—such that members of his culture will not hesitate in affirming that he has seriously transgressed. It is surely grotesque to think that what is wrong with Jack's actions is the self-harm being generated. The wrongness of torture, for example, surely derives chiefly from the harm being inflicted on *others*! Moreover, this "self-harm view" falls apart in the face of the universal truism that if Jack's actions are sufficiently wicked then he deserves punishment for them—for what sense is there in the view that if a person suffers the unpleasantness of self-harm this warrants (or even demands) the infliction of further harm upon him? Again, I would be astonished if presented with any culture whose moral practices indicated that *self-harm* was the principal concern, and that harming others was only a derivative crime. It is possibly true that most moral transgressions do result in self-harm of one sort or another, but the fact that moral judgments remain in place even with self-harm subtracted (even if only in imagination), plus the fact that we are inclined to respond to transgressive self-harm by administering *more* harm, shows that the applicability of moral judgments does not depend on that self-harm.

The realization that moral judgments pertaining to action are typically not pieces of advice appears to amount to the view that they are typically categorical imperatives. This was Kant's term for a practical imperative that does not depend for its legitimacy on some goal aimed at by the subject of the prescription ((1783) 2002: 216). "Shut the window" will usually admit of an addendum (usually only tacit) along the lines of "if you want to keep warm." If the addressee turns out to lack that desire, then the imperative will usually be retracted. This is a hypothetical imperative. The moral judgment "Don't kill innocent people," by contrast, does not appear to depend on any end had by the person to whom it is addressed. A person cannot evade a moral imperative by citing unusual desires or aberrant goals. Someone who responded to the proscription against killing with "But I really enjoy killing innocent people—in fact, it's my main project in life" would *not* meet with the retraction "Oh . . . well . . . I guess that it's not the case that you ought not kill innocent people after all." Moral imperatives rarely depend on the goals of those to whom they are addressed. Even if, as a matter of fact, it is in our nature to have a certain end (as Kant thought, claiming that Mother Nature provides each of us with a desire for his or her own welfare ((1783) 2002: 217)), the hypothetical imperative advising us how to satisfy that end would still not have the kind of practical oomph we require of a moral imperative, for moral imperatives are not merely the ones that people *do not* evade by citing special goals, they are the ones that people *cannot* evade by citing special ends. This is what makes them *inescapable*.

I am not claiming that all moral judgments involve imperatives, or that all moral imperatives are categorical imperatives. I am just observing that categorical imperatives appear to be central to any moral system, to such a degree that if faced with an alien value system that had no place for evaluating actions in this manner we should have doubts whether it counts as a *moral* system at all. Kant's conception of a categorical imperative is laden with theoretical impedimenta, and represents a philosophical exposition of a concept already heavily elaborated within the Judeo-Christian cultural tradition, so in claiming that categorical imperatives appear in all moral systems I don't mean to import all the Kantian trappings. In emphasizing this I hope to assuage any who would protest that my giving pride of place to categorical imperatives is a projection of a certain modern and Western moral tradition onto morality simpliciter. My understanding of the notion is minimal: an imperative that does not recommend a means to an end. I don't see how anyone can seriously deny that moral imperatives frequently have this status, and I will make another confident anthropological claim that this is a cross-cultural phenomenon: All cultures recognize certain acts of harming others as wrong, but no culture thinks that the wrongness of all such acts depends upon a primary harm that the perpetrator does by frustrating his own ends. (And I caution strongly against taking the assertions of the moral philosophers of a culture as representative of that culture's actual moral commitments.)

In a 1972 article, the ethicist Philippa Foot drew attention to a kind of imperative (or "ought" sentence[6]) that appears to fall between the cracks of Kant's distinction. A rule of etiquette—e.g., "Do not speak with your mouth full"—is not withdrawn when it is revealed that the person to whom it is addressed cares nothing for etiquette. Irrespective of a person's feelings for etiquette, he or she ought not speak with a full mouth. It is important not to misread Foot on this point. She is not advocating the prudish view that etiquette must be followed irrespective of the situation. If you notice that your dinner companion is about to eat a wasp, and there is no time for you to swallow your own mouthful before she does so, then clearly the right thing to do is warn her, even if this means speaking with your mouth full. Foot's point is that the rule of etiquette doesn't "cease to be" in such a situation; it remains true, in some sense, that you ought not speak with your mouth full. This is seen by reflecting on the fact that it would be natural for you later to say "I had to violate etiquette in order to stop my friend being stung." The fact that you recognize that you *broke the rules* shows that "the rules" were still there, for if the rules ceased to hold in such situations, then you couldn't have broken them.

Foot hedges her bets by calling such rules "non-hypothetical imperatives," but by my minimal definition they count as categorical. Foot doesn't want to consider them as full-blown categorical imperatives, because they lack the practical oomph with which categorical imperatives are usually imbued. Here is a good place to introduce some clarifying terminology from David Brink (1997). Moral *inescapability* is the quality had by categorical imperatives (including institutional rules, such as etiquette): of being legitimately applied to a person irrespective of her ends. But many moral philosophers (with Kant leading the charge) have wanted more from moral imperatives—some extra practical oomph that distinguishes them logically from etiquette. They have wanted moral *authority*. Let us say (as a first approximation) that an imperative has authority if the subject would be irrational in ignoring it, or at least the subject has a reason of genuine deliberative weight to comply. Moral normativity, it might be thought, has both inescapability and authority. Lacking a word for this conjunction, let me decree that a normative system enjoying both features has *practical clout*.[7] (From here on I will use these as terms of art; though perhaps I should add that the term "oomph" will remain in a usefully vague and vernacular role. That morality has practical oomph is a simple observation; whether that oomph should be cashed out as *clout* is a philosophical problem.)

Moral authority is a philosophically controversial topic (though those opposed to it often confusedly express this as a hostility toward the doctrine of moral categoricity instead), but I must confess to having a lot of sympathy with the Kantian intuition that there is *some* kind of extra authority in addition to inescapability with which we typically imbue our moral claims (though whether any defensible sense can be made of this authority is another matter entirely). The intuition can be motivated by considering just how wimpy categorical imperatives (inescapable normativity) can be. Suppose that some strange cult in Idaho believes that everyone ought to dye their hair purple. This isn't, let me stipulate, a piece of advice; they aren't saying that we ought to do this in order to avoid the wrath of the Great Purple Lizard God or whatever. Rather, it is, like etiquette, just a set of rules that is applied to people irrespective of whether they care. If you were to say to one of these cult members "I'm not going to dye my hair because I don't care about your silly cult," he might reply "There is nothing in the rules about their depending on whether you care about them; you simply must dye your hair purple." It is obvious that you would (and should) remain unmoved. You need not *deny* that the cult rules demand that you dye your hair purple; it's just that the weight that this imperative carries in your practical deliberations is proportional to your independent interest in following the cult rules in general: zero.

We do not, I suggest, think of moral requirements as like this. No human culture allows the authority of its moral rules to be so easily shrugged off. Now, it is possible that, despite this observation, moral imperatives really are just a species of Foot's non-hypothetical (i.e., inescapable but non-authoritative) imperative, but we're all just too deeply embedded within the "morality cult" to recognize this (for presumably the cult members from Idaho will also not agree that you are free to opt out from their normative system). But the price of accepting this is to acknowledge that the authority of morality is an illusion, that people who genuinely don't care about it are as a matter of fact as legitimately free to ignore it as we are all free to ignore cult members telling us to dye our hair purple, that if we were able to see things as they really stand we'd recognize that it may be perfectly reasonable for a person to scoff "Morality, schmorality!" Insofar as we are motivated to avoid this conclusion (even if this motivation is just the result of our being immersed within a particular normative framework), we are motivated to try to make some sense of moral clout.

Whatever kind of practical oomph moral prescriptions are imbued with, it doesn't have its source in internal or external sanctions, nor in some institution's inviolable rules, nor in the desires or goals of the person to whom it is addressed. In this respect ordinary thought distinguishes moral requirements from conventional and prudential requirements. (There is a large body of empirical evidence, to be discussed in chapter 4, demonstrating that even very young children make these distinctions.) This is not to say that the distinction must be crisp and simple; I'm sure it is a vague and multifaceted distinction but an important one nevertheless. And to complicate things further, many actions are judged to be prescribed or proscribed both morally *and* by human convention—indeed, a person may judge herself to be morally required to respect some conventional framework (e.g., judge that it is morally correct to obey the law, in which case she may see driving on the right-hand side of the road as morally required)—so in many cases it may be hard to tease them apart.

As admitted above, it may be that as a matter of fact morality is just a matter of human convention; the point is that this is not how we think of it (when we are "within it," so to speak); we think of it as having a convention-transcendent practical clout. How exactly this clout is ultimately to be cashed out is a philosophical problem stretching back to Plato, and no doubt beyond. At present we are not trying to defend it or provide a theory that accounts for it, but are simply acknowledging its presence in a moral judgment in an attempt to understand the basic features of these judgments. The whole issue of moral authority, and whether it can be accommodated in a naturalistic framework, is something we will return to much later in this book.

2.5 The Subject Matter of Moral Judgments

By the "subject matter" of moral judgments I mean the range of things to which moral predicates can be sensibly applied. Are there constraints regarding this? One kind of possible constraint would be that in order for a value system to count as a *moral* system, some particular predicate(s) must be applied to some particular subject(s). For example, it might be held that any value system that failed to endorse "Infanticide is wrong" simply wouldn't be a moral framework. A weaker kind of possible constraint would be that in order for a value system to count as a moral system, the predicates must range over a certain *type* of subject matter. For example, it might be held that if a value system endorsed only prescriptions concerning footwear, then it simply wouldn't be a moral framework. Philippa Foot once claimed that to regard a person as bad merely on the grounds that he runs around trees in a particular direction, or watches hedgehogs by the light of the moon, is not to have evaluated him from a *moral* point of view; it's just the wrong *kind* of thing to be morally bad (Foot 1958: 512). Against this, anthropologists have reported finding some pretty surprising things condemned in what appears to be a moral way: The Semang of Malaysia judge it sinful to comb one's hair during a thunderstorm, or to throw a spear in the morning (Murdock 1980: 89).

I am not confident that there are any constraints of the first sort, for the reason that much and perhaps all of morality can be disputed. If it were to be claimed that, say, a proscription against infanticide is a necessary feature of any moral system, then this would exclude the very possibility of having a moral debate over the permissibility of infanticide. It is important that our arguments not be infected with parochialism; throughout history, many communities that have found infanticide, at least in certain circumstances, to be an acceptable (and in some circumstances obligatory) behavior. I am not claiming that the views of such cultures are just as "valid" as our own; for all that is being said, views permitting infanticide may be completely false and pernicious. All that is being claimed is that they at least count as false and pernicious *moral* views. We would only hamper our understanding if we insisted, as a way of underlining our own moral view that infanticide is intolerable, that such value systems don't even deserve to be considered "moral." (This said, I am not excluding the possibility of there being constraints of this sort, but I wouldn't wish to suggest what they might be.)

Regarding the second kind of constraint I am willing to be somewhat more bold. We can start by noting the kinds of things to which moral predicates are typically applied. First, they are applied most naturally to *actions* and *persons*. We morally assess both particular actions ("Your lying to your mother last Thursday was mean") and general action types ("Lying for self-gain is wrong"). We also appear to assess persons in both the particular and general, though arguably when we evaluate persons in the general ("All liars are wicked") it is a character trait or a type of action that is really being assessed. More contentiously, we appear sometimes to morally assess *states of affairs*: "A world with no slavery therein is a morally better place than a world with slavery." I am not insisting that these three categories are exhaustive. We may describe a belief as pernicious, or an artwork as morally debauched. We might describe an institution, a law, or a whole society, as corrupt. Certain cultures have employed a concept that we might call "moral pollution": a quality that can reside in ordinary *objects* or *places*, passing contagiously to anyone who encounters them.

Despite an apparent abundance of kinds of things to which moral predicates are sensibly applied, it seems that certain generalizations can be drawn. A number of comprehensive cross-cultural studies have unanimously found certain broad universals in moral systems: (1) negative appraisals of certain acts of harming others, (2) values pertaining to reciprocity and fairness, (3) requirements concerning behaving in a manner befitting one's status relative to a social hierarchy, and (4) regulations clustering around bodily matters (such as menstruation, food, bathing, sex, and the handling of corpses) generally dominated by concepts of purity and pollution. (For discussion and references, see Haidt and Joseph 2004.) The first three categories involve interpersonal relations, encouraging one to draw the conclusion that a large chunk of any moral system will be devoted to prescriptions and values that seem designed to protect and sustain social order, to resolve interpersonal conflicts, and to combat the rampant pursuit of individual welfare. In particular, a great deal of the moral domain is devoted to matters pertaining to how humans may harm each other. (For references to empirical support for this claim, see chapter 7 of Nichols 2004.) Morality seems to be designed to serve society. The fourth universal appears to pertain to self-regarding actions, though it should be borne in mind that this appearance is made problematic by the fact that what seems self-regarding from a Western viewpoint is often not perceived to be so from the perspective of the culture in question. (In other words, it is as much an error to project a parochial conception of *harmfulness* or *self-directedness* onto other cultures, as it is to project a parochial conception of the moral realm.[8]) This is not to deny that people do make purely self-regarding moral judgments—e.g., that cleaning the toilet with the national flag is wrong[9]— but it seems safe to say that the bulk of any moral system involves our relationships with each other.

In saying this I don't purport to be putting forward a conceptual claim about a necessary feature of any moral system, but rather am just making an observation. Perhaps Robinson Crusoe could make up an entire system of imperatives that are wholly self-regarding ("Going to the southern part of the island is forbidden," etc.) but which would still count, in virtue of their characteristic authoritativeness, as moral. Or it might be instead insisted that any such normative system invented by Crusoe wouldn't count as a "morality" precisely because it wouldn't be other-regarding. To be honest, I could go either way on this; I doubt very much that the meaning of the English word "moral" is determinate enough to settle on an answer. But we can still draw a useful conclusion by noting just how bizarre Crusoe's entirely self-regarding "moral" system seems. A morality that governs interpersonal relations seems natural and necessary, while a "morality" that has nothing to do with interpersonal relations (if such a thing is possible) is outlandish and cries out for explanation. We are interested in the hypothesis that *human* morality is the product of natural selection, not in the extravagantly implausible hypothesis that *any* morality *must* be the product of natural selection. So the observation that human morality takes interpersonal relations as its central subject matter is a worthwhile piece of evidence, unaffected by the fact (if it is a fact) that the concept of *morality* is sufficiently vague around the edges to permit the imagination of "moralities" that take some other subject matter entirely.

2.6   Desert

If an important part of the purpose of morality is the sustenance of social order, then we might expect to observe that deviations from moral requirements will prompt a negative response from one's fellows as a way of reinforcing the norms. We might expect that embedded in the very idea of a moral judgment is a reference to a special relation holding between transgressive acts and the negative responses that they provoke (and compliant acts and the rewards that they provoke). I believe we do find such a relation centrally incorporated in moral systems: We think that certain behaviors *deserve* certain responses. The idea of desert is so familiar to us that it can be difficult to stand back and see what a strange notion it is; it is so obvious that it can be blindingly so.

Suppose there were a community of social creatures who employ imperatives that largely govern their interpersonal relations ("Don't steal for self-gain," "Keep your promises," etc.), and, moreover, they appear to make these claims categorically: They continue to press them irrespective of whether the subject of the prescription cares, treating them as demanding of practical consideration regardless of the subject's desires. So far, these creatures might be us. But they are unlike us in the following respect. If someone fails to follow one of these prescriptions—say, one of them doesn't keep a promise, out of selfishness—her fellows don't subject her to criticism. It's not that they don't understand criticism: They criticize each other for practical foolishness, like locking the keys in the car, or drinking too much coffee before going to bed. But they don't see this criticism as something that the situation *demands*. Let's say that this imaginary community has no concept of *desert* at all. Granted, if someone breaks one of these social rules in a dramatic way—say, by killing a few of his fellows—then it may be decided that he should be shut away for the good of the community, or it may be that by establishing a probabilistic connection between killing and the unpleasantness of imprisonment these people hope to discourage future law-breakers. Penalties administered for these kinds of reasons may be "a good idea," they may be expedient, but they are not *demanded* by the act of wrongdoing. The person who is subject to the penalty has done something that his fellows don't like, and perhaps also they consequently don't like him, and perhaps his imprisonment thus gives them a certain satisfaction—but at no point does the idea enter anyone's head that he is getting *what he deserves*.

I think it is quite clear that this is not a tiny difference between us and them. It is difficult to estimate, but it would appear that in stipulating that they have no concept of *desert* one is thereby by implication stipulating the absence of a great deal more. One major implication of this conceptual lacking is that these creatures must also lack a central element of the notion of *justice*: the element pertaining to getting what one deserves. Such creatures would not be troubled if told of the expedient public chastisement of a person who was innocent of a crime but who was widely believed to have committed it. If we were to protest "But that's *unjust*; he didn't *deserve* to be treated that way!" they simply wouldn't know what we meant. Without a sense of *desert*, moreover, these creatures can have no sense of *guilt*—for what is guilt, if not an emotion that involves the judgment that one deserves some kind of penalty for one's actions? (More on this in the next chapter.) Without guilt, these creatures cannot have the faculty that we refer to as "a moral conscience." It might even be speculated that they could have no real appreciation of typical Hollywood movies, or Jane Austen novels, for they would gain no satisfaction from the way that just deserts are distributed in the final scenes.

The fact that these imaginary creatures have no grasp of such concepts casts doubt, I believe, on the proposal that they are making *moral* judgments at all. Without desert, justice, guilt, and conscience in the picture, their categorical imperatives—for all their apparent authoritativeness and interpersonal importance—suddenly seem very alien to us. What is the force of the imperative "Don't kill" if made within a framework of thought that doesn't include these concepts? Perhaps it would be like us addressing the imperative "Don't kill humans" to an animal. Suppose you hear a story of a crocodile that killed someone and then fled the scene, never to be heard of again. Perhaps evidence comes forward confirming that it never again harmed a human. Compare the feelings with which the story leaves you with those you'd have if the story had instead concerned a *human* who killed someone, and fled the scene, never to be heard of again. Our imaginary creatures lacking the notion of desert could not feel that difference; they would not be able to grasp the distinction between the human killer who got away *with something* and the croc that simply got away.

When we examine our ordinary concepts of *desert* and *justice*, what we seem to find is an idea of the world having a kind of "moral equilibrium." When a wrong is done this equilibrium is upset, and the administration of the appropriate punishment is seen as the procedure that will effect its restitution. This restoration of balance appears to give us satisfaction, and we are proportionally unsettled by the idea of wrongdoers going free. (See Lerner 1980; Vidmar and Miller 1980.) In the realm of fiction, few themes give as much raw gratification as when the wicked character finally gets his or her unpleasant and richly deserved comeuppance. And it's not the "removal of the danger" that gives us satisfaction, nor the fact that the villain coming to a rotten end sets an example for other would-be villains. Let's face it; the pleasure comes from seeing him get what he damn well deserves! Whether any real sense can be made of this idea of an "equilibrium" is not our present concern. I grant that when one examines it critically—especially if unwilling to invoke supernatural forces—it all sounds highly mysterious. But we are not now trying to defend or attack the idea; all we are trying to do is gain an understanding of, or even just a "feel" for, what is distinctive about human morality.

A strong way of putting this point would be to assert that morally judging that somebody ought to do something involves the thought that she deserves some form of punishment if she doesn't do that thing. Such deserved punishment would not need to involve formal chastisement, like imprisonment or fines, for one can morally trespass in relatively minor ways (e.g., standing on someone's foot and not apologizing), but perhaps we think that even lesser moral offences deserve criticism, or even just a cold shoulder. We may have no firm idea at all of what negative response is called for, but nevertheless have some inchoate impression that the person "deserves her comeuppance." We may, moreover, decide that all things considered it is better that it isn't administered at all, while still judging that some negative consequence is deserved. We may even think that we are required to "turn the other cheek," believing that punishments will be doled out accordingly by a supernatural being on Judgment Day.

But perhaps this is too strong. Maybe we could find instances of token moral judgments of wrongdoing for which no one thinks that the wrong-doer deserves to suffer any repercussions. Perhaps if the misdemeanor is trivial enough this is so. But it remains plausible to claim that such judgments will make sense only against the background of a conceptual framework within which much more serious wrongs are recognized: wrongs for which punishment is demanded. Could there be a "moral" system in which *all* wrongs are just minor misdemeanors, where nothing deserves a firm response, where the concept of *desert* doesn't figure anywhere? I doubt it.

In this discussion of desert the subject of *guilt* has cropped up several times. We will discuss it at greater length in chapter 3, but I do want to say something about it here since there seems an important relation. The connection is that both are centrally involved in the notion of *redress* or *making amends*. If a person has done wrong, then equilibrium may be restored if she receives the punishment she deserves, but it may also be restored if she undergoes an appropriate course of repentance, in which we expect guilt to figure principally. In fact, the former without the latter leaves us uneasy. We are disquieted by the thought of a criminal who serves his time then returns to the community explicitly and utterly lacking any contrition over his former misdeeds, even if he clearly has no intention of reoffending. We may accept that he has paid his dues to society, but nevertheless harbor uneasiness that the punishment hasn't really "worked." The development of this tendency can be tracked through childhood. When asked to rate the "badness" of the face of a moral transgressor, most 6-year-olds and all 8-year-olds rated a smiling face as worse than a sad face, while 4-year-olds made no such distinction (Nunner-Winkler and Sodian 1988). Appropriate guilt (i.e., having a sad face) is a crucial step on the road to moral improvement for creatures like us, and for everyday moral faults we think that guilt often is sufficient for atonement. A person with no capacity for guilt we consider potentially dangerous, and certainly possessing a vice, even if all his actual actions seem morally impeccable. An incapacity to feel guilt amounts to the absence of an "internal self-punishment system"—something we think of as an important mechanism for reliably guiding moral conduct.

2.7 Summary and Preview

This chapter started out showing how it is a relatively straightforward matter to understand how humans might be biologically designed to have prosocial emotions like love, altruism, or sympathy; an appeal to kin selection suffices. (This is not to deny that these emotions may have evolved via other processes as well.) The real point of that discussion was to draw attention to how far short any such explanatory framework falls from successfully explaining the capacity to make moral judgments. This led us directly to the question "What, then, *is* a moral judgment?" and the remainder of the chapter has highlighted several important characteristics of human moral judgments. Here is a summary of the points made:

• Moral judgments (as public utterances) are often ways of expressing conative attitudes, such as approval, contempt, or, more generally, subscription to standards; moral judgments nevertheless also express beliefs; i.e., they are assertions.
• Moral judgments pertaining to action purport to be deliberative considerations irrespective of the interests/ends of those to whom they are directed; thus they are not pieces of prudential advice.
• Moral judgments purport to be inescapable; there is no "opting out."
• Moral judgments purport to transcend human conventions.
• Moral judgments centrally govern interpersonal relations; they seem designed to combat rampant individualism in particular.
• Moral judgments imply notions of desert and justice (a system of "punishments and rewards").
• For creatures like us, the emotion of guilt (or "a moral conscience") is an important mechanism for regulating one's moral conduct.

Something to note about this list is that it includes two ways of thinking about morality: one in terms of a distinctive subject matter (concerning interpersonal relations), the other in terms of what might be called the "normative form" of morality (a particularly authoritative kind of evaluation). Both features deserve their place, and any hypothesis concerning the evolution of the human moral faculty is incomplete unless it can explain how natural selection would favor a kind of judgment with *both* these features.

Some of these features can be thought of merely as observations of features of human morality, whereas others very probably deserve the status of conceptual truths about the very nature of a moral judgment. But by and large this delicate philosophical distinction is something that doesn't need to be settled in this book, and so I am content to leave it be. Thus I am not claiming that this list succeeds in capturing the necessary and sufficient conditions for moral judgments. It is doubtful that our concept of *a moral judgment* is sufficiently determinate to allow of such an exposition. The sensibly cautious claim to make is that so long as a kind of value system satisfies *enough* of the above, then it counts as a moral system. A somewhat bolder claim would be that some of the items on the list (at least one but not all) are necessary features, and enough of the remainder must be satisfied in order to have a moral judgment. In either case, how much is "enough"? It would be pointless to stipulate. The fact of the matter is determined by how we, as a linguistic population, would actually respond if faced with such a decision concerning an unfamiliar community: If they had a distinctive value system satisfying, say, four of the above items, and for this system there was a word in their language (say, "woogle values"), would we translate "woogle" into "moral"? It's not my place to guess with any confidence how that counterfactual decision would go. All I am claiming is that the above items would all be important considerations in that decision. (We will run up against this issue again in section 6.4.)

It is possible that there are some important characteristics missing from the list. Some may simply not have occurred to me; others I have left out on purpose. It has been argued, for example, that one of the distinctive features of a moral judgment is that it is a *universal* prescription. (See Hare 1952, 1963.) I have always found this a dubious assertion, both as a conceptual claim and as an empirical observation. Having our moral prescriptions be universalizable may well be a worthy goal, but saying this is very different from holding that they necessarily must be universalizable or else they don't even count as "moral." Many communities have value systems that we don't hesitate to call "moral," but which allow for *particular* judgments. For example, many (if not most) moral systems allow for strong distinctions to be made between community members and outsiders. Such distinctions *can* be supported by a universal judgment—e.g. "Anybody has special duties toward members of his or her community"—but it seems unlikely that they actually typically are derived from such a universal support. The Yanomamö people were once notorious for thinking nothing of killing any foreigners encountered. Who is to say that they conceived of "foreigner" as a universal category? Perhaps it just meant *anyone who is not a Yanomamö,* and perhaps this amounted to *anyone who is not descended from the blood of Periboriwa.* The fact that I don't know whether their understanding of "foreigner" was universal or ineliminably particular doesn't mean that I should remain correspondingly uncommitted about whether their rule "It is permissible to kill foreigners" counted as a *moral* liberty. (I also worry about whether the alleged moral virtue of patriotism is really consistent with a universal moral code.)

Now we have some idea of what a moral judgment is—or, at least (what I hope amounts to the same thing) how the phrase is to be understood throughout this book—we can return to our real task. Is the human tendency to employ such judgments the product of biological natural selection? One reason that a person might have been inclined to think "No" is that what we have seen of moral judgments reveals them to be strongly authoritative *prosocial* prescriptions, whereas biological natural selection, it might be thought, can favor only self-serving behavior. But chapter 1 has already amply demonstrated that such a view is mistaken; natural selection may very well in some circumstances prefer creatures with prosocial traits. The hypothesis in which we are interested is that the tendency to make moral judgments is one such prosocial mechanism within the human repertoire.

Questions that remain to be addressed are the following. *When* did the moral sense evolve? I will argue in chapter 3 that the emergence of language places an a priori constraint on the emergence of moral concepts and certain moral emotions. *Why* might the moral sense have evolved? Chapter 4 argues that moral judgments can serve as commitments at both the personal and interpersonal level in such a way as to advance the reproductive interests of those making the judgments. *How* might the moral sense have evolved? Chapter 4 also discusses empirical evidence supporting the hypothesis that it was through modifying emotions that natural selection forged the human moral sense, and speculates more precisely that the act of "projecting emotions" onto the world lies at the heart of our capacity to make moral judgments. The chapter ends with a review of some of the empirical evidence (largely from developmental psychology) indicating that the major hypothesis of this book up to this point—that the human moral sense *is* the product of biological natural selection—is something to be taken seriously; it is more than a mere just-so story. Chapters 5 and 6 can be considered as the second part of this book, addressing the question of what metaethical conclusions may be drawn from the hypothesis advocated in the first part.

3 | Moral Language and Moral Emotions

3.1 The Normative (but Non-Moral) Mental Life of Animals

When I was a child, we used to keep the family dog fenced in the back yard much of the time. The dog was forever trying to escape into the exciting world of the neighborhood, though he knew it wasn't allowed. He would saunter over to the fence, as if investigating an interesting smell, keeping an eye on the window to make sure he wasn't being observed. If satisfied that no one was watching, he would launch himself at the foot of the fence, pushing and digging with all his might. If disturbed just before attempting his breakout, he would carry on with the pretense that he was just checking out that interesting smell, though looking rather sheepish in his non-chalance. If grabbed in the middle of the escape, he would be overcome with guilt and disappear submissively into his kennel. And if discovered when within inches of freedom, then, after an anxious backward glance and a swift calculation of how long it would take the approaching human to cross the yard, he would redouble his assault on the fence—often with success.

In a sense this is a perfectly true story from my childhood; my dog used to act in just this way. But in another sense—a sense that it would be tedious to insist upon in any context other than philosophy—it isn't true. Speaking strictly, I don't believe that my dog "knew that it wasn't allowed" or that he genuinely had "guilt." He knew that he would be punished, granted, and he didn't want that. He had internalized a rule of the household, but he didn't know it *as* a rule. His mind, though impressively devious in many ways, and clever enough to respond to words like "walk" and "sit," did not have the capacity to form a thought about escape from the yard, or anything else, as being *prohibited*.

The aim of this chapter is to back up this assertion. I will first explore what kind of normative thoughts animals may have, before presenting an argument that they cannot have *moral* thoughts. The basis of this argument is the contention that *language* is a prerequisite for having moral concepts. This will be followed by a discussion of moral emotion, and here my main intention will be to show that certain emotions are conceptually rich. The upshot is that language is a prerequisite for having certain moral emotions—most prominently, guilt. This tells us something about *when* the moral sense evolved—not in terms of years, but in terms of its relation to the emergence of other traits.

I started out talking about dogs, but it may be more fruitful to focus on the trickier case of chimpanzees, since it is reasonable to hold that in many ways they resemble a point in human development, and so discussion of what chimpanzees have or lack in the moral sphere promises to cast light on the question of when the capacity to make moral judgments appeared in the hominid line.[1] Some have claimed that the undoubted social complexity displayed by chimpanzees, and the fact that they appear to follow rules, suffice for chimpanzees to be granted a moral sense (Sapontzis 1987; Harnden-Warwick 1997; Waller 1997; see also Gruen 2002). I will argue that this is mistaken. In so arguing I don't take myself to be defending a minority viewpoint. I suspect that most people will readily agree that chimpanzees do not make moral judgments, yet few have offered better than a vague answer as to why they do not.

For clarity, let's first distinguish three questions that might be asked about an animal's relation to morality. One question is whether animals are moral *subjects*—that is, beings whose nature is such that they make moral demands upon us. This, though a very important practical matter, is not something in which we are interested here; I raise it merely to distinguish it from other questions. A second question is whether animals are moral *agents*—beings whose nature is such that their actions count as morally blameworthy or praiseworthy. Though in everyday language we often describe animals in terms of moral assessment ("Bad dog!"), the serious view that such appraisals are to be taken literally appears to be very much a minority one. Note that I am speaking only of *moral* appraisal. Evaluating an animal according to its satisfying some specifiable criteria—say, a "good race horse" or "a good dog" in the sense of a *well-behaved* dog—is not problematic. A third question—the one in which we are interested—is whether animals themselves make moral judgments. This is not unrelated to the second question (as was noted in the introduction), since one might well argue that a being's actions can be judged morally praiseworthy or blameworthy only if that being knows the difference between right and wrong, which requires the capacity to make moral judgments. As a matter of fact I doubt that this intuitively plausible connection holds (see section 2.2), but the argument I will pursue will not depend on it one way or the other. I prefer to focus directly on this third question.

A useful starting place is a distinction made by the primatologist Frans de Waal between *descriptive* and *prescriptive* social rules (1992; the page references below are to this article). Descriptive social rules are just regularities in an organism's responses to its conspecifics, which may be assigned even to fish and insects. Prescriptive social rules, by contrast, are regularities that are not merely *followed*, but which individuals "respect because of active reinforcement of others" (244). Talking of the rule of avoiding a mother's hostility in defense of her offspring, de Waal says that it becomes prescriptive when "members of the group learn to recognize the contingencies between their own and the mother's behavior and to act in a way that minimizes negative consequences" (ibid.). Such prescriptive rules, for de Waal, appear to be a necessary but not sufficient condition for being ascribed a moral system. They do suffice (it would seem) for what de Waal calls "a sense of social regularity," defined as "a set of expectations about the way in which oneself (or others) should be treated and how resources should be divided, a deviation from which expectations to one's (or the other's) disadvantage evokes a negative reaction, most commonly protest in subordinate individuals and punishment in dominant individuals" (242). (De Waal thinks that the parenthetical "others" mentioned in the definition are most likely to be kin.) De Waal is confident that chimpanzees possess this "sense," but he adds later that "it is unclear" to what extent the fact that chimpanzees distinguish "accepted and unaccepted behavior" should be taken as evidence that they have "an awareness of 'good' and 'bad' or 'just' and 'unjust'" (254). Non-human apes, he writes, lack the capacity "for the cognitive formulation and communication of abstract rules," insofar as they cannot use verbal language (241). Thus de Waal grants apes the "precursors" or "building blocks" of morality, but not the real McCoy. (See also de Waal 1996; Flack and de Waal 2001.)

It seems to me that the above definition of "a sense of social regularity" fudges something. The ambiguity arises from what might be meant by saying that someone "*expects* that such-and-such *should* happen." "Should," as we all know, is used very differently in different contexts. Here are three distinct uses:

(i) It should rain tomorrow.

(ii) If you want to get up early tomorrow, you should go to bed soon.

(iii) One should refrain from killing innocent people.

All three cases could be easily reworded to accommodate an "ought" instead of a "should." The first is an instance of what is sometimes called "a 'should' ('ought') of prediction," indicating that evidence suggests the likelihood of something occurring. This is an "ought" that TV weather forecasters use every evening. Since any animal with the capacity for even the most rudimentary associative learning can form expectations about what will happen, any such animal can be properly described as having expectations about what should happen. The "should" doesn't really add anything, for saying "X expects that such-and-such should happen" (where this is the "should" of prediction) is no different than saying "X expects that such-and-such *will* happen." If, on the other hand, we read the "should" as something more obviously evaluative—as a moral "should," for example—then the natural wording would be "X *judges that* such-and-such should happen." In other words, either one *expects* that something *will* occur, or one *judges* that it *should* occur; but, upon reflection, the idea of someone *expecting* that something *should* occur is rather an odd one.

The point of these pedantic observations is not to criticize de Waal, but rather to forewarn the reader that though it may be permissible to ascribe animals certain mental states whose contents involve the word "ought" or "should," this may do nothing to establish the legitimacy of ascribing to them *moral* judgments. One could argue that animals cannot have beliefs involving the moral "ought" because they have no beliefs at all. But this is not my strategy. In what follows I am very carefully *not* going to offer any particular theory about animal cognition, since it is a very controversial topic, and for this book to take a general stand on it would only prejudice my case. I am prepared to grant to my potential opponent a liberal view, such that chimpanzees and other animals may count as having all sorts of beliefs, but I will argue that they still don't have beliefs concerning moral matters.

On the assumption that to have an expectation is to have some kind of belief state, we have already seen that animals may be ascribed beliefs involving the "ought" of prediction. Can they also be ascribed beliefs involving the hypothetical "ought"? It would be interesting if the answer were affirmative, since such beliefs would more obviously be deserving of the label "normative," whereas those involving the "ought" of prediction surely are not. As was mentioned in chapter 2, a hypothetical imperative—such as (ii) above— is a prescription the legitimacy of which depends on the subject having a certain end (Kant (1783) 2002: 216). If it turns out that the subject doesn't have that end, the "ought" claim is retracted. So, regarding (ii), if it turns out that the addressee is planning to sleep till noon tomorrow, then the imperative "You should go to bed soon" must be withdrawn. Suppose, though, that Jim believes (1) that Molly desires to get up early, and also believes (2) that going to bed early is the best means of Molly satisfying her desire. The question, then, is whether Jim believes (3) that Molly ought to go to bed early. The answer depends on how we settle a crucial distinction. On the one hand, perhaps (3) merely *follows logically* from (1) and (2)—in which case although Jim *ought* to believe (3) he may actually fail to do so (for people frequently fail to believe the logical consequences of their beliefs[2]). On the other hand, perhaps believing (1) and (2) is *constitutive* of believing (3), such that given that Jim believes (1) and (2) he already *does* believe (3). We have already seen an example of this: If someone believes that it will probably rain tomorrow, we can legitimately describe her as believing that it ought to rain tomorrow (where this is the "ought" of prediction). The latter ascription isn't a second belief that accompanies or follows from the first; rather, they are just two ways of describing one and the same belief. I have to admit that regarding the relation between (1) + (2) and (3) it is not clear to me which option is correct.

If chimpanzees cannot form beliefs about what individuals desire, all this is beside the point. However, there is some evidence—controversial, it is true—suggesting that they can form higher-order beliefs about the mental states of others (Premack and Woodruff 1978; Premack 1984; O'Connell 1995). In addition, they seem capable of forming beliefs about how desires can best be satisfied. Therefore, it is possible that a chimpanzee could have beliefs of the form (1) and (2) above. For example, if Floyd the chimp is watching a young female chimp struggling to reach the food hanging from a high branch, maybe he knows that she wants the food, and he also knows that the only way she is going to get the food is to poke it with a long stick. If, then, the relation between (1) + (2) and (3) is a constitutive one, we may attribute to Floyd the belief that the youngster ought to use the stick. If, on the other hand, the relation is not constitutive, then we don't appear to be forced to this conclusion. There isn't any real need for us to pursue any lengthy discussion trying to establish one over the other; let us just allow for the sake of argument—if only to make concessions to those who are liberally inclined in their mentalistic assignments—that chimpanzees can be ascribed beliefs containing the hypothetical "ought," which, we have accepted, may count as a kind of normative judgment. The real point I want to establish is that even if we go this far in our ascription of normatively loaded psychological content to chimpanzees (and I am not necessarily arguing that we should) we are still a long way from attributing to them anything like a *moral* judgment.

3.2   No Moral Judgments for Chimps

In describing the chimpanzee's use of prescriptive social rules, de Waal chose his words carefully. They are, he wrote, aware of "accepted and unaccepted" behaviors. This is very different from an awareness of accept*able* and unaccept*able* behaviors—the difference being that the former implies only knowledge that certain behaviors *will* provoke hostility, whereas the latter implies a judgment that these behaviors *merit* hostility. (The suffix "-able" frequently should not be taken literally. "Desirable" does not mean "able to be desired," but rather "worthy of desire." The fact that certain people have desired genocide proves that genocide *can* be desired; but acknowledging this hardly forces us to agree that genocide is desirable.) I argued in the previous chapter that the notions of *merit* and *desert* lie close to the heart of the moral judgment. Without them there can be no sense of justice, no guilt, and no moral conscience. Without them "moralistic aggression" can be only a metaphor. In fact, a stickler might reasonably insist that without the notion of *desert* the term "punishment" should be avoided in favor of something more neutral, like "negative response."

Can a chimpanzee be properly attributed a belief that certain behaviors *merit* certain responses? Consider the way that chimpanzees practice "moralistic aggression" against misbehavior (bearing in mind that in this phrase, which is from Trivers 1971, "moralistic" is pure metaphor). Male chimpanzees, when fighting with females, generally refrain from using their large canine teeth, with which they could do a great deal of harm. It has been observed that on the rare occasions that a male did employ his dangerous canines against a female, the victim's protesting tone of voice changed—a change to which the whole colony responded with barks of complaint, and sometimes with a group of females chasing off the aggressor (de Waal 1992: 247). Isn't this a case of the members of the colony judging that using canine teeth in this manner *deserves* a certain punitive response, and therefore might it not involve a moral judgment? I don't believe so, for I maintain that we can smoothly explain the full repertoire of chimpanzee behavior while ascribing to chimpanzees only aversions, inhibitions, and desires—at no point do we run up against anything that requires us to credit them with thoughts about *transgressions* or *prohibitions* or *deserved punishments* or any other moral concept. Moreover, I think there are a number of reasons why we shouldn't ascribe such concepts to them. I will first mention two inadequate answers before briefly mentioning two much better answers; I will then present my own somewhat eccentric view on the matter.

First, it might be thought that moral concepts are too abstract to be ascribed to animals; one might think that language is necessary for abstract concepts. But once we have opened the door to animal beliefs, there seems to be nothing that would prevent us from allowing them beliefs with abstract contents. Chimpanzees can learn to distinguish between stimuli that are the same and stimuli that are different, even when the particular items in question are entirely novel (Premack 1983), as can pigs (Keddy-Hector et al., forthcoming), and this, it has been argued, permits ascription of beliefs involving the non-perceptual relational properties *sameness* and *difference*. Monkeys seem to recognize mother-offspring bonds in general—apparently permitting ascription of beliefs involving the relational property *being the mother of* (Dasser 1988; Cheney and Seyfarth 1990). Darwin noted that dogs employ the general concept *dog*, since "when a dog sees another dog in the distance, it is often clear that he perceives that it is a dog in the abstract; for when he gets nearer his whole manner suddenly changes if the other dog be a friend" ((1879) 2004: 105).³ Many other examples could be provided suggesting that language is not a necessary condition for being ascribed abstract beliefs.

Another reason that people may be disinclined to ascribe moral judgments to animals (or perhaps to non-language-users in general) is the vague thought that moral concepts are too complex. But I am not confident that my understanding of the notion of "complexity" goes much beyond a gut feeling. Is the concept of *prohibition* really more complex than the concept *banana*? Complex in what way? In any case, it is far from clear exactly what it is about language that opens up the realms of conceptual complexity. The relational concept *being-the-same-as* strikes me (intuitively) as very complex, yet some non-language-users seem to have it.

If it is neither the complexity nor the abstract nature of morality that explains why we shouldn't ascribe moral judgments to chimpanzees and other animals, what is it? There are a number of possible (and possibly complementary) answers to this largely neglected question. Marc Hauser (2000, chapter 9) argues that animals lack moral concepts and moral emotions because they lack self-awareness (to be distinguished from self-recognition, which experiments involving mirrors show some animals to possess). Geoffrey Sayre-McCord (forthcoming, and personal communication) argues that in order to represent things as *better* or *worse* creatures must deploy concepts which "must be sensitive not just to whether things satisfy a certain standard but also whether that standard itself is justified (which is to say, at least roughly, that the standard itself is such that it satisfies the standard of value in play—and its use as a standard is sensitive to its satisfying this test)." In order to employ a normative concept it is not enough simply to justify one's behavior according to a certain standard; one must have sensitivity to the question of whether that standard is itself justified. Upon discovering that the items one had treated as falling under the concept in fact do not provide reasons for performing or refraining from actions, one must be disposed to revise the criteria used in deploying that concept. Since animals lack this degree of flexible cognitive sophistication (it seems safe to assume, though Sayre-McCord doesn't assert it), we must conclude that they don't truly evaluate their world or one another at all. Both of these arguments are perfectly plausible. My own pet theory is rather different, and, as experience has taught me, it is unpopular among philosophers. Still, it would be tedious to write a book in which *everything* is obviously correct, and so I ask the reader to indulge me for a few paragraphs while I sketch an idiosyncratic diagnosis of why non-language-users don't make moral judgments. (This can be bracketed off from the main argumentative thread of this book, so if the reader is willing to grant me the widely accepted view that moral judgment requires language then no harm will be done if he or she skips ahead to section 3.4.)

We can start by noting that there's a whole range of words that we don't use in describing animal beliefs, even if we are liberally inclined in our ascriptions. No matter how much the antelope dislikes the lion, we don't seriously claim that it thinks the lion is "a heartless bastard"; nor does the lion believe that the antelope is "a pathetic wimp." Lions may desire raw meat, but they don't think "This is yummy" when they catch it. These terms—"bastard," "wimp," "yummy"—are what philosophers call "thick evaluative terms" (Williams 1985), which we encountered in chapter 2 in the discussion of pejoratives such as "kraut" and "slut."[4]

A very good question—and one about which surprisingly little has been said—is "Why don't we (seriously) use terms such as 'slut,' 'wimp,' and 'bastard' when describing animal beliefs?" Why do such concepts seem unavailable to them?

My thoughts on this matter crystallized upon hearing the following lines from the movie *Ghost World*:

Rebecca (to Seymour):   "Enid thinks you're a dork."
Seymour: *"Is that what she said?!"*

Seymour didn't ask whether Enid liked him or respected him; it seems that in order to know whether she thought him a dork he needed to know whether she had used that *word* to denote him (or at least that she had shown some willingness to use that word). Had the reply to Seymour's query been "Well, Enid certainly doesn't like or respect you," then, however depressing that may have been for Seymour, it seems that he may at least have taken heart in the fact that whether Enid actually thought him a dork remained open.[5]

Let us consider a slightly more straightforward example. Again, compare teaching someone the word "German" and teaching someone the word "kraut." The former could be achieved without *mentioning* language at all. One could just say "Someone is a German if and only if he or she is a native or inhabitant of Germany." (Other purely descriptive nouns can be taught by pointing to exemplar objects, though pointing at German persons is unlikely to succeed in identifying the intended salient characteristic.) By comparison, in order to teach the word "kraut" one can say all that one says for "German," but one must add "and 'kraut' is an offensive term"—in other words, one must say something about the word itself. Indeed, this distinction is enshrined in dictionary entries for obviously pejorative terms. The *Oxford English Dictionary* tells us that "kraut" is "derogatory"—a comment that doesn't seek to describe what the word denotes, but rather describes a convention of usage that requires "semantic ascent" in order to state. ("Semantic ascent" is a phrase, coined by W. V. Quine, denoting a "shift from talking in certain terms to talking about them. . . . It is [e.g.] the shift from talk of miles to talk of 'mile'" (1960: 271).) Were we to line up all our platitudes surrounding the concept *kraut* and all those surrounding our concept *German*, the former list would differ from the latter in its inclusion of platitudes necessarily involving semantic ascent; the former will have to say something about the conventions surrounding *the word* "kraut," such as "It is a derogatory term; it is a word used to insult people." (For a discussion of "lining up platitudes," see chapter 2 of Smith 1994.) The significance of this distinction is that non-linguistic creatures might have the concept *German* but not the concept *kraut*. Of course, I don't think that animals actually do have either concept, but the reasons differ in each case. Animals lack the concept *German* because in order to have it they would have to be able to distinguish German people from non-German people (which would involve ascertaining where they were born, checking passports, etc.—discriminatory powers that animals simply lack). But *in principle* (in some broad sense of the notion) a non-linguistic creature might have such powers. By contrast, to have the concept *kraut* one needs to know something about *the word* "kraut"—that it is a means of expressing disdain—so non-linguistic creatures necessarily cannot have the concept. This knowledge may be implicit, dispositional, procedural, or knowledge-how rather than knowledge-that; all that matters here is that it is knowledge concerning language.

Another example comes from Frege ((1897) 1997: 240–241): "dog" vs. "cur." Darwin may be correct that dogs themselves have the general concept *dog*, but no one thinks that dogs need to know anything about the word "dog" (or "chien," etc.) for this to be true. Colin Allen (1999; see also Allen and Hauser 1991) argues that in order for an animal to have a concept of X it must (i) be able to systematically discriminate some Xs from some non-Xs, (ii) be capable of detecting some of its own discrimination errors between Xs and non-Xs, and (iii) be capable of learning to better discriminate Xs from non-Xs as a consequence of its capacity (ii). Maybe dogs can do this with dogs. But, I am arguing, someone—whether human or dog—most know something about language in order to be granted competence with the pejorative concept *cur*. If (simplifying things slightly for illustrative purposes) we assume that asserting "It is a cur" is a way of both expressing the belief that it is a dog *and* expressing contempt for it, it no longer can be maintained that it is necessary for having the concept *cur* that one can reliably and flexibly discriminate curs from non-curs. Curhood just isn't a property that may be picked out in the world in the way that doghood may be; thus, Allen's otherwise plausible criteria seem inadequate for such evaluative concepts. Nor does it suffice for believing that something is a cur that one believes that it is a dog *and* has contempt toward it. After all, some dogs themselves seem to satisfy these criteria (my family dog despised the neighbor's dog), but we still don't seriously ascribe them beliefs involving concepts like *cur*. The concept *cur* is one whose surrounding platitudes will include some requiring semantic ascent in order to state. Since knowledge of these platitudes (albeit possibly knowledge-how) is by definition necessary for being granted conceptual competency, linguistic knowledge is necessary for concept possession.

Perhaps all this talks of dorks and krauts and curs has been distracting. The point is that what goes for these obviously derogatory terms also goes for a dominant chunk of moral language, as I argued in section 2.3. Just as one cannot be counted competent with the word "kraut" unless one knows that it is a derogatory word, one cannot be counted competent with moral language unless one knows that in using it (seriously) one expresses subscription to certain practical standards. Thus a perfect dictionary would recognize such well-entrenched linguistic conventions by including something akin to "*derogatory*" in its entries for moral terms. Thus the platitudes surrounding moral language—those which capture what one needs to know in order to be granted conceptual competency—require semantic ascent in order to state. Thus moral judgments cannot be legitimately and seriously ascribed to a non-language-user.[6] Ergo, no moral judgments for chimps.

This conclusion is consistent with the previous provisional acceptance that chimpanzees may have mental states that are legitimately described using other kinds of "ought." Consider these statements:

It ought to rain tomorrow. But I subscribe to no normative standard that commends its raining tomorrow.

You want to stay warm, and the open window is keeping you cold, so you ought to shut the window. But I subscribe to no normative standard that commends your shutting the window.

These are both slightly odd statements, in that it is hard to imagine a context in which someone would say them, but it is a very different kind of oddness than that manifested by the similar numbered examples presented in chapter 2. There is no temptation to read the "But I subscribe" part as nullifying or canceling the preceding speech act; the oddness has nothing to do with Moore's paradox. Therefore these uses of "ought" are apparently not used to express condemnation or commendation. I would say the same about various other normative words, such as the comparative terms appearing in "This is the best banana" or "This is a good tree to climb up." Just as one can acknowledge "Tony is the best assassin around" without thereby subscribing to the standards of the Assassins' Guild, so too one's assertion of "This is the best banana" does not express any conative attitude. For this reason I am not arguing that normative terms—such as "ought," "mustn't," and "good"—can never appear in the beliefs we ascribe to non-language-users, only that the distinctively *moral* uses of these terms cannot.

3.3   Realism versus Instrumentalism about Moral Beliefs

There are a couple of follow-up clarifications to this argument that must briefly be made. In everyday language the term "moral judgment" sometimes denotes a mental activity and sometimes a linguistic utterance. Nothing I have said disallows this, but I have argued that just as the attribution of a slut-belief depends upon the subject's abilities regarding the word "slut," so too moral judgment as a mental activity is in a sense secondary (which isn't to say *less important*), in that its attribution depends on the subject having relevant linguistic capabilities. (One might say that whereas we tend to regard speech as a noisy form of thinking, for certain subject matters it is the other way around: Thinking is a quiet way of talking.) This raises the question of whether beliefs with such contents can be construed *realistically*.

Realists about beliefs think that when we say that Joe believes that *p* we are claiming that there is a genuine state that Joe is in—presumably a state of Joe's brain—which is causally implicated in his behavior, and which could (at least in principle) be empirically investigated. Instrumentalists, by contrast, think that to say that Joe believes that *p* is merely to evince commitment to the fact that Joe's behavior is most usefully predicted and explained by ascribing such a belief to him. (See Dennett 1987.[7]) If an ape performs behaviors that can best be explained and predicted by ascribing to it mental states, then the instrumentalist will take this as all there is to the ape having mental states, whereas the realist will take it as, at best, good evidence that the ape has mental states.

I hope my readers will understand my reluctance to get unnecessarily tangled up in this complex debate. In any case, my view is that both theories are, after a fashion, acceptable. Sometimes when we ascribe mental states to an entity we do so with realist commitments: We are saying that the entity really does stand in a relation to something that can be called "a belief," and this belief interacts causally with other mental states, with the autonomic nervous system, and ultimately with the world. Paradigmatically, this is what we do with humans. However, there is no reason to insist that our talk of mental states is always laden with such realist commitments. If we want on certain occasions to relax our standards—to say that a chess computer wants to get its queen out early, or that a computer believes that its printer port is free—that's fine. Some complex systems can be usefully thought of and spoken about as if they had mental states, without our worrying about whether they really do. (For a detailed and cogent account of the compatibility of realism and instrumentalism, see Godfrey-Smith 2004.)

A familiar and popular version of realism for beliefs—championed by Jerry Fodor (1975, 1994) and Steven Pinker (1994)—holds that beliefs exist as "sentences in the head"—sentences in the language of "Mentalese." But how can *dork*, *slut*, or *evil*—concepts that require the subject to have acquaintance with the how the words "dork," "slut," and "evil" function *in a public language*—be expressed by terms in Mentalese? What sense can be made of the idea that some entries in the Mentalese dictionary might contain "derogatory"? The answer, I believe, is that Mentalese cannot contain terms that smoothly translate such English words. This is not to say that Fodor's theory fails, only that it will have to make room for a special story to be told concerning such evaluative beliefs. But it probably comes as no surprise that the nature of the truth conditions of "Lucy believes that the cat is brown" (the kind of simple case that the realist has traditionally focused on) is going to be rather different from those provided for "Enid believes that Seymour is a complete dork." But if I am correct that what it takes to have the belief that Seymour is a dork is (roughly) the ability (and perhaps the willingness) to assertorically apply the word "dork" to Seymour, then this is no hindrance to realism, for it is reasonable to assume that this ability (and this willingness) is a genuine causally efficacious state that may be empirically investigated.

The second clarification concerns instrumentalism about beliefs. If it is of predictive and explanatory value to ascribe to non-language-users beliefs involving evaluative terms, then aren't we permitted to do so? If, for example, it serves our explanatory practices to ascribe to bees the belief that wasps are complete bastards, then instrumentalism, it would seem, permits us to do so. To address this I need to say a bit more about the relation between instrumentalism and realism about beliefs.

Although on occasions we may speak in an instrumentalist manner, saying things like "The computer thinks that the printer port is free, but it's not," it strikes me as exceedingly implausible that all our mental-state ascriptions are like this, that we never speak with realist commitments. (See Lycan 1987 for criticisms of generalized instrumentalism; see also Yu and Fuller 1986.) If someone says "The computer thinks that the printer port is free, but it's not," she can nearly always be encouraged to retract or qualify the claim if pressed with appropriately serious grilling: "Okay, but does it *really* have beliefs about its printer port?" (Some philosophers with exceedingly liberal realist views of what it takes to have beliefs and desires are, no doubt, exceptions.) By comparison, there is no such tendency to back down from assertions concerning what humans believe (unless, of course, there exists some doubt of the everyday sort about whether the human in question does indeed have the belief). If I claim that Caesar believed that the Rubicon was made of water, the query "Okay, but did he *really* believe that?" would just confuse me; I wouldn't know what the questioner was driving at. Seen in this light, instrumentalism appears to be a "convenient fiction" in which we sometimes allow ourselves to participate. Compare more familiar fictive discourse. If I say as part of a fairy tale "The princess lived in a castle made of rubies," then I will be willing to retract the claim if pressed in an appropriately serious way. To the query "But you don't *really* think there ever was a castle made of rubies, do you?" I will answer something like "No, of course not, but you're missing the point." But if I say assert something seriously—"Princess Elizabeth of Bohemia corresponded with Descartes"—then upon being pressed in this way I will stick to my guns. The fact that we apparently know that in saying "The computer thinks that the printer port is free, but it's not" we are doing something different from saying "Sally believes that the printer port is free, but it's not"—the fact that we generally will abandon the former claim if pressed, and admit that it is "just a way of talking"—suggests that when we ascribe beliefs on instrumentalist grounds we are indulging in a harmless and useful piece of fictionalizing.

But if this is the correct understanding of the role that instrumentalism plays in our belief ascriptions, then the worry that bees might turn out to believe that wasps are complete bastards is not a major problem. Or if we want to credit a male chimpanzee—one who is watchful of his mate because she is sexually receptive to other males—with the belief that she is *a slut* (while ascribing to her the belief that the other males are *hunks*), fine. In the same way, if we want to ascribe chimpanzees with beliefs that certain behaviors are *demanded*, that some behaviors *merit* punitive response, and that some character traits are *praiseworthy*, that's fine too. There is no great harm in doing this on instrumentalist grounds so long as we remain aware that it is a form of make-believe, a shorthand justified by the need for conversational expediency. But—just as with pretending that Santa Claus comes down the chimney—we shouldn't take what is said seriously. As to the question of whether bees *really* believe that wasps are bastards, or whether a chimp might *really* believe that another chimp is a slut or a hunk, or whether a non-language-user might *really* judge an action to be morally required, etc.—the answer to all of these questions is "No."

3.4 A Language of Reciprocity

In section 3.2 I presented an a priori argument to the conclusion that language is a prerequisite for making moral judgments. Could there be an argument for the converse: that language requires the capacity to make moral judgments? Well, I don't see much hope for supporting it as a logical implication, but one might reasonably make the case that contingently, as a matter of fact, human language developed in order to permit the making of evaluations. To see this we must turn to the evolution of language.

Precisely when our ancestors started talking to one another is something about which at present we can only theorize.[8] We should bear in mind that nothing very precise can be expected. What counts as "a language," as opposed to a system of signals, as opposed to noises made in order to arouse attention, as opposed to noises that happen to arouse attention, is a thoroughly vague affair. Even if we were magically granted full observational access to our ancestors, including all neuroscientific data, and were able to trace all developments over millions of years, we would still disagree dramatically about when language developed, for the problem isn't just over our limited knowledge (though there is certainly that problem), it is also an inevitable imprecision over what we mean by the word "language." This vagueness shouldn't bother us—our language is full of useful and benign indeterminacy—but we should be aware of it. The best we can aim for is a theory that states "At n years ago our ancestors didn't have a language, and at $n - m$ years ago they did." (And if confronted with an intermediate date, to the demand "Did they have a language *then*?" the correct answer would be "Sort of.")

More interesting than the *when* question is the *why* question. There is no reason to think that the answer must be singular; there may have been numerous problems facing our ancestors for which linguistic communication offered a useful solution. But here I am going to highlight one plausible hypothesis about the original "purpose" of language, derived in particular from the work of the anthropologists Robin Dunbar and Leslie Aiello (Aiello and Dunbar 1993; Dunbar 1993, 1996).[9] The hypothesis follows from two empirical observations. First, it is noted that in non-human primates social cohesion is maintained through closely monitored interactions between individuals—the usual currency of regulation being grooming behavior—and that there is only so much time that an individual can allot to this activity before its pursuit of other important goals (foraging, etc.) becomes compromised. It turns out that an individual primate has a maximum "social budget" of about 20 percent. Second, it is observed that among extant social primates there is a significant correlation between neocortex ratio (the ratio of neocortex volume to the volume of the rest of the brain) and group size—the larger the group, the larger the neocortex ratio—strongly suggesting that one of the primary functions of the neocortex is to process social information. Not only do creatures need a bigger neocortex in order to remember who's who, and who is a friend or an enemy to whom, but also to make more accurate and "higher-order" attributions of mental states (e.g., "She believes that I know what he wants), enabling better anticipation of others' responses (Mithen 1996: 108).

This second observation allows us to draw (provisional) conclusions about the size of the groups in which our various types of ancestors were living, based on examination of their fossilized crania. By this means Dunbar and Aiello surmise that australopithecines, for example, lived in groups about 67 strong, *Homo habilis* in groups of about 82, *Homo erectus* in groups of about 111, and so on. (Various hypotheses exist as to why group size was growing. Richard Alexander, for example, supposes that intergroup conflict provided the primary advantage of large group size

(1987: 79–81).) These data then permit us to estimate how much time an individual of each kind of hominid would need to devote to grooming in order adequately to maintain bonding interactions with every member of his or her group: australopithecines about 18 percent, *Homo habilis* about 23 percent, *Homo erectus* about 31 percent, *Homo neanderthelensis* about 41 percent. The conclusion is that in the course of human evolution an increasing pressure was developing in favor of there being some new and more efficient means for exchanging information about the behavior and relationships of one's interactants. The pressure was first upon *Homo habilis*, and subsequently became so acute that we can assume that some solution must have been struck upon. Language, it is argued, is that solution. One way to find out about another individual's trustworthiness is to observe her interactions with others; but if you are simultaneously trying to observe dozens of prospective interactants, then you are in trouble. But if one can *talk* to others who have interacted with the individuals in question, then a lot of information can be gathered very easily. Spending 20 percent of one's time gossiping is sufficient to learn a great deal about the social minutiae of a great many individuals. By the same token, one can spread flattering information about oneself to a much larger audience. (Networking has been around a long time.) This "gossip hypothesis" about early language receives corroboration from the fact that we still expend an enormous amount of our conversational energies on "reputation management"—60–70 percent, according to the psychologist Nicholas Emler (1990, 1992). And I think that an important truth lies behind Truman Capote's defense of his novella *Answered Prayers* (an unflattering portrait of well-known individuals): "My book isn't gossip. Except in the sense that all literature is gossip."

Moreover, with gossip one can do great damage to another's reputation at a distance with virtually no effort, thus making the administration of punishment virtually risk-free while also greatly extending one's sphere of punitive influence. (This observation speaks against the need for an appeal to group selection in order to explain the evolution of punishment strategies; see section 1.7.) Note that this well-known "gossip hypothesis" about the evolution of language amounts to the claim that human linguistic faculties were selected for in order to serve reciprocal exchanges when the groups got large. A language of gossip is a language of reciprocity.

The importance of reciprocity in increasingly large groups created a growing pressure for the development of language not only because of the advantages of gossip but also because language permits and facilitates more complex and subtle exchanges. Leda Cosmides and John Tooby (1989: 64) make the point nicely:

If I want to exchange an axe for something, how do I indicate what I want? Let's say that I point to the pear you are holding in your hand. What am I referring to by pointing at the pear? Do I want that particular pear? Any pear at all? Five bushels of pears? A fruit of some kind, not necessarily a pear? To be led to the site where you found such good pears? Do I want you to hold a branch-ladder so I can climb into a tree that has pears? Or a tree with some other kind of fruit? Do I want to use my axe to core the pear, in exchange for half the pear?

Trading concrete goods would have been increasingly important as the material culture advanced. This may also be indirectly related to group size, insofar as a larger group allows and encourages division of labor, which is a spur to technological advance. Let us, then, adopt this as a working hypothesis: that the first conversations concerned exchanges—both the arranging of complicated or precise trades and the discussion of how others have conducted themselves in their interactions. (See Paine 1967; Barkow 1992; Enquist and Leimar 1993.)

Any hypothesis concerning what the first language was *for* entails conclusions concerning what the first language was *about*. What are the basic constituents of a language of gossip and trade likely to be? There will have to be ways to refer to specific individuals, to the items and commodities exchanged, and to the relations among the individuals. But we should also expect that evaluative terms will appear at the start. Our ancestors didn't just want to *describe* the fact that someone failed to reciprocate; the purpose of their gossip was that other individuals could be *criticized*. The evolutionary point of having sensitivity to the reputations of others is that someone with a poor reputation can be avoided, ostracized, or actively punished. Effective (juicy) gossip involves more than mere *descriptions* of who did what to whom; it embodies praising and condemnatory language—perhaps along the lines of "Ogg never repaid Gak for that axe: the *scoundrel!*" (to choose a rather quaint translation) or "Klug always repays a favor: He's a great guy!" Self-promotion is also more effectively served by evaluative language, as anyone who works in advertising will tell you.

A natural thought is that humanity's first language consisted primarily of nouns and verbs—a kind of "Me Tarzan, you Jane" vocabulary—and that evaluative language came later. I am suggesting that, on the contrary, it follows from Dunbar's research that evaluative language was a central part of our linguistic repertoire from the very start, that a dictionary of that first language would have to contain entries with something equivalent to "*derogatory*." This may appear extravagantly speculative, but it follows pretty directly from an empirically well-supported theory of the original function of language. No one thinks that grooming among primates is merely a means of removing parasites; it is a currency of social bonding, a way of assessing one's associates and evaluating one's relations with them. If language is primarily a device that steps in for grooming when the group grows, then language has the same function. And since we may safely assume that language fulfills this function largely through its content (rather than, say, through its prosodic qualities, or the exercising of the larynx), then we come to the conclusion that an important evolutionary function of language is to convey certain types of social evaluative content.

3.5 Taking Stock of the Strategy

Claiming that a language contains social evaluations is not the same as saying that it contains *moral* terms, for we know from chapter 2 that moral judgments are a special class of evaluations. It might seem reasonable to think that moral terms *would* emerge as a means of discussing reputations, arranging exchanges, plugging self-promotion, condemning transgressors, etc., because a language the purpose of which is to discuss fairness, cheating, punishment, desert, greed, ownership, etc., will not get very far if it lacks the words "fairness," "cheats," "punishment," "desert," "greed," "ownership," etc. (or, more precisely, words that translate into these English terms). However, we have no business translating our ancestors' linguistic grunts into such English terms (in their moral sense) unless we can also be confident that our ancestors imbued such judgments with the kind of practical clout that was discussed in section 2.4—and nothing that has yet been said warrants this. I think that in fact moral language *will* serve reciprocal exchange much better than non-moral evaluation—I think, for example, that Gak will do much better at inspiring his fellows to punish Ogg's non-reciprocation if he can assert that Ogg has violated a convention-transcendent norm that must be respected whether one likes it or not—that Ogg *deserves* to be punished—than if he merely expresses his own anger at Ogg's actions. This claim, however, requires further argumentation which will be deferred till the next chapter.

Let me pause to summarize some of the main points I have made. We want to know how and why the human tendency to employ moral judgments might have evolved. It is reasonable to take a look at our primate cousins, some of whom live in complex social systems, and wonder about which of the building blocks of morality they have and which they lack. I have argued that the apparent rule following that we observe in chimpanzees can be explained without crediting them with any capacity to make moral judgments. They have certain inhibitions, aversions, and inclinations (whether innate or learned), they respond negatively to certain behaviors (or certain omissions), and they can delay meting out the negative response if they cannot administer it at the time of transgression. They are clever enough to anticipate being the recipient of such negative responses, they probably ascribe mental states to one another, and, I am willing to concede, they probably "internalize" a lot of these connections to the extent that they behave in certain ways (prosocial ways, let's say) out of habit. De Waal's label for this, "a sense of social regularity," seems suitable. Insofar as I have also conceded for the sake of argument that chimpanzees may be ascribed judgments involving the hypothetical "ought," I see no reason to deny that their social lives are to a large degree governed by "normative" considerations.

But where's the morality? None of the above attributions, nor the sum total of them, amount to a chimpanzee thinking of a negative response as *deserved*, or supposing an act to be a *transgression*, or judging a behavior to be *appropriate*, or considering a trait to be *virtuous*, or assessing a division to be *fair*, or believing that an item is *owned* (i.e., that certain individuals enjoy special *rights* over the item). In section 3.2 I offered a diagnostic argument as to why this is so—why, in fact, a chimpanzee *cannot* think such things— based on language being a prerequisite for such thoughts. I am aware that my diagnosis may leave some readers unpersuaded, but even if this is so the principal general point still stands: Chimpanzees may have building blocks for morality, but there are other crucial building blocks that they lack. We should focus our attention on this evolutionary transition carefully. How does one move from having inhibitions to making judgments about prohibitions: from disliking to disapproving, from desiring to regarding-as-desirable? Of course the evolutionary process will be gradual, but noting this doesn't alleviate the puzzle. A red animal may have evolved from a yellow ancestor, but explaining the forces that brought about yellowness and then pointing out that there is a gradual continuum between yellow and red still leaves one wondering how and why the evolutionary color change to red took place. The building blocks of morality possessed by chimpanzees—to the extent that they can be understood entirely as inclinations, aversions, desires, and inhibitions—cannot be assembled or reshuffled in order to get a moral judgment. (Arrange the yellow blocks however you like; you can't construct a red building.) That the transition cannot occur until language is on the scene is interesting, but it doesn't answer the question.

So far I have largely avoided mentioning the role of emotion. There is a natural thought that my claim that chimpanzee social life is governed by inhibitions and inclinations might be translated into the proposition that chimpanzee social behavior is governed by emotions. And this popular thought is supplemented by another: that the reason that chimps don't make moral judgments is precisely that moral judgments require cognitive and conceptual sophistication, and emotions just aren't going to provide this. I think that there is more wrong than right about these familiar thoughts, but I do think that emotions are a crucial part of the transition on which we want to focus, so it is to emotions that we now turn.

Many emotions are relevant to our moral lives: anger, gratitude, indignation, disgust, sympathy, contempt, shame, guilt, pride, schadenfreude—the list might be long, and I don't propose to discuss them all, or even to develop a very precise account of what an emotion is. (See Haidt 2003a; Fessler and Haley 2003.) I will defend a view no more detailed than is necessary for me to make a point that I am keen to make: At least some of these emotions are cognitively rich, and among the concepts necessary for having certain emotions are evaluative concepts. It is for this reason that this discussion of emotions follows on the heels of the argument that language is a prerequisite for moral judgment. The two discussions establish two premises that entail an interesting conclusion: that language is necessary for certain emotions and that the evolution of language made certain moral emotions accessible. The main focus in the rest of this chapter will be one the emotion of guilt, though other emotions will be mentioned in the course of the discussion.

3.6 Emotions

Many theories have been put forward concerning the emotions—indeed, so vastly different are the theories that one wonders whether there is even a stable subject matter about which the theorists are talking. Robert Plutchik (1980) identified 27 different definitions of emotion! But thankfully there has been a degree of convergence in the field in recent years. The emotions—at least, the "basic" emotions—are widely acknowledged to be adaptive mechanisms, each designed by biological natural selection to perform a task that involves physiological, psychological, and behavioral elements of the organism in such a way as to encourage it to respond adaptively to recurrent types of fitness-relevant threats and opportunities in the environment. On this view, there is no such thing as an "emotional faculty" in the brain; each basic emotion "does its own thing," more or less oblivious of the others, employing different neurological structures (if need be), looking out for its own special kinds of stimuli, and implementing its particular range of behavioral responses. Evidence for this comes from truisms concerning the emotions: They are notorious for lying outside voluntary control; they often ignore our attempts to reason with them; they respond seemingly of their own accord to particular types of stimuli; they affect motivations and thus behavior. Moreover, roughly the same range of basic emotions is recognized across all human cultures throughout known history—for example, ancient Indian dramaturgic scholars came up with a list of "eight fundamental feelings" that would not look in the least surprising coming from a North American psychologist in the 21st century (Ghosh 1967: 121–125).[10] There is some evidence that particular emotional responses may be impaired by neurological damage, leaving others intact (Damasio 1994; Calder et al. 2000; Adolphs et al. 2003).[11] We can, moreover, construct plausible evolutionary hypotheses concerning the function of each emotion, though admittedly theorists continue to argue over the details. Some see their advantage in terms of physiological arousal (regarding which our "experience" of them is but a side effect of our happening also to be conscious creatures); others emphasize their role in memory, motivation, attention, planning, and learning; others emphasize the communicative aspect of the emotions. Insofar as natural selection loves to kill two birds with one stone, it is perfectly conceivable that all these benefits (and others) may have figured in the evolution of the emotions, perhaps in differing degrees for different emotions.

Despite the overwhelming advantages enjoyed by the Darwinian account of the emotions, it is unlikely that every type of emotion that we recognize is directly produced by an innate, discrete mechanism aimed at solving an ancestral problem. It is much more probable that, given an evolved suite of emotions, cultural factors enter into the picture and allow novel and finer distinctions to be drawn. This means that different cultures, and different historical moments, will recognize different emotions. For example, a whole range of Chinese words, allowing finely tuned emotional differentiation, all get translated into English as "shame" (Wang and Fischer 1994). But no anthropologist—despite the fact that many of them clearly relish the challenge—has ever produced an example of an emotion recognized by another culture that is so alien to us that we just don't have any grasp of it. The very fact that we can smoothly group together all those Chinese emotion words and label them "varieties of shame" is in itself telling. We never hear of a foreign word that denotes a kind of furious sympathy, tinged with jealousy, elicited by snowfall and prompting laughter. What cross-cultural variation there is arises from the facts that emotions may be prioritized differently by different cultures (sometimes shame, for example, is a central organizing principle), that emotions may have varying culturally determined elicitors and expected behaviors, and that the emotional field may be taxonomized differently, allowing for more or less nuanced distinctions to be made. None of these observations undermine the hypothesis that there is an innate set of underlying emotional universals. A lot of argument has focused on just which emotions are the innate or "basic" ones, and on how much of human emotional life is a cultural overlay on an innately constrained foundation (and, of course, there are still those around who cling to the once-fashionable view that it's *all* cultural). On this empirical matter the jury is still deliberating, and the arguments presented in this book do not require us to take sides in the general debate. Another important thing to note is that all these evolutionary considerations still leave wide open the question of what an emotion really *is* (the ontology of emotion, if you like). Are they feelings, physiological changes, neurological events, dispositions to act, beliefs, something else entirely, or some combination of the above? This too is something we need not take a stand on.

What I am keen to emphasize is that some emotions involve a degree of cognitive sophistication. Consider disgust. The psychologist Paul Rozin and his colleagues have argued that "core disgust" is associated with food rejection, which was Darwin's view ((1872) 1999: 255–260). The distinctive facial expression of disgust indicates expulsion of food from the mouth, and at its most extreme the emotion elicits a gagging response, even when the object of disgust is not being consumed. Yet disgust, Rozin et al. argue (2000), is more than distaste: It includes a feeling of offensiveness and a sense of contamination. The latter is well documented by experiments showing subjects to be reluctant to wear a sweater that has been used by a stranger even after it has been scrupulously laundered—their willingness plummeting further if the previous owner of the sweater is believed to have had an amputated leg, or to have committed murder (Rozin et al. 1994). Rozin (1999: 33) states:

Disgust is closely linked to sympathetic magical thinking. Disgusting entities contaminate the things they touch, illustrating the sympathetic magical law of *contagion*: "once in contact, always in contact" [Frazer (1890) 1925: 11]. . . . Responses to disgusting entities are so strong that disgust often generalizes to entities that are not inherently disgusting, but look like disgusting things. Thus, people feel disgust towards objects like imitation feces made of plastic or chocolate . . . or a synthetic mucuslike liquid, even though the observer knows the objects are not what they seem.

On this basis, Rozin et al. (2000: 646–647) conclude that animals and infants do not have disgust, since "the notion of invisible entities and the notion that appearance is distinct from reality are cognitive achievements of considerable abstraction. . . . This cognitive limitation may be the principal barrier to a full childhood acquisition of disgust." (See also Rozin and Fallon 1987.) And the observable evidence supports this hypothesis; though animals and infants obviously find certain foods distasteful, they exhibit none of the symptoms of extreme offended repulsion that we associate with disgust.

Guilt is another emotion that emerges relatively late in an infant's repertoire. This in no way undermines the hypothesis that guilt is an innate emotion, for not all "design features" are intended to appear at birth—just consider puberty. Happiness, sadness, anger, and fear are the emotions that seem to appear first (Emde 1980), and when children begin to use language it is the names of these emotions that they understand and use before others. One study found that over 90 percent of children aged 30–35 months understood the term "scared," but at 54–59 months still only 23 percent understood "guilt" (Ridgeway et al. 1985). Needless to say, children may have the capacity to experience guilt before they are competent with the term, and some rudimentary elements of the emotion may be found in very young infants (see Zahn-Waxler and Kochanska 1989; Barrett 1995), but it remains reasonable to conclude that guilt arrives on the scene after other emotions, and the probable reason for this is that guilt, like disgust, involves a certain conceptual capability that takes some time to develop (see Kagan 1984; Damon 1988; Lewis 1992). We must not be diverted from this conclusion by the fact that guilt, like many other complex traits, develops gradually. Certainly we can in relaxed conversation point to a 2-year-old who has some of the elements of full-blown guilt and describe her as having "guilt," just as we can point to a 1-year-old who has mastered "mama" and "dada" and describe her as "talking." But just as it would be crazy to conclude on the basis of the latter observation that the 1-year-old really satisfies the necessary and sufficient conditions for having language, and that all the sophisticated combinatorial abilities she will subsequently develop are strictly unnecessary components of language, so too is it mistaken to assume that the cognitive elements of guilt and disgust are unnecessary. Our emotion words are designed primarily to apply to normal adult humans, and the fact that on occasions we may find it conversationally useful to extend them to other subjects who satisfy *some* of the criteria for having these emotions hardly shows that the criteria which are not satisfied by such subjects are not really criteria at all.

In calling attention to the fact that some emotions require conceptual sophistication, I am not supporting the view that such emotions require beliefs. A lot of people have thought that beliefs are a crucial part of emotions. The ancient Stoics, in fact, thought that emotions just *are* beliefs. I think this is mistaken, and if you don't agree then just go and see a decent horror movie. (Analogous advice for an ancient Stoic: Go and see a decent tragedy.) Suppose the movie is about vampires, and it scares you. Some philosophers would deny even this possibility. So tied are they to the thought that emotions must involve beliefs that when forced to consider engagement with fiction—where one doesn't really believe what one is witnessing—they deny that we have real emotions at all: Horror movies don't frighten us, tragic novels don't make us sad, gross-out movies don't disgust us. Next they will be telling us that fictional characters can't be sexy or funny! Common sense can of course be mistaken, but when what would prove it mistaken is a shaky philosophical thesis—one that offers no explanation of why common sense would be so misguided—then most likely it is the philosopher who has it wrong. (For a more detailed discussion of this point, see Joyce 2000a.)

But our emotional responses to fiction are nevertheless puzzling. In the case of a horror movie, exactly what are you frightened of? You might claim that images of vampires have reminded you of actual threats, such as serial killers, and it is these that you are really frightened of. But this seems mistaken. You are certainly not aware of thinking of serial killers—all your fearful thoughts concern bloodthirsty vampires—and so the proponent of this "mnemonic view" must hold that the real object of your fear is subconscious. Not an incoherent view, maybe, but highly implausible. No, you are frightened of *vampires*, and yet you don't believe that they exist; you don't believe that anything is threatening you (or anyone real), even for a moment. If you did believe it, you would get yourself a string of garlic and a wooden stake. However, even if you don't *believe* that vampires are out for your blood, you can still *entertain the thought* of this. As you lie sleeplessly in bed, nervously listening to the branch scratch the windowpane, the proposition "Vampires are after me" is being *thought* by you but not affirmed by you. One might say that you are scared *by* the thought, but you are not scared *of* the thought (Lamarque 1981, 1991; Joyce 2000a). The thought as a mental state with content (as an intentional state) provides the content of your fear: vampires. The thought as a brain event is what causes your fear. The important point to note, given what was argued above, is that thinking *p* involves the deployment of the same concepts as does believing *p*. So the thesis that an emotion may require cognitive sophistication is not threatened by the phenomenon of emotional reactions to fiction.

Can one have *any* emotion in response to a fiction? This may seem an unnecessary question for us to engage with, but in fact the answer is important to matters that will be discussed toward the end of this book, and now is a good time to address it. It does seem that there are certain emotions that we don't typically have in response to fiction. Jealousy has been cited as one (Radford 1995; Neill 1995). But in fact I see no reason why one might not have jealousy in response to a fiction, though I admit that it is rare. Suppose that a single person were just *imagining* himself to have a girlfriend, and then went on (somewhat gloomily) to imagine her affections being won by a younger and more dynamic suitor. Couldn't the mere thought of this get his blood up? Couldn't it be jealousy that he is feeling? It seems to me that the positive answer is most natural. This imaginative person is still jealous *of* someone, but it is not a real person; he doesn't *believe* that another is winning the object of his affections, but he is entertaining the thought of this occurring. The reason that jealousy of a fictional character is an unusual phenomenon is that it is an emotion that cannot be vicarious, for it involves the conception of oneself standing in a relation to another—a very particular kind of relation—and books and movies don't typically encourage this. Reading *Anna Karenina* may involve the act of make-believe that Anna exists, but it doesn't normally involve the act of make-believe that one is going to interact with her. I don't spend much time worrying about what I would say to Anna, or what she would think of the way I dress, or whether I am going to be able to find a decent espresso in nineteenth-century St. Petersburg. This is not to deny that one *might* think these things. One might like the character so much that one starts to imagine oneself in a relationship with her, and one might accordingly feel jealous when Vronsky comes along. The claim is only that this is not a direction that fictions typically encourage one's imagination to take, and so it is rather unfamiliar.

In the same way, it is unusual to feel the emotion of guilt when engaged with a fiction, for guilt is usually aroused when one believes that one has wronged someone, and fictions generally don't invite the audience to entertain such acts of make-believe. But, as before, it doesn't seem that guilt *must* involve beliefs. If I sit and think in vivid detail about, say, my committing an act of reprehensible infidelity toward a friend (whether a real or imaginary friend)—not necessarily an act that I am in the least tempted to perform—then it seems that I can get a glimmer of guilt going. It is not the same as guilt directed at real-life wrongs, any more than fear of Hollywood vampires is the same as fear of dying in a car crash, but saying that it is "not the same" doesn't have to amount to "it counts as a different type of emotion altogether" or "it doesn't count as a real emotion at all." Everyday language uses the same terms for both kinds of scenarios, and all the empirical evidence we have about the neurology of emotions tells us that on this occasion common sense is correct. If emotions are designed by biological natural selection to deal with real-life problems, then one may wonder why it is they can also be triggered in response to mere imaginative acts. One explanation is, in the words of two eminent psychologists, simply that "the cognitive evaluations that engender emotions are sufficiently crude that they contain no reality check" (Johnson-Laird and Oatley 2000: 465)—just as, I suppose, the human system of sexual arousal need not check whether the object of excitement is a real person or a piece of colored paper in a magazine. Alternatively, one may think that the human tendency to enjoy fictional engagement served some positive adaptive purpose in the ancestral environment.[12]

One final general comment I want to make about emotions is to re-emphasize that nothing that has been said takes sides on the question of what an emotion *is*. The only theoretical options that have been excluded are those that would make beliefs necessary to emotions—thus, emotions cannot *be* beliefs. (So much for Stoic psychology.) All I have claimed is that for *some* emotions the deployment of concepts—sometimes within beliefs, sometimes within thoughts—is necessary. To the question "Necessary in what way?" I offer no answer because nothing in this book hinges on how it is answered. But one observation is worth making: From the fact that a type of emotion necessarily involves a certain type of belief or thought, it does not follow that when we refer to that emotion (using words like "pity," "disgust," and "guilt") we thereby in part denote that belief or thought. To understand what I mean, consider the concept of a *scar*. I happen to have three small marks on the palm of my right hand that look very much like a scar. And yet they are not a scar, since I was born with them; they were not caused by damage from an external source. To be a scar requires a certain causal history. This is an a priori necessity; it is something that we *mean* by the word "scar." Despite this, the event that is necessary to make a bodily mark a scar is not part of the referent of the word "scar"—in fact, it is hard to see how it could be, since it is what caused the scar. When I refer to "the scar on my ankle" (where I do have a scar from putting my foot through a window), I am referring to something that is *on my ankle*—something that can be seen and touched—not a weird hybrid entity made up of both a physical object and a window-smashing event that occurred years ago. (See Thalberg 1978; Shaffer 1983; Green 1992.)

Perhaps the relation between beliefs/thoughts and emotions matches the relation between events involving bodily damage and scars: a necessary accompaniment (and the cause) of the thing that the emotion word denotes. If so, then this leaves wide open the question of what the actual emotion *is*. Perhaps it is a feeling, or perhaps it is a neurological or physiological event. On the other hand, perhaps the belief/thought *is* part of the emotion (i.e., emotions are hybrid entities). Or perhaps it really is the emotion itself, and the feelings and physiological events are just unnecessary accompaniments. Fascinating as this question may be, to pursue its answer here would only be a distraction.

3.7 Guilt

What is interesting about guilt is that, along with shame and embarrassment, it is a self-directed emotion that guides one's moral conduct "from the inside." Whereas most of our discussion so far has tended to focus on other-directed moral judgments (Gak condemns Ogg for stealing his spear, etc.), it is clear that self-regulation is a vital feature of our moral lives and that it also requires explanation. Indeed, it is a tempting thought that a creature cannot be legitimately described as having a moral sense unless it has "internalized" prescriptions, and cannot be reasonably described as having internalized prescriptions unless disposed to apply them to itself; that is, unless it has a conscience. Darwin thought it reasonable to identify the "moral sense" with a conscience:

> . . . any animal whatever, endowed with well-marked social instincts, the parental and filial affections being here included, would inevitably acquire a moral sense or conscience, as soon as its intellectual powers had become as well developed, or nearly as well developed, as in man. ((1879) 2004: 120–121)

Context makes it apparent that the disjunction "moral sense or conscience" is not intended to specify two separate things but rather indicates broadly synonymous or co-referential terms; it is like saying "New York or the Big Apple," not "New York or Philadelphia." Just a few sentences earlier, Darwin has made the striking claim that "of all the differences between man and the lower animals, the moral sense or conscience is by far the most important" (120).

Darwin's first pronouncement leaves us with a puzzle. How does the addition of "intellectual powers" to prosocial sentiment lead to moral judgment? Why does an "intellectualization" amount to a "moralization"? One thing about which Darwin is obviously correct (and which I emphasized in sections 2.1 and 2.2) is that *something* must be added to prosocial inclinations before we can speak literally of a "moral sense," for a conscience requires a fair degree of cognitive sophistication. Though we speak of the "prickings" and "stabs" of conscience, this is just figurative; feeling the emotion of guilt is not really much like feeling pins and needles. Nor is the conscience just a series of strong, motivation-engaging inclinations. Having a conscience is not just a matter of not wanting to perform certain actions, or of disliking them; it is not wanting to perform them *for a certain reason*: because they are judged to be transgressions. It is no accident that the word "guilt" denotes both an emotion and a relation in which one can stand to a norm violation (as in "He is guilty of the crime"), for when one has the emotion of guilt one judges oneself to be guilty. In the absence of any such judgments, mere desires or inhibitions, no matter how firm and reliable, do not constitute the emotion of guilt.

We are thus already in a position to deal with at least one element of Darwin's puzzle. Something that seems odd about his claim that an intellectualization might amount to a moralization is that we naturally think of the conscience as being mediated largely by guilt—but guilt is an emotion, not an "intellectual power." If what I have said above is correct, however, this thinking relies on an uncomfortable dichotomy. Certainly guilt is an emotion—I am not denying this—but it is an emotion that involves "intellectual powers," if by this we mean that it requires the deployment of concepts.

What is the conceptual burden of guilt? It may be useful first to compare it briefly with the emotion of shame. Guilt seems most naturally to associate with the judgment that the person has performed a wrongful action for which amends might be made; shame seems to associate with a judgment that the person is "wrong in himself," and perhaps nothing can be done about it. One feels guilty for having told a lie, but one feels shame for being a liar. Guilt concerns transgressions; shame involves shortcomings. Guilt urges reparative action; shame encourages social withdrawal. One may feel shame about one's lowly upbringing, or one's enormous nose, or one's accidental defeat at the hands of a lesser rival, but one would not feel guilt about such things. (For useful discussion and further references, see Tangney and Fischer 1995; see also Niedenthal et al. 1994.) Though intuitively these seem to be promising ways of drawing the distinction, it would be pointless to expect any crisp line between the two, and in many instances a person can properly be described as having both emotions at once. Some languages apparently do not mark the distinction clearly at all (Levy 1973: 342), and some cultures do not elaborate guilt to the extent of shame, but neither of these observations implies that guilt does not exist in such cultures. Anthropologists have sometimes found it useful to distinguish "shame cultures" from "guilt cultures," and occasionally the implication is assumed to be that the former kind of cultures—in which shame is terribly important and intricately elaborated—do not recognize guilt at all. But when one goes back to the intellectual origin of this distinction—the work of the anthropologist Ruth Benedict—what one finds is shame being contrasted with "an internalized conviction of *sin*" (Benedict 1946: 223). Being connected to a framework of sin and redemption is just one way in which guilt can be culturally elaborated—it is a major strand of the Christian tradition—but it is a parochial mistake to assume that this is all there is to guilt, and thus it is a parochial mistake to conclude that any culture unfamiliar with that framework therefore has no concept of *guilt*.

Psychologists give us a more complex image of guilt. (See Zahn-Waxler and Kochanska 1988; Baumeister et al. 1994.) They reveal that guilt is overwhelmingly elicited by episodes of harming others (Hoffman 1982; Tangney 1992), the strength of the guilt being proportional to the perceived importance of the social relationship with the victim (Fiske 1991; Baumeister et al. 1994). Thus, it is not surprising that guilt is typically associated with moral transgressions (Tangney 1992). We all know that people can feel guilty over non-moral and self-regarding transgressions, but the fact that such instances seem to require the most socialization to instill and the fact that they are the easiest to extinguish suggest that they are the instances most derivative from "core guilt."

Freud (1929: 123) claimed that guilt "expresses itself as a need for punishment"—an astute comment from someone who said a lot of harebrained things about the development of guilt. Note how different this is from the *fear of* punishment. One can fear punishment without feeling guilty, and one can feel guilty without fearing punishment. A person may know that she has broken some rules, and fear that punishment is looming, but unless she in some sense endorses those rules (even if she doesn't all-things-considered endorse the rules) she won't feel guilty. Guilt requires that she judge not that she might be punished but that she deserves to be. This, I think, is an improvement on Freud's view of guilt as involving *the need* for punishment, for one might feel the need for punishment without judging it to be deserved, and one might judge it to be deserved without feeling the need for it.

Note the parenthetical comment above that a person may endorse rules without *all-things-considered* endorsing the rules. A former Roman Catholic may feel guilty about using contraception even though she no longer supports the doctrine of the Catholic Church. However, clearly these values continue to have some kind of hold over her; the thought that contraception is some kind of transgression is still active in her psyche; the rule remains endorsed by one fragment of her mind, even if it doesn't represent her all-things-considered judgment. The denial of this—the view that the emotion of guilt is just some kind of concept-less anxiety or conditioned raw aversion—doesn't stand up to scrutiny. Of course a former Catholic *might* be left with nothing but a non-cognitive aversion toward certain activities, but with no accompanying thought of *transgression* or *desert* or *blameworthiness* entering her head (even if it is just an annoying whisper from the back of her head against her better judgment) it won't count as guilt. Similarly, well-documented cases of "survivor guilt" might be supposed to be a counterexample to the claim that guilt involves thoughts of "transgression," but again I would emphasize that, although such subjects may know very well at a rational level that they are not responsible for the harm that befell others, they cannot shake the feeling that they have "done something wrong." It is precisely because their experience has this phenomenology that we are inclined to call their distress "guilt."

Let me draw two major conclusions from the foregoing discussion. First, if guilt necessarily involves the making of self-oriented moral judgments, then to the extent that we decide guilt is an innate mechanism we must conclude that the capacity to make moral judgments is innate. But this conclusion is probably a bit too strong, since we must acknowledge that occasionally guilt involves non-moral transgressions. The safer and more cautious conclusion is that to the extent that we decide guilt is an innate mechanism we must conclude that humans have an innate capacity to judge certain actions to be transgressions of endorsed normative frameworks, meriting reparative or punitive response. Second, we can now put together the results of the second half of this chapter with the results of the first half, to draw the conclusion that non-language-users cannot have the emotion of guilt. Language is a prerequisite for the ascription of certain evaluative concepts, and such concepts are necessary for having certain moral emotions. My childhood dog—for all his submissive behavior and awareness of potential negative reactions—did not and could not have the emotion of guilt. He probably had something going on in his canine brain that bore some resemblance to what goes on in a human brain when the human experiences guilt, and that "something" might well have modified his behavior, and may even count as an emotion. But it wasn't *guilt*. We would do better to call it "proto-guilt," or to treat it as a whole new emotion-type: "dog-guilt" or "animal-guilt." This may sound pedantic to the point of silliness, but I am not arguing that such exactitude should be respected in ordinary conversation. I *am* arguing that when we are speaking in a careful and reflective way about animal cognition—which is precisely what we are doing in this book—then such expressions need to be qualified or dropped.

What, then, has become problematized is the common, simple assumption that the social life our distant ancestors was regulated by prosocial emotions such as love, anger, contempt, disgust, and guilt, and that the capacity to wield sophisticated abstract concepts then somehow arrived on the scene and made moral judgment possible. Rather, the emergence of certain prosocial emotions, the "arrival" of certain concepts, and the advancement of language all are entwined, making the evolution of the human moral sense an untidy affair. This is not to deny that certain prosocial emotions—such as love and sympathy—might antedate both language and moral judgment (I as much as argued this in section 2.1), for I haven't insisted on the strong claim that *all* emotions require concepts, and a fortiori I haven't argued that they all require evaluative concepts. I am doubtful that all the things we categorize as emotions are susceptible to a neat unified analysis (though I confess to having in the past succumbed to the temptation to provide one: see Joyce 2000a). All I have claimed with assurance is that *guilt*, an emotion that is central to the moral conscience, comes with evaluative concepts. If pressed to name other emotions of which this is also true, shame, indignation, and "moral disgust" would be among the first I would mention.

But, as was noted earlier, the observation that the emergence of these emotions is wrapped up in the evolution of language and the moral sense still leaves us wondering about some big questions. We cannot just conveniently stipulate that when language arrived on the scene so too, as if by magic, did this idea of "a transgression meriting reparative or punitive response." We still need to appreciate how and why the tendency to think something like *that* would arise. Then and only then will we have in hand a hypothesis about how the capacity to make moral judgments developed through biological natural selection. Let us now turn to these questions.

4　The Moral Sense

4.1　Preview

What are the practical advantages of moral thinking? Irrespective of one's views on the evolution of a moral sense, this is a good question to ponder. It is important that the question be tensed correctly here, for we are not trying to discover how morality is adaptive, but rather how it might have come to be an adaptation—that is, how it *was* adaptive. Unless we have a credible working hypothesis of why a trait was useful to our ancestors, in the sense of advancing their reproductive fitness, we can never be comfortable with the claim that natural selection produced it. (Of course, no such hypothesis is sufficient; from the fact that we can tell a plausible story about how a trait could have been fashioned by natural selection, it hardly follows that it was thus produced.) Whether morality continues to be useful is another matter, and is something that has been denied by certain radical thinkers. (Nietzsche may be interpreted this way; see also Hinckfuss 1987 and Garner 1994.) It is possible that a tendency to make moral judgments is like the human sweet tooth, which was adaptive relative to ancient environments where sweetness was a rare commodity and a safe bet for nutritional value but which has become a life-threatening hindrance to many people when the temptations are abundantly present and easily accessible. I say that this is possible, but I don't think it is likely. Understanding how moral thinking enhanced the reproductive fitness of our ancestors is likely to reveal something about how it continues to be generally useful to us, and vice versa. (This is not to claim that it will reveal that morality continues to be *adaptive*; the term "useful" in the previous sentence is a vernacular one that has little to do with the replicative powers of genes.)

I think it clarifies matters to begin by subdividing the problem into distinct questions (though in fact later we will find cause for re-merging two of these questions). First, there is the issue of whether the moral sense evolved via group selection or individual selection. If group selection is the principal process we need to ask why having individuals engaged in moral thinking might be beneficial to the group, whereas if individual selection is the principal process we must ask why making moral judgments might enhance an individual's fitness. Second, we should distinguish the benefits that might arise from morally judging *others* from the benefits that might arise from regulating one's *own* behavior by moral deliberation, for it is quite possible that these are separate adaptations for distinct evolutionary purposes. Thus there are four possible questions worthy of investigation:

In what way might judging others in moral terms benefit one's group?
In what way might judging others in moral terms benefit oneself?
In what way might judging oneself in moral terms benefit one's group?
In what way might judging oneself in moral terms benefit oneself?

Note that it is not incumbent on the moral nativist to answer *all* these questions in a positive manner; his answer to up to three of them might be "It doesn't." As a matter of fact, however, I think that all can be plausibly answered. In what follows (sections 4.2 and 4.3) I will concentrate on outlining an answer to the fourth question, since it seems intuitively the most challenging. Our interest here is in a *why* question: Why would a moral sense evolve by natural selection? (Why might a moral sense be adaptive?) The second task of this chapter is to direct attention to a naturally concomitant *how* question: *How* did a moral sense evolve?—What did natural selection do to the human brain to enable moral judgment? The hypothesis to be advocated in section 4.4 is that the human tendency to project emotions onto the world lies at the heart of our moral sense. As to the further reasonable question "What did natural selection do to the human brain to enable this projection of the emotions" I have little to say. Eventually our explanations peter out at the limit of what we know about how brains work.

The completion of these two tasks later in the chapter will find us with a big fat just-so story about the evolution of morality on the table. Since I am averse to leaving matters at that, my third task in this chapter (section 4.5) is to conclude with a review of some empirical evidence in support of the story, thus turning it into a respectable scientific hypothesis.

4.2 Conscience as a Personal Commitment

Why might judging oneself in moral terms—that is, having a conscience—enhance one's reproductive fitness relative to competitors lacking such a trait? My thinking on this matter is dominated by the natural assumption that an individual sincerely judging some available action in a morally positive light increases the probability that the individual will perform that action (likewise, mutatis mutandis, judging an action in a morally negative light). If reproductive fitness will be served by performance or omission of a certain action, then it will be served by any psychological mechanism that ensures or probabilifies this performance or omission (relative to mechanisms that do so less effectively). Thus self-directed moral judgment may enhance reproductive fitness so long as it is attached to the appropriate actions. We have already seen that the "appropriate actions"—that is, the fitness enhancing actions—will in many circumstances include helpful and cooperative behaviors. Therefore it may serve an individual's fitness to judge certain prosocial behaviors—*her own* prosocial behaviors—in moral terms.

Our focus should be on the premise that moral judgment engages motivation and thus probabilifies action. Many modern philosophers have endorsed a thesis known as "motivation internalism": that moral judgment involves motivation to act *as a matter of a priori necessity* (to be contrasted with motivation externalism). Often this view is associated with non-cognitivism, though I have argued elsewhere (2002; forthcoming a) that this connection is problematic. Recall from chapter 2 that when a non-cognitivist claims that moral judgments express some kind of conative, motivation-implicating state, the expression relation in play is not a causal one but a conventional one. Thus non-cognitivism does not entail that moral judgments are necessarily accompanied by motivation, any more than the fact that apologies express regret entails that there is no such thing as an insincere apology. Nevertheless, my qualified endorsement of non-cognitivism in section 2.3 does imply some kind of a priori relation between moral judgment and motivation: A "canonical moral judgment" (as we might call it) is accompanied by motivational states. A canonical speech act is one in which the speaker actually has all the mental states expressed by the speech act at the time of utterance. So if the public moral judgment "Stealing is wrong" expresses both the belief that stealing is wrong and a conative acceptance of a standard condemning the activity, then a canonical token of this judgment is one made by a person who has both these mental states. And since "conative acceptance" denotes a motivation-implicating state, it follows that a canonical moral judgment involves motivation.[1]

One doesn't have to accept this metaethical view in order to agree that moral judgment affects motivation—a purely contingent psychological connection will suffice to make the point. That there is such a connection can be brought out by considering the phenomenon of weakness of will. Consider how we humans, though pretty good at calculating long-term benefits, are notoriously poor at getting our motivations in line with the output of these deliberations. Even when it is abundantly clear that the pursuit of short-term gain is going to harm us in the long run, we still find ourselves tempted and succumbing to temptation. We eat junk food, we stay up too late, we grade our students' essays at the last possible moment, we accumulate an assortment of barely used exercise machines in the attic, we procrastinate endlessly on nearly everything. Some of us are worse offenders than others, and no doubt there are a few godlike individuals who might reasonably claim freedom from such practical vice, but no one could deny that the inability to get one's motivations in line with what one judges to be prudent, the tendency to surrender to instant gratification while trampling the inner voice of practical reason, is a marked feature of human psychology.

I confess to painting a one-sided picture here in order to draw attention to a phenomenon; humans are, of course, at the same time spectacularly prudent compared with other animals. But there certainly appears to be an important gap between the output of our mechanism for prudential reasoning and the springs of motivation and action. Prudential calculations in favor of a course of action ("I should order the salad for the sake of my health") simply do not reliably result in pursuit of that course of action. Most of us know this from personal experience, and there is abundant empirical evidence available in support (Schelling 1980; Elster 1984; Ainslie 1992). This demands an explanation; why has natural selection left us with a design flaw that so often handicaps the pursuit of our own best interests? Presumably it is the result of different psychological faculties, each with its own agenda, tugging for satisfaction in the behavioral realm. But though this "competing faculties" view is likely to be correct (as even Plato recognized), we might still wonder why natural selection would not rectify such a glaring problem. The probable answer is that weakness of will is the inevitable price to pay for some other valuable end. That end might be the ability of a creature to calculate subjective preferences in a flexible way. A creature that in any circumstances conceives of a banana as the highest good will be at a constant disadvantage to a creature that is able to reassess the value of the banana depending on circumstances. A banana isn't worth much when you are full; when you are on the brink of starvation it may in fact be the highest available good. But the inevitable price of any such plastic system of goal assessment (i.e., practical intelligence) is error. Just as biological natural selection cannot create a creature that has a flexible belief-formation system *and always forms true beliefs*, nor can it build a creature that has a flexible capacity for assessing the subjective value of things *and always does so correctly*. Weakness of will, according to this view, is a particular type of this sort of practical error, where the lure of tangible short-term profit—this allure itself the output of an innate mechanism—causes a subject to make a mistake, to "rationalize" a poor choice.

Suppose there was a realm of action of such recurrent importance that nature did not want practical success to depend on the frail caprice of ordinary human practical intelligence. That realm might, for example, pertain to certain forms of cooperative behavior toward one's fellows. The benefits that may come from cooperation—enhanced reputation, for example—are typically long-term values, and merely to be aware of and desire these long-term advantages does not guarantee that the goal will be effectively pursued, any more than the firm desire to live a long life guarantees that a person will give up fatty foods. The hypothesis, then, is that natural selection opted for a special motivational mechanism for this realm: moral conscience. If you are thinking of an outcome in terms of something that you desire, you can always say to yourself "But maybe forgoing the satisfaction of that desire wouldn't be *that* terrible." If, however, you are thinking of the outcome as something that is *desirable*—as having the quality of *demanding* desire—then your scope for rationalizing a spur-of-the-moment devaluation narrows. When a person believes that an act of cooperation is *morally* required—that it *must* be performed whether he likes it or not—then the possibilities for further internal negotiation on the matter diminish. If a person believes an action to be required by an authority from which he cannot escape, if he believes that in not performing it he will not merely frustrate himself, but will become *reprehensible* and *deserving of disapprobation*—then he is more likely to perform the action. The distinctive value of imperatives imbued with practical clout is that they silence further calculation, which is a valuable thing when our prudential calculations can so easily be hijacked by interfering forces and rationalizations. What is being suggested, then, is that self-directed moral judgments can act as a kind of *personal commitment*, in that thinking of one's actions in moral terms eliminates certain practical possibilities from the space of deliberative reasoning in a way that thinking "I just don't like X" does not.

In saying this I am in part agreeing with Daniel Dennett (1995), who argues that moral principles function as "conversation-stoppers": considerations that can be dropped into a decision process (be it a personal or interpersonal decision) in order to stop mechanisms or people from endlessly processing, endlessly reconsidering, endlessly asking for further justification. "Any policy *may* be questioned, so, unless we provide for some brute and a-rational termination of the issue, we will design a decision process that spirals fruitlessly to infinity" (Dennett 1995: 506). In deciding how to treat a criminal, the consideration "He has a moral right to a fair trial" seems to close off further discussion. In deciding whether to shoplift, the consideration "It is wrong to shoplift; I mustn't do it" puts an end to deliberations. "Faced with a world in which such predicaments are not unknown," says Dennett, "we can recognize the appeal of . . . some unquestioning dogmatism that will render agents impervious to the subtle invasions of hyper-rationality" (ibid.: 508). (Dennett's views will be discussed further in chapter 5.)

Imagine a person with no capacity to engage in moralized thinking. Assume that it is in his interests to maintain a reciprocal relationship with someone, and he does so either because he consciously desires the profits brought by the exchange or because he has been endowed with sympathy (albeit conditional sympathy) for his partner. Suppose, though, that he reneges on a deal for some arbitrary reason—perhaps the lure of short-term profit overwhelms him in a moment of distraction. (And why shouldn't it? Ex hypothesi, his reluctance to cheat is not based on a principle.) How does he now feel? The fact that he has broken a habit may surprise him. The fact that he has hurt someone he didn't want to hurt may cause him disappointment and distress. But the important thing is that he can feel no *guilt*, for guilt requires the thought that one has transgressed against a norm. With no moral concepts in play, this person does not have access to the thought that he deserves to be punished for his action. He regrets, but he cannot repent. His active sympathy may prompt in him a desire to alleviate the victim's suffering (he may even feel a desire to compensate the injured party); however, since he has no thought that he *must* do something to make amends, if he is distracted by other matters, causing his sympathy for the victim to fade, then there is nothing to propel his deliberations back to the resolution that "something must be done." In the end, he has just done something out of character that he wishes he hadn't done. "Sympathy," James Q. Wilson once wrote, "is a fragile and evanescent emotion. It is easily aroused but quickly forgotten; when remembered but not acted upon, its failure to produce action is easily rationalized. The sight of a lost dog or a wounded fledgling can upset us greatly even though we know that the woods are filled with lost and injured animals" (1993: 50).

By comparison, a person who in addition to being sympathetic judges that cheating is morally wrong will feel very differently if on occasion she succumbs to temptation. She can tell herself that she has done something *wrong*, that her action was *unfair* or *unjust*, that she *must* make amends, that she not only has risked punishment but *deserves* it. The emotion of guilt is available to her. In addition, she can judge that other offenders deserve punishment too—a thought that was unavailable to our previous non-moralized agent. The fact that these more robust forms of self-recrimination are available to the moralized thinker when she does cheat strongly suggests that when she is behaving herself her motivation not to cheat is more reliable and resolute than that of her non-moralized counterpart. Although in the preceding I have put a certain spin on the thesis—from my armchair, as it were—plenty of empirical evidence confirms the hypothesis that self-directed moral judgments influence behavior (Keltner et al. 1995; Bandura et al. 1996; Bandura 1999; Ferguson et al. 1999; Tangney 2001; Beer et al. 2003; Keltner 2003; Covert et al. 2003; Ketelaar and Au 2003).

Note that the argument doesn't depend on comparing someone who is motivated by non-moralized sympathy with someone who is utterly unsympathetic but has a robust rational sense of moral duty—a thought experiment familiar to students of Kant. First, we are granting the moralized person all the sympathies and inclinations of the non-moralized person; the argument is just that moral judgment *adds something* to that motivational profile, that it gives her an edge. Nor is the claim that moral thinking always does better than prudential thinking, for a lot of the time prudential thinking is completely resolute (the knowledge that crossing the highway will result in your death is probably more motivationally engaging than the judgment that jaywalking is morally forbidden); the argument is just that moral judgment can step in on those occasions when prudence may falter (in particular when the prudential gain is a probabilistic long-term affair). Also it must be remembered that moral judgment is not being conceived of here as the cool intellectualized affair that Kant fancied it to be; among the things moral judgment contributes to a person's mental life, for example, is the emotion of guilt. When I say that moral judgment promotes motivation, I am including the motivational efficacy of certain moral sentiments. The term "moral sentiment" can lead to confusion in this debate, since sometimes it refers to emotions that are considered morally laudable or broadly prosocial (such as love or benevolence), which I have set aside from our discussion, and sometimes it refers to emotions that can *involve* moral judgment (such as guilt). Part of what is being advocated is that moral sentiments of the former kind will be reinforced in a motivation-bolstering way if supplemented by moral sentiments of the latter kind.

The hypothesis, then, at its first approximation, is that a judgment like "That wouldn't be right; it would be reprehensible for me to do that" can play a dynamic role in deliberation, emotion, and desire-formation, prompting and strengthening certain desires and blocking certain considerations from even arising in practical deliberation, thus increasing the likelihood that certain adaptive social behaviors will be performed.[2] Needless to say, a moral judgment in favor of an action is no *guarantor* that the action will be performed, but so long as it at least increases the likelihood of the performance then this may be its evolutionary function. Of course, ultimately what determines whether a person acts is the strength of her desires in favor of acting compared with her desires against acting. This last observation, however, raises a worry about the whole preceding argument. It may be true that moral judgment does bolster motivation, and that typically it does so better than ordinary prudential deliberation alone; however, as the biologist and philosopher David Lahti (2003) points out, this still leaves us with the question of why natural selection did not simply make humans with stronger desires that directly favor cooperation in certain circumstances. After all, for some adaptive behaviors this is precisely what evolution has granted us. Protective actions toward our offspring, for example, appear to be regulated by robust raw emotions, not primarily by any moralistic sense of duty. These emotions are by and large stoutly resistant to the lures of weakness of will: Few are tempted to rationalize a course of action that promises short-term gain while resulting in injury to their beloved infant. Moreover, insofar as our hominid forebears already had in place the neurological mechanisms for such strong desires, it is something of a mystery why the inherently conservative force of natural selection would not press into service these extant mechanisms in order to govern any novel adaptive behavior, rather than fabricating a "radically different" and "biologically unprecedented mechanism for a purpose which is achieved regularly in nature by much more straightforward means" (Lahti 2003: 644). Lahti's challenge must be addressed.

Whenever an evolutionary psychologist hypothesizes about the presence of a specialized mechanism functioning to govern an adaptive behavior, the following question can always be raised: "Why would natural selection bother with that mechanism? Why wouldn't it simply create an overwhelmingly strong desire to perform that behavior?" That there is something fishy about this question is revealed if we consider some non-moral cases. Think instead about the psychological reward systems that have evolved in humans regarding sex and eating. One might ask why natural selection bothered giving us all that complicated physiological equipment needed for having an orgasm—why not design us simply to *want* to have sex? It seems a misguided question. Natural selection *did* make us want to have sex, and one of its means of ensuring this desire was precisely the human orgasm. Similarly, natural selection made us want to eat food, and one of its means of achieving this was to create a creature for whom food tastes good. And perhaps natural selection has made us want to cooperate, and granting us a tendency to think of cooperation in moral terms (where this includes the capacity for guilt) is a means of securing this desire. That natural selection may employ a distinctive *means* for creating and strengthening a type of fitness-advancing desire is no more mysterious in the moral case than in the other two cases. Granted, in the moral case we are considering a "biologically unprecedented mechanism"—something that evolved uniquely in the hominid line—but insofar as human social relations *are* radically different from those of other animals, a radically different solution may have been necessary. Note also that despite the conservatism of natural selection, there is an obvious reason that distinct fitness-advancing behaviors will often require different mechanisms motivating them: If eating or promise-keeping were rewarded with an orgasm, an individual might not bother with sex.

It is still reasonable to inquire what special features a moral judgment might have that render it suited to the evolutionary task we are speculatively assigning it here. An important part of the answer, I think, concerns the public nature of moral judgments. That we are now focusing on self-directed moral judgments shouldn't lead us to assume that we are talking about a private mental phenomenon. There can be private other-directed judgments (e.g., ruminating quietly to oneself "John's such a bastard"), just as there can be publicly announced self-directed judgments ("I want you all to know that I'm thoroughly ashamed of what I did"). A moral judgment, even a self-directed one, is essentially communicative; indeed, if my argument of chapter 3 is correct—that moral judgment as a mental phenomenon is dependent on moral judgment as a linguistic phenomenon—then the very idea of a wholly private moral judgment is problematic. A moral judgment is something that may be asserted in the course of collective negotiation, may be employed to stake a claim, to justify a decision, to provide warrant for a punishment, to criticize or praise another's conduct or character, or to present evidence of one's own character. The manner in which thinking of a possible course of action in morally positive terms promotes the motivation to perform it cannot be divorced from this public sphere. Even when my private conscience guides me to refrain from cheating with the thought "Cheating is wrong," I am aware that this is a consideration that might be brought into the domain of public deliberation if I am required to justify my actions; I am accepting that, were I to cheat, punishment from others would be warranted. By comparison, the proposition "I just don't like cheating" may be brought forward to *explain* one's actions, but it lacks the normative *justificatory* force of a moral consideration.[3]

For clarity let me locate myself relative to a slightly different debate. On what is arguably the common-sense view, in everyday life people make moral decisions through a process of reasoning, and their emotions and motivations respond appropriately: Mary reasons that Fred's action was morally wrong, this judgment causes her to feel indignant, and this emotion prompts her action of slapping Fred's face. An alternative view—championed most cogently by the psychologist Jonathan Haidt (2001)—says that common sense has things the wrong way around. Rather, Fred's actions prompt in Mary the emotion of indignation (say), which causes her to slap his face, and her reasoning concerning why his action is morally wrong is a kind of post hoc construction. The view for which I am arguing may look at a glance as if it is opposed to Haidt's, but it is not (which is a good thing, since Haidt presents plenty of persuasive empirical evidence, some of which will be discussed later in this chapter). I haven't made the claim that moral *reasoning* prompts moral judgment or moral behavior. Rather, the hypothesis is that moral judgment (however it is arrived at— e.g., whether through reasoning, emotion, or gut intuition) plays a role in motivating behavior. Remember that a moral judgment may well be "embedded" in an emotion, so when I speak of moral judgment prompting action I include the motivational effects of guilt, disgust, approval, etc. Even if it is true that many moral judgments are produced by post hoc rationalization, this doesn't imply that they have no motivational role to play. Perhaps Fred's action initially prompts Mary's indignation, which leads to her slapping him, and only subsequently does her reasoning produce the new moral judgment "Fred is a sexist pig." But this new moral judgment, though a "rationalization," may serve a practical purpose. It may bolster Mary's resolve to avoid Fred even more effectively than would the raw indignation alone. More importantly, it gives Mary something to say in the public domain to justify her slapping of Fred and to provide others with a deliberative consideration against him. Haidt himself highlights this link, emphasizing that a moral judgment "is not just a single act that occurs in a single person's mind. It is an ongoing process, often spread out over time and over multiple people. Reasons and arguments can circulate and affect people, even if individuals rarely engage in private moral reasoning them- selves" (2001: 828–829). This is no less true of self-directed moral judgments than it is of Mary's other-directed judgment concerning Fred. A person's resolve to act (or not to act) is importantly affected by her conception of how others will receive her decisions, her confidence in to whom she can justify herself, her perception of herself as acting from considerations that would also move her fellows—in short, her experience of herself as a social being. Lahti's puzzle is solved when we realize that a moral judgment affects motivation not by giving an extra little private mental nudge in favor of certain courses of action, but by providing a deliberative consideration that (putatively) cannot be legitimately ignored, thus allowing moral judgments—even self-directed ones—to play a justificatory role on a social stage in a way that unmediated desires cannot.

This reasoning leads me to supplement the simple hypothesis with which we started (i.e., that the evolutionary function of moral judgment is to provide added motivation in favor of certain adaptive social behaviors). Morally disapproving of one's own action (or potential action)—as opposed to disliking that action—provides a basis for corresponding *other*-directed moral judgments. No matter how much I dislike something, this inclination alone is not relevant to my judgments concerning *others* pursuing that thing: "I won't pursue X because I don't like X" makes perfect sense, but "You won't pursue X because I don't like X" makes little sense. By comparison, the assertion of "The pursuit of X is morally wrong" demands both *my* avoidance of X and *yours*. Near the beginning of this chapter, I distinguished between the question of what benefits self-directed moral judgments bring and the question of what benefits other-directed moral judgments bring. These two questions, I am now observing, are not independent of each other—which should hardly be surprising. To be sure, we should now see that one of the adaptive advantages of moral judgment is precisely its capacity to unite these two matters. By providing a framework within which both one's own actions and others' actions may be evaluated, moral judgments can act as a kind of "common currency" for collective negotiation and decision making. Moral judgment thus can function as a kind of social glue, bonding individuals together in a shared justificatory structure and providing a tool for solving many group coordination problems. Of particular importance is that although a non-moralized strong negative emotional reaction (e.g., anger) may prompt a punitive response, it takes a moral judgment to *license* punishment, and thus the latter serves far more effectively to govern public decisions in a large group than do non-moralized emotions, especially when such emotions may (at the end of a long day's hunting and gathering) be listless, distracted, or divided. Guilt—involving a self-directed judgment that punishment is deserved—may serve the individual by inhibiting his own usual defensive mechanisms, prompting him to submit to punishment or at least to apologize, and thus quickly get back on a good footing with his fellows. (See Trivers 1985: 389.)

Although for brevity's sake I have spoken of moral judgments as bolstering the motivation to cooperate, I don't mean to imply that we are designed to be *unconditional* cooperators. The moral sense is not a proclivity to judge cooperation as morally good in any circumstance—something that looks like a recipe for disastrous exploitation. By the same token, the fact that we have innate mechanisms dedicated to making us want to eat, rewarding us with pleasure for doing so, doesn't mean that we eat unconditionally and indiscriminately. We may be designed to be very plastic with respect to cooperative strategies. How generous one can afford to be, or how miserly one is forced to be, will depend on how resource-rich is one's environment. Who is a promising partner and who is a scoundrel is something we learn. One can moralize a conditional strategy, such as "Be trusting, but don't be a sucker." One can moralize non-cooperation, seeing it as forbidden in certain circumstances. The idea being advocated is that there are adaptive benefits to be had by moralizing the whole plastic social structure. Doing so prevents under-performance, which is not to be confused with encouraging over-performance. It is true that there is a sense in which any boost to the motive to cooperate on a token occasion means that one may be encouraged to commit a practical error—to stick with an exchange relation when one's fitness would really be better served by cheating. (Think of where Thomas More's moral convictions took him.) But this is the same sense in which any natural reward system can lead us to occasional and even disastrous error: The craving for food can lead someone to eat a poisonous plant, and the pleasures of sex can result in making powerful enemies.

4.3 Conscience as an Interpersonal Commitment

In the previous section I argued that thinking of an action as morally required will frequently have a positive impact on a person's motivations. How much benefit this brings to the individual depends on which actions she is moralizing: If she is moralizing prudent actions—the focus of the above discussion—this will be a very good thing for her; but if she is seeing self-harming actions as morally required this may be disastrous for her. However, another argument allows that an individual strengthening her resolve to perform even *imprudent* actions may, in certain circumstances, be to her advantage. Since moralized thinking is, I have argued, motivationally resolute thinking, this is a further argument in favor of the thesis that it may be in a creature's best interests to have a moral conscience. The argument is due to the economist Robert Frank (1988).

Consider the inconvenient lengths to which a person might go in order to secure a refund of $10 for a faulty consumer item. If it is pointed out that this inconvenience far outweighs the cost of simply buying a new item, the response will usually be "Yes, but *it's the principle of the thing.*" What sense can be made of this apparently irrational attitude? One answer is that in behaving in this way a person establishes a reputation for herself, and thereby reduces the chances of being cheated in the future. But this has only limited applicability, for we often pursue things "on principle" even knowing that our future interactants will know nothing of this behavior. Frank's answer is that such behavior is governed by emotions—in this case, an emotion we might call "indignant anger"—and such emotions act as guarantors that certain behaviors will be pursued even to the point of self-harm, overriding prudent calculations. Consider a shopkeeper's point of view. If he is faced with a customer who always calculates prudently, and he also knows that it will cost this customer more than $10 worth of inconvenience to return an item, then he can without a care sell a defective $10 item. But if faced with a second customer whom he knows will pursue the matter of a faulty item to great lengths, who will sacrifice an *irrational* amount of energy on seeking redress, he will ensure that the $10 item he is selling is in good working order. Now ask yourself which kind of customer you would prefer to be: one who continually gets ripped off, or one who gets good service. The irony is that the latter kind of customer—the one who will go to self-destructive lengths to attain justice—will typically not need to go to such lengths (so long as she is able to communicate her "irrationality" to the shopkeeper), and will thus be better off.

According to Frank, a moral conscience is an emotional faculty that acts in a similar way as this emotional resolve to return a $10 item: as a guarantor that good conduct will be pursued even when it may be irrational to do so. Which kind of person would you want as a companion in a dangerous cooperative venture: someone whose cooperative behavior is governed by an ongoing prudent deliberative procedure, or someone who can *commit* to cooperating and will continue to do so even when it may be prudentially irrational? No one has put the answer quite as succinctly as the cartoon character Homer Simpson: "We don't need a thinker, we need a doer—someone who will act without considering the consequences!"[4] If your survival depends on your being selected as a partner in cooperative ventures (including your being selected as a mate), then it will be rational for you to choose to be the second kind of person. In other words, in circumstances where cooperative exchanges are important it is often rational to choose to have a faculty that urges you to what would otherwise be irrational behavior. That faculty is a conscience—a repertoire of judgments and emotions (most notable, guilt) that motivate behavior in accordance with accepted standards of conduct even when external sanctions are absent. (Obviously, people don't really *choose* to have a conscience at some early point in their lives; rather, biological natural selection has done the choosing. The point is that, hypothetically, a prudent person *would* choose to have a conscience.)

Frank's theory forces us to draw a distinction between the value that derives from being able to communicate to others your steadfast willingness to do something and the value that comes from actually doing it. The former is the primary source of value. In the case of the defective $10 item, the value came from being able to communicate to the shopkeeper a willingness to pursue the matter to great lengths. This caused the shopkeeper to think twice about defrauding you, and so you got the item replaced and weren't forced to pursue things to great lengths. But what if the shopkeeper calls your bluff? Then your commitment to pursue the matter will lead to you actually pursuing the matter (of course); you may end up with your $10 item replaced, but only after having gone to more than $10 worth of trouble. And surely, in this case, your commitment has backfired, forcing you to perform an irrational action? Not necessarily. Frank recognizes a secondary source of value: By performing the action in question, you have strengthened and sustained your commitment, rather than undermined it, and so placed yourself in good stead for future interactions. In other words, the presence of some mechanism of commitment may alter whether the action in question really is irrational for you perform. Going to enormous lengths to get a $10 item replaced may be irrational for a non-committed person, but it need not be irrational for a person who already has in place an emotional commitment to go to great lengths. This secondary value need not always be available, for the commitment may involve a resolve to perform an act that is not merely inconvenient but self-destructive. (A good example of a commitment is brandishing a grenade and threatening to blow yourself up along with your enemies unless they comply with some request.) In such cases, yes, the commitment in question is a guarantor that an irrational action will be performed, and the only value in play is the primary kind of value. But across a range of cases the presence of the commitment alters the cost-benefit structure, since it introduces the potential benefit of *strengthening the commitment*. In order to cover both kinds of cases, it is preferable to describe Frank's theory as claiming not that it may be in a person's best interests to show a firm willingness to perform irrational actions, but rather that it may be in a person's best interests to show a firm willingness to perform actions that would *otherwise* be irrational. The advice is not "Act imprudently" but rather "Restrict the role of prudential calculation in your decision procedure."

There is a limitation in Frank's presentation of his theory that we are in a position to improve upon. He takes himself to be explaining how it might be to an individual's advantage to have a conscience, but he treats the conscience seemingly just as a set of communicable motivation-engaging *feelings* in favor of and against certain courses of action. ("Consider, for example, a person capable of strong guilt feelings. This person will not cheat even when it is in her material interests to do so. The reason is not that she fears getting caught but that she simply does not *want* to cheat" (Frank 1988: 53).) But we have seen that such raw aversions alone, without associated moral cognitions—e.g., "I would deserve punishment if I did that"—don't suffice for the emotion of guilt, and thus don't suffice for having a conscience. Although Frank succeeds in explaining why natural selection may favor a creature able to demonstrate its commitment to what would otherwise be imprudent practices, he doesn't explain why conceiving of certain actions as "morally forbidden" is a more effective sort of commitment device than just having strong emotional inhibitions against these actions.

But we now have the resources to provide this explanation. The argument pursued in the previous section proposed that moral judgments can act as effective personal commitments better than mere inhibitions, providing a kind of motivational bulwark. It follows that if someone is able to communicate to others that he is thus personally committed, then moral judgments can also act as effective *interpersonal* commitments. Accepting this line of reasoning leads us somewhat away from Frank's model. Because Frank has an impoverished view of conscience—seeing it as merely a set of aversions—then his task is to explain how such aversions might be communicated persuasively to others. His answer is that human life is replete with *emotional* communicative displays that to a significant extent are resistant to counterfeit signaling (tone of voice, facial muscles, pupil dilation, perspiration, blushing, trembling, laughter, crying, eye movements, yawning, posture, breathing rate, etc.).[5] But although I don't by any means wish to ignore the central emotional ingredients of morality, I think it is important also to emphasize its cognitive element. Therefore my task is to explain how such moral judgments (even ones made in the absence of emotion) might be communicated persuasively to others.

Thankfully, this is not a difficult burden to discharge. Suppose, just to clarify things, that for a moment we put aside entirely the emotional side of morality. Emotions are by no means the only way in which interpersonal commitments might be made. One can make a public commitment by rearranging external constraints—e.g., by burning bridges behind you (literally) as you advance, or by undertaking an arduous initiation rite, or by signing a binding contract. Churchill was making such a commitment when he declared to the world "I would rather see London in ruins and ashes than . . . tamely and abjectly enslaved." The important thing about a commitment is that it forecloses future possibilities in order to bring about a desirable end by altering others' choices (where "others" includes future time slices of oneself[6]). It can be purposeful or involuntary (perhaps even hardwired), absolute or probabilistic.

Moral judgments—even without emotional backing—can serve effectively as such interpersonal commitments. The very fact that abiding by morality is in general a conspicuously costly undertaking gives it obvious potentiality for serving as a public commitment. (With these costs, at a certain point the price of faking moral commitment becomes higher than simply being genuinely committed.) Declaring "For me to pursue X would be wrong" is like a contract: It is an acceptance that punishment is appropriate if one does pursue X. One can signal one's moral commitment in a myriad of ways beyond just declaring it. Acting in accordance with it (i.e., never pursuing the temptations of X) will usually involve sacrifice; confessing and submitting to punishment if you do succumb to temptation will be harmful; going to great lengths to administer punishment to others who break the norm may bring risks; raising one's children to have this value takes trouble. In all these ways one signals to others in a costly manner that one is committed to guiding one's own actions by this moral judgment, that one is not going to pursue X. Others who accept this may consequently alter their actions toward the morally committed individual, choosing him for cooperative ventures—deciding that he is a promising mate, a good trading partner, or simply a valuable member of society.

These observations should be seen as supplementing Frank's own account rather than disagreeing with the heart of it. Emotions certainly *are* central to our moral lives, and emotional displays are probably an important way of signaling interpersonal commitments. But there is much more to morality than emotions, more to conscience than mere aversion, and more to interpersonal commitments than emotional giveaways lying beyond our volitional control. This is particularly important to emphasize, I think, in light of the fact that the emotion of guilt (which surely lies at the core of the moral conscience) does not seem to have been designed with physiologically mediated communication in mind to quite the extent that fear, anger, disgust, and joy have been: Studies have not found a distinctive facial expression associated with guilt (Keltner and Buswell 1996).

In section 4.2 I made the case that moral judgments serve as personal commitments, meaning they need not be signaled at all. In this section I have made the complementary case that moral judgments also serve as interpersonal commitments, meaning that some kind of honest or costly signaling is required, but I have downplayed the centrality of *emotional* signals. Both kinds of commitment have a paradoxical air, in that the benefit of the commitment is attained only by *not* aiming deliberately at it. In the case of personal commitments, replacing clear-headed prudential calculation with coarse-grained and unquestioning moral thinking will, on many occasions, serve one's prudential welfare better. In the case of interpersonal commitments, prudential welfare will often be best served if one can commit to performing what appear to be, and may in reality be, downright imprudent actions. (The point is that the act of signaling that one is so committed may remain prudent, especially since if everything goes according to plan the consequence of this signaling is that the threatened imprudent action need never actually be performed.) Although these two ideas have been teased apart for clarity, my response to Lahti in section 4.2 suggested that the two types of commitment are in fact psychologically entwined; the way in which a private moral judgment affects one's resolve cannot be properly understood in isolation from the way in which its public declaration would affect the resolve of others. When we think of ourselves in moral terms we are thinking of ourselves in social terms, we are evaluating actions against the background of a collective justificatory framework.

We now have a plausible hypothesis concerning the adaptive value of having a conscience. It is a complex view, but since the phenomenon is complicated this should be judged to be a virtue.

4.4 The Projection of Emotions

I have been addressing a "why" question: Why would natural selection come up with the trait of moral thinking? But even a complete answer to this (which I am sure the above considerations do not provide) would leave us with a further question: *How* would natural selection bring about moral thinking? The ideal answer would be given in neurological and genetic terms. I won't feel bad about not being able to supply such an answer, since no one else is now in a position to do so either; our best science is simply not up to the challenge. Nevertheless, recent empirical research does point us in a definite direction, revealing that emotions play a central role in moral judgment and thus suggesting that, if natural selection had a direct hand in shaping the human moral sense, the modification the brain's emotional architecture was its principal means. (The evidence also suggests neurological links between moral processing and long-term planning abilities, thus perhaps providing some support for the adaptational hypothesis presented above in section 4.2.) Taking these empirical data as my starting point, I devote most of this section to presenting a philosophical metaphor that may be fruitful in helping us to understand what the prehistoric human mind started doing that enabled it to make moral judgments. I do not pretend to contribute to the question of what was going on at the neurological level (let alone the genetic level) to allow this.

After centuries of philosophical debate about the respective roles of emotion and rationality in moral thought, recent scientific advances have yielded concrete results. The landmark example is the celebrated case of Phineas Gage, who, in a terrible industrial accident in 1848, suffered massive neurological trauma when a long iron rod an inch and a quarter in diameter was blown through his head, entering below his left eye and exiting at the top of his skull. (The best overview of the case is to be found in Damasio 1994.) To the amazement of all, Gage survived the wound and seemed to recover in all physical respects but for blindness in one eye. However, it quickly became apparent that his personality had undergone a radical shift: Previously temperate, likable, and conscientious, after the accident Gage was crude, irresponsible, imprudent, and disrespectful of moral considerations. In more recent times, subjects with similar injuries have undergone more precise testing (Saver and Damasio 1991; Damasio 1994; Anderson et al. 1999). Such subjects, suffering from what has been called "acquired sociopathy" caused by damage to the ventromedial prefrontal cortex, become hopelessly imprudent and irresponsible, especially regarding social decisions. They exhibit self-destructive behavior, lie for no good reason, fail to form affectionate relationships, can't hold down a job, are incapable of formulating reasonable plans for the future, and fail to express any regret or remorse for their misconduct and gross incapability. When tested under laboratory conditions with a series of tasks that mimic real-life situations, such individuals show an inability to forgo short-term satisfaction for proportionally greater long-term gain. Also noteworthy is a dramatic dampening of emotional response. (Whether this was true also of Gage is not clear.[7]). When shown pictures that in ordinary subjects will provoke a distinct skin-conductance response (pictures of nudity, injury, death), subjects suffering from acquired sociopathy remain unmoved.

These lesion studies suggest a strong link between moral deliberation (and its implementation in moral behavior) and emotional capacity. Studies of psychopaths confirm this pattern too; roughly speaking, the moral impairment exemplified by a psychopath is associated with an emotional deficit but not with a rational deficit (Blair 1995; Blair et al. 1997). It is important here to note that the psychopath's "moral impairment" is not just a matter of behaving in an anti-social manner; it includes an incapacity to make moral judgments in the normal way (if at all). Psychopaths are unable to distinguish moral transgressions from conventional ones—something that gives normal 3-year-olds little trouble. (See section 4.5 below.) And we get even more impressive confirmation from fMRI studies, which reveal that subjects asked to make moral calls on tricky situations often show marked activity in the emotional regions of the brain, especially for problems that are "personal"—that involve, say, the thought of doing direct injury to a person (Greene et al. 2001; Greene and Haidt 2002; see also Moll 2002, 2003). Neuroimaging research on persons playing the "ultimatum game" also reveals activated emotional centers when subjects decide to punish an opponent for defecting (Sanfey et al. 2003; see also Pillutla and Murnighan 1996).[8]

All this evidence gives us a very coarse-grained answer to what natural selection did to the human brain to enable moral judgment: It manipulated emotional centers. This is not to say that every moral judgment is the product of an emotional episode, or that there is no such thing as clear-headed moral reasoning, or that moral judgments cannot be justified by rational methods (hence moral rationalism is not undermined), or that public moral judgments function to express these emotions (hence non-cognitivism/emotivism is not supported).[9] But I do think that these data provide some support for a certain philosophical view that has been around for a long time: *moral projectivism*. (In this I am in agreement with Joshua Greene (2002).)

No one has described this thesis quite as eloquently as David Hume, who spoke of the mind's "great propensity to spread itself on objects" ((1740) 1978: 167) and who claimed that "taste" (as opposed to reason) "has a productive faculty, and gilding and staining all natural objects with the colours, borrowed from internal sentiment, raises in a manner a new creation" ((1751) 1983: 88). Suppose, for example, that you are confronted by a suffering animal, and you feel the emotion of pity. If you then "project" this emotion onto the scene you may see the suffering animal as having a quality of "demanding pity," or being pitiful. This property of *pitifulness* is, in Hume's words, the "new creation" that your mind has "raised"; it seems as if this is a feature of the situation, that your pity is a response to this property (rather than being actively implicated in its creation), and that someone who looks on indifferently, feeling no pity, is missing something and thus is subject to criticism. The projection of the emotions does not mean that moral experience is quasi-perceptual—that we *see* evil in the same way that we see red; it means that our experience of the world is as of considerations that bind us irrespective of our interests and attitudes, that it seems to us to be a brute fact that, say, killing babies is morally wrong. But although this may capture the phenomenology of the experience—that the pitiful nature of the event is the parent of the sentiment—in fact, according to the projectivist, it is the emotion's *child* (Blackburn 1981: 164–165). Nothing is literally projected, of course, which is why we should consider it a metaphor; the idea is just that certain qualities that appear to be in the world owe this appearance to the nature of the perceiver's mental life.

It is often assumed that projectivism about morality and non-cognitivism go hand in hand (indeed, they are sometimes used as if synonyms), but this is mistaken. Suppose those who are projecting this property of *demanding pity* onto the world decide to give the apparent property a name: They call such things "pitiable," say, and go around pointing to bits of the world saying "That's pitiable," "That's not pitiable," "That's a little bit pitiable," and so on. From the fact that its seeming to them as if the situation has the property of being pitiable is to be explained by the situation having prompted in them the emotion of pity, it does not follow that their way of articulating things—uttering "The situation is pitiable"—*functions to express* that emotion of pity. My previous adamant arguments to the conclusion that the relevant *expression* relation is conventional, not causal, suffice to establish this (section 2.3). It is, in fact, hard to see how projectivism and pure non-cognitivism even could go happily together. The crucial thing to notice is that projectivism implies an account of how the world *seems* to those who are doing the projecting: It seems to them as if it contains certain properties. Since we can assume that the language with which they discuss the matter will reflect their experience, then when they say things like "That animal's suffering is pitiable" we can assume that they are asserting that the situation instantiates this property. But if they are *asserting* such things—that is, expressing their beliefs on the matter—then they cannot simply be expressing their emotions.

Projectivism, according to Hume, extends far beyond morality. It is also his favored story for sounds, colors, heat and cold, and (famously) causation. He knows that this is counterintuitive—"Philosophy scarce ever advances a greater paradox in the eyes of the people, than when it affirms that snow is neither cold nor white: fire hot nor red" ((1762) 1986: 416)—yet, in view of what was said in the previous paragraph, projectivism is *necessarily* counterintuitive. A projectivist view of, say, heat and cold implies how these features appear to us: as if they are in the world, real properties of fire and snow. Thus any philosophical view revealing the projection for what it is will be deemed farfetched by ordinary lights; thus projectivism is, ex hypothesi, counterintuitive.

"Vice and virtue," Hume asserts, "may be compar'd to sounds, colours, heat and cold, which, according to modern philosophy, are not qualities in objects but perceptions in the mind" ((1740) 1978: 469). The orthodoxy to which Hume is appealing here is that of the eighteenth century, inspired by Galileo, Newton, and Locke—all of whom have been interpreted as favoring projectivism about color. Whether projectivism is the ubiquitous phenomenon that Hume took it to be remains a live question. (For a modern defense of projectivism regarding color, see Boghossian and Velleman 1989.) But I do think that evolutionary science lends at least some credibility to the projectivist case, since it provides us with an understanding of how we are designed by a process for which practical success rather than accuracy is the summum bonum. Obviously in very many areas of life accuracy is the best route to practical success: The most useful beliefs to have concerning whether there is fruit in the tree, and how many pieces of fruit there are, and in what direction they lie, are the true beliefs. But regarding other areas—most notably the sensory modalities like color, sound, etc.—utility may best be served at the expense of truth. In order to visually distinguish ripe fruit from unripe fruit, for example, it may be better if one's experience exaggerates the difference. And in fact this appears to be what has happened. The colors red and green as they appear to our sensory consciousness are much more distinct than are the associated light frequencies in reality—almost certainly a reflection of a frugivorous past where identifying the ripeness of fruit was of prime importance (Johnston 1999: 14–15).

Why would natural selection encumber us with these projectivist tendencies? The tempting answer is that it is not an "encumbrance" at all—on the contrary, it appears to be the most efficient way of designing a perceiving creature. Consider first a perceptual quality that *isn't* projected onto the world: pain. When you stick a fork in your leg, the subsequent pain presents itself as something mental; you don't for a second think of the pain as a quality that resides in the fork, passing into your leg upon sudden contact. That pain is non-projected is presumably to be explained by reference to the fact that the whole point of pain is to signal to the organism a problem with the body. What is of primary importance is that *I* am in pain, not that a fork has pain-producing qualities. But imagine how odd it would be if all our sensory perceptions presented themselves like this. Your experience of a hot, red, crackling fire would not be as of a real fire having these qualities, but rather as of your having hot-sensations (caused by some feature of the world), and red-sensations (caused by some feature of the world), and crackling-noise-sensations (caused by some feature of the world). I don't see anything incoherent with this possibility—we can probably imagine creatures whose perceptual relation to the world is like this—but it is clear that it is not how things appear to *us*, and it is clear why this is so: There would be no fitness advantage in experiencing the world like that. A perfectly adequate and simpler solution is if our experience presents itself as being *of the world*: of the fire being hot, red, and crackling. The least complicated setup (ceteris paribus) is for a creature's perceptual experiences to be as of a direct acquaintance with aspects of the world, as if one's senses are but open windows to reality, as if the way things reliably seem is the way things really are. For finding ripe fruit, avoiding leopards, locating and impressing prospective sexual partners, raising children, knapping a tool, and so on, sensory experience that wore its mentalistic nature on its sleeve would be a pointless extravagance and a distracting hindrance. Projectivism, on this view, far from being an extravagance, is the predictable result of natural selection's tight-fisted efficiency.

The above, of course, is hardly a complete argument; the philosophical intricacies of the debate are daunting. The intention is not to assert with any assurance that Hume was correct about snow not being white, fire not being hot, etc., but just to acknowledge that an understanding of the process of natural selection lends some prima facie support to the doctrine. On the matter of *moral* projectivism, however, I think we can do a little better. Let me make clear that I am not arguing that the evidence *establishes* moral projectivism—that it excludes all other theories—only that it sits very comfortably with a projectivist interpretation, such that adopting projectivism as a working hypothesis may prove fruitful in our bid to understand what our ancestors' brains started doing that allowed them to make moral judgments.

What kind of empirical evidence would support moral projectivism? First the evidence would need to sustain a claim about moral phenomenology: that in some sense moral attributes seem to be "in the world." Then there is a claim about etiology: that the moral appearances are in fact caused largely by emotional activity. A corollary is that appearances are to some extent deceptive; though our judgments are in fact prompted by emotional activity, our phenomenology is one as of the emotional activity being a response to attributes instantiated the world. Perhaps in addition we should add a negative requirement: that there is no evidence that the moral sense functions to detect a realm of genuine moral facts. As I say, I doubt that the satisfaction of these requirements suffices to *establish* projectivism, but it certainly makes it a serious contender. Some of this evidence we have already seen; some I will mention briefly here and will discuss in detail later.

First, it would seem that the requisite thesis concerning moral phenomenology is supported. Research reveals that "common-sense morality" does include certain claims to objectivity. One study (Nichols and Folds-Bennett 2003; Nichols 2004) looked at young children's responses concerning properties such as *icky*, *yummy*, and *boring* and compared them with their attitudes toward moral and aesthetic properties. Here are two examples of the questions these 4–6-year-olds were asked:

Now, think about a long time ago, before there were any people. There were still grapes, just like the grapes now. Way back then, before there were people, were grapes yummy?

You know, I think it was good for the monkey to help the other monkey. Some people don't like it when monkeys help each other when they're hurt. They don't think it's good when monkeys do that. Would you say that when one monkey helps a hurt monkey that is good *for some people* or that it's good *for real*?

The children treated the instantiation of all properties as existentially independent of humans (i.e., before anyone was around, grapes were yummy, roses were beautiful, and so on), yet made a striking distinction between properties that depend on preferences and those that did not: Things that are yummy or icky are yummy and icky *for some people*, whereas things that are good are good "for real." Having reviewed such evidence, Shaun Nichols (2004: 176) comes to this conclusion: "The data on young children thus suggest, as a working hypothesis, that moral objectivism is the default setting on common-sense metaethics."[10] These findings complement a large body of literature in developmental psychology showing a robustly cross-cultural tendency to distinguish between transgressions that are independent of any authority and those that depend upon someone's decree. (I will discuss this literature in section 4.5.) Larry Nucci (1986, 2001) has even found that among Mennonite and Amish children and adolescents *God's* authority does not determine moral wrongness. When asked whether it would be OK to work on a Sunday if God said so, 100 percent said "Yes";

when asked whether it would be OK to steal if God said so, over 80 percent said "No." Such findings contribute to a compelling body of evidence that moral prescriptions and values are experienced as "objective" in the sense that they don't seem to depend on us, or on any authoritative figure.

Second, it would seem that the requisite thesis concerning moral etiology is supported. I have already mentioned evidence from psychopathy, lesion studies, and neuroimaging, all of which suggests that moral and emotional faculties are linked. The empirical research also suggests, however, in which direction the linkage typically goes: from emotion to moral judgment. Jonathan Haidt musters a great deal of evidence in favor of this hypothesis. (See especially his 2001 paper.) In one study (Wheatley and Haidt 2005), highly hypnotizable participants were given a post-hypnotic suggestion to feel a pang of disgust whenever they read an arbitrary word ("often" or "take"). They were then asked to read a variety of fictional vignettes—some involving moral transgressions and others involving no transgression at all, some using the target word and others not using it. In cases where disgust was prompted, the subjects' moral condemnation was heightened. Even in the non-transgression story, subjects who felt disgust were often inclined to follow up with a negative moral appraisal. This is striking when one considers that there was nothing in the story remotely to support such a judgment:

Dan is a student council representative at his school. This semester he is in charge of scheduling discussions about academic issues. He [tries to take] ⟨often picks⟩ topics that appeal to both professors and students in order to stimulate discussion.[11]

Disgusted subjects nevertheless reported that "it just seems like he's up to something," or "he's a "popularity-seeking snob," or "it just seems so weird and disgusting," or "I don't know [why it's wrong], it just is." This is evidence that a great deal of the time it is our emotions that are driving our moral judgments, but it certainly doesn't seem this way "from the inside." Haidt's studies have repeatedly shown that people are frequently largely unaware of what is prompting their moral evaluations; they grope for reasons and justifications, and will bend over backwards to avoid admitting "I judge it to be wrong simply because it makes me angry, and that's all there is to it."

This evidence concerning (on the one hand) what really causes moral judgment and (on the other hand) how it seems to us virtually adds up to a statement of moral projectivism. There is no evidence that the human moral sensibility functions anything like a perceptual organ, detecting moral properties in the world. In all our discussion thus far in this book concerning why moral judgment might have been adaptive, nowhere did the story require or imply that moral judgments operate to depict a realm of objective moral facts; nowhere has it been hinted that the function that natural selection had in mind for moral judgment was anything remotely like *detecting a feature of the world*, but rather something more like *encouraging successful social behavior*. Yet it was also a feature of that hypothesis that moral judgments would serve this purpose only if they seem like they *are* depicting a realm of objective moral facts, at least in the sense of providing practical considerations with inescapable and authoritative force. (A "conversation-stopper" will not serve effectively as a conversation-stopper if you are thinking of it *as* a conversation-stopper.) So the evolutionary hypothesis that was presented in sections 4.2 and 4.3 concerning the adaptive function of moral judgment in itself suggests projectivism. It describes an area of our lives where natural selection is unconcerned with detection, but for which a detection-like phenomenology is paramount.

Moral projectivism also promises to make sense of what might otherwise seem a perplexing phenomenon: intractable moral disagreement. If moral judgment were a matter of detecting a realm of facts, then shouldn't we be able to come to some kind of agreement? Not always, perhaps, but at least we should be able to decide upon procedures for settling disputes. But the phenomenon of disagreement is unusual in its tenacious *intractability*. Let me put it boldly: No moral judgment has ever been made by a human being for which there has not been another perfectly intelligent and informed person disposed to interpret it as false, pernicious, biased, and narrow-minded. And the striking thing is that we have no agreed-upon means of settling such disputes. An American president can talk confidently about "the existence of evil," though no one can tell us what kind of property it is, by what means we detect its presence, or how the truth of the claim might be tested. As a result, persistent disputes abound with no hope of resolution; often the best that can be hoped for is that both parties "agree to disagree." But even when a degree of toleration is achieved, each party often continues to interpret the other as mired in false ideology and/or selfishness (though confident that they themselves are seeing things clearly and correctly)—while those of us in the fortunate position of disinterested onlookers will often suppose that *both* disputants are thus mired. What are we to make of this? It is *possible* that moral judgments really are in the business of detecting moral facts and that emotions just interfere, yet it seems to me that the far more plausible explanation of the acrimony and futility surrounding our moral disputes is that emotions are in the driving seat, and that moral judgment is a matter of these emotions being projected on to the individual's experience of her social world (Haidt 2001: 823). In other words, although it is conceivable that if we were able (per impossible, perhaps) to strip ourselves of emotions then all our moral judgments would become clearer and truer (and there would be much more moral agreement), in fact it seems more likely that without emotions we would no longer make any moral judgments at all.

In pressing the case for moral projectivism I don't mean to suggest that every moral judgment humans make is the product of an emotional episode. The claim is primarily genealogical: that the emergence of a projectivist faculty in our ancestry is a principal component in the explanation of the human capacity to make moral judgments. This genealogical thesis is consistent with the possibility that we can on occasions—and perhaps frequently—come to moral judgments through other methods. (See Haidt 2003b.) The same thing might be said regarding a projectivist account of color. Suppose I ask you now to state what color the carpet is in my hallway at home. You can't say? Well, I'll give you a big clue: It is roughly the same color as ripe tomatoes, blood, and raspberries. You shouldn't have much trouble judging that the carpet is red. You have made a particular color judgment, but no act of "Humean projection" was involved. Nevertheless, it is fairly obvious that this color judgment is in some sense parasitic upon "paradigmatic" color judgments, where one has the normal phenomenological visual experience of red while looking at the appropriate kind of object (such as a tomato). And it is this paradigmatic color judgment (a Humean would say) that involves an actual act of projection. Something roughly analogous, I believe, should be allowed by the moral projectivist. Certainly people make moral judgments, and sincere ones, without emotional activity. But in some sense (a sense that on this occasion I will leave unspecified) such judgments are parasitic upon paradigmatic judgments which are accompanied by emotional episodes. Just as it is true that if there were no one making paradigmatic color judgments then there would be no one making *any* color judgments, so too if there were no one making paradigmatic moral judgments—involving the projection of the emotions—there would be no one making any moral judgments at all.[12] (These claims are not intended as conceptual or necessary truths.)

The puzzle we started out with was how natural selection might bring about the capacity to make a moral judgment. What might have been done to our brains to get us thinking in terms of *obligations, fairness, desert, property, cheating*, and so on? I submit that we can plausibly understand this transition in projectivist terms. As we saw earlier, mere aversions and inclinations will not suffice for such thinking; to dislike an outcome is very different from disapproving of it. What is needed is a movement from desiring something to finding it desirable, from feeling contempt for something to judging it contemptible, from praising something to regarding it praiseworthy, from not accepting something to considering it unacceptable, from demanding something to deeming it demanded. This is precisely the changeover that projectivism is well placed to explain. And with such concepts as *desirable, contemptible, praiseworthy, unacceptable,* and *demanded* in play (concepts, incidentally, that are available only to language users), a whole domain of normative concepts that are less obviously to be explained in projectivist terms becomes available: desirable but not demanded, inappropriate but not forbidden, heroic, miserly, cruel, just, depraved, hospitable, heartless, rude, etc., etc. To the extent that a projectivist tendency can be called an "intellectual power" in virtue of enabling this expansion of a person's conceptual space, we can finally make sense of Darwin's puzzling assertion (quoted in section 3.7) that an intellectualization of prosocial sentiment can amount to a moralization (not that I'm suggesting that this is what Darwin had in mind.)

One may still reasonably ask "But *how* did natural selection bring about this projectivist transition?" (How in neurological terms? How in genetic terms?) This, though a great question, is simply beyond our present capabilities to answer. But the absence of a complete and satisfying theory here is not unusual; the landscape is littered with such unanswered questions. How in neurological or genetic terms did natural selection bring about the human linguistic faculty, or our preparedness to find snakes frightening (as opposed to guns), or our ability to distinguish between male and female faces, or even something so basic as our interest in sex? The fact that we don't know the complete answer to any of these questions should stimulate our inquiry rather than nourish suspicion that such phenomena are not the direct product of natural selection at all.

4.5 A Big Fat Just-So Story?

Well, it's a nice story. But is it anything more than what Stephen Jay Gould (1978) famously accused of being a "just-so" story (after Kipling's charming tales about how the leopard got its spots, how the elephant got its trunk, etc.)? I must own up to disliking Gould's phrase—and disliking it all the more so for its casual popularity. For a start, Kipling's stories are flights of sheer fantasy—nothing like serious and plausible explanatory hypotheses. If the complaint is simply that a hypothesis remains to be tested, then let that be the observation—why stoop to a generic rhetorical smear? Second, it should be remembered that Gould's accusation was primarily against the "adaptationist program": the view that every trait of an organism is a perfect adaptation, and thus the only issue is *how* it evolved, not *whether* it did. Whether anyone has ever held the extreme view that Gould was attacking is something I will leave for others to decide. (For historical details of the debate, see Segerstråle 2000.) It suffices here to declare for the record that I am not assuming that all organisms are perfectly adapted, or that every phenotypic characteristic is an adaptation. I take seriously the hypothesis that human morality is a trait that was not selected for. It may be akin to one of Gould's spandrels: a fortuitous by-product of natural selection, with no evolutionary function (Gould and Lewontin 1979). It may be what Dennett (1995: 77–78, 485–487) calls "a Good Trick": something so obvious that any bunch of humans of average intelligence can be expected to invent it. Though I take these hypotheses seriously, I happen to think that they are unlikely to be true—but far from this verdict being the result of my preferring a plausible but empirically ungrounded and untestable fairy tale, it is what the weight of evidence indicates. It must be recognized that on such matters we will never have a deductive argument from demonstrably true premises; we will never have, nor should we hope for, *certainty*. My fear is that "merely a just-so story" is such a habitual retort in some quarters that it will be leveled at any genealogical explanatory hypothesis whose evidential support falls short of verification. If this is so, then we may continue to hear Gould's memorable sneer applied to perfectly respectable and well-confirmed scientific theories.

I take it that the crucial prerequisite for avoiding any legitimate application of Gould's censure is that a hypothesis be *testable*. A hypothesis may be at present untested, but that is no ground for a mocking condemnation. What is crucial about an untested hypothesis is that we accept it for what it is; the tendency to embrace a plausible but unconfirmed hypothesis as *true* is of course as much a vice here as it is anywhere in science. Gould is quite right that something is amiss in any field of inquiry when "virtuosity in invention replaces testability as the criterion for acceptance" (1978: 530). And so, with this in mind, let me clearly state that I am not putting this hypothesis forward as *true*. It is a hypothesis that is plausible, coherent, and testable—and its truth remains to be established. There is, however, good reason for looking favorably upon it. Let me, in this final section of the chapter that completes the first task of this book, review some of the evidence that supports it.

Morality (by which I here mean *the tendency to make moral judgments*) exists in all human societies we have ever heard of. Moral precepts are mentioned in the Egyptian Book of the Dead and in the Mesopotamian epic of Gilgamesh. To the extent that trade implies a grasp of ownership, and ownership implies some kind of comprehension of *rights*, we find the physical traces of morality far back in the archaeological record, at least into the early Upper Paleolithic (Mellars 1995: 398–400), and perhaps far beyond (McBrearty and Brooks 2001). There is not a shred of evidence that morality (or trade in particular) is a de novo artifact of modern civilization that spread from one or more points of cultural invention. Rather, like language, it is ubiquitous and ancient.

Moreover, morality exists in virtually every human individual. It develops without formal instruction, with no deliberate effort, and with no conscious awareness of its special features. For example, very young children are able to distinguish moral norms from prudential norms (Tisak and Turiel 1984)—yet no one explicitly teaches them this, since even most adults are not overtly aware of the distinction (and even many philosophers who have thought hard about such things fail to see it). This is not to say that moral judgment develops *inevitably* in the human child; as with language acquisition, exposure to certain environmental features is necessary. But all the evidence suggests that the infant mind is "prepared" for moral judgment, in much the same way as, say, a bird's brain is prepared to learn songs[13] (Seligman 1970, 1971). The course of moral development in the human child exhibits an extremely reliable sequence, it gets underway remarkably early, its developmental pathway is distinct from the emergence of other skills, and its unfolding includes abrupt maturations. On this last point, Haidt (2001: 826–827) describes the findings of the anthropologist Alan Fiske (1991) as follows:

> . . . children seem relatively insensitive to issues of fairness until around the age of 4, at which point concerns about fairness burst forth and are overgeneralized to social situations in which they were never encouraged and in which they are often inappropriate. This pattern of sudden similarly timed emergence with overgeneralization suggests the maturation of an endogenous ability rather than the learning of a set of cultural norms.

When I talk here of "moral development" I don't just mean prosocial behavior or even simply prosocial emotions; I mean genuine cognitive (though perhaps still emotionally embedded) moral judgments. There is a large body of research in developmental psychology illuminating the emergence of this trait. First, we know that children as young as 3 years manifest the same dissociation as do adults in their capacity to process indicative versus deontic conditionals. For example, when presented with a model house and some toy mice—some of which squeak when squeezed and some of which don't—preschoolers have trouble picking which mice should be squeezed to test the indicative conditional "All the squeaky mice are in the house" (Cummins 1996a). But when a task with the same underlying logic is posed in deontic terms—i.e., the children must pick which mice should be squeezed to test the rule "All squeaky mice must stay in the house"—their performance is twice as good. (Research by Harris and Núñez 1996 supports these results.) Similar tests on adults reveal this effect to be robustly cross-cultural (Cummins 1996b; Sugiyama 1996; Sugiyama et al. 2002[14]).

Young children do not merely show improved reasoning when dealing with deontic matters; at a remarkably early age they are able to discriminate among different kinds of deontic rules.[15] Most notably, their capacity to distinguish moral from conventional transgressions emerges as early as the third year (Smetana 1981; Smetana and Braeges 1990)—and this is an impressively cross-cultural phenomenon (Nucci et al. 1983; Hollos et al. 1986; Song et al. 1987; Yau and Smetana 2003). Even children raised in abusive and deprived environments continue to make the moral/conventional distinction (Smetana et al. 1984); as a matter of fact, about the only individuals who can't make it are psychopaths (Blair 1995), whose characteristics have little to do with upbringing but almost certainly result from neurological aberration (Wootten et al. 1997; Laakso et al. 2001; Kiehl et al. 2001).

Researchers on the emergence of the moral/conventional distinction largely follow the psychologist Elliot Turiel in making the distinction along several dimensions: Moral transgressions are taken to be more serious, more generalizable (e.g., wrong in other countries too), are justified differently (e.g., with reference to harmful consequences), and are considered independent of authority (Turiel 1983, 1998; Turiel et al. 1987). Whether all four criteria reliably come together or form a natural kind may be doubted (Shweder et al. 1987), but certainly Turiel and his colleagues have succeeded in uncovering some sort of deep developmental distinction. Of particular interest is the last dimension, which is understood in counterfactual terms. Concerning a conventional transgression, such as a boy wearing a dress to school, when asked "But what if the teacher were to say it's OK?" children will allow that the rule is no longer binding. But concerning a moral transgression, such as punching another student, children will tend to maintain that it is wrong regardless of what the teacher says on the matter. (This dissociation has been observed in children not yet 3 years old (Smetana and Braeges 1990).) This observation meshes well with all I have claimed about the special "practical clout" of moral judgment. (It also dovetails with Nichols and Folds-Bennett's experiment, reported in the previous section.)

These results from developmental psychology strongly suggest that the tendency to make moral judgments is innate. No one would deny that cultural learning plays a central role in determining *the content* of the moral judgments that an individual ends up making; the claim is that there is a specialized innate mechanism (or series of mechanisms) designed to enable this type of learning. The cross-cultural nature of these findings should impress us. Cross-cultural universality doesn't imply innateness, and nor does innateness imply cross-cultural universality. But innate features will tend to produce cross-cultural traits *absent any environmental variation to cause divergence*. And, conversely, cross-cultural universals do require explanation; thus, when we locate them we must always ask whether there is some plausible alternative hypothesis that can do the job. Opponents of the moral nativist case (e.g., proponents of Dennett's "Good Trick" hypothesis) will, I submit, struggle to provide an alternative account to explain these robust findings. It is exceedingly unlikely that across the wide variety of human social ecologies there is some stable exogenous characteristic that may be plausibly appealed to as the explanans of this exceptionally regular ontogenetic sequence that characterizes the moral development of the human child. The logic of the argument is inference to the best explanation, and, as things stand, innateness is our best explanation.

This argument is supported by the observation that it is difficult to see how a general learning mechanism even *could* learn to make a moral judgment. The problem here isn't just that the environment doesn't offer *enough* data for a child to grasp the necessary distinction; it's that it is puzzling what there even *could be* in the environment—even a rich and varied environment—for a generalized learning mechanism to latch on to in order to develop the idea of a moral transgression. Mid-twentieth-century social learning theorists may have been correct that punishment is the road to norm-internalization, but they didn't address the question of how punishment leads to anything other than fear of punishment and aversion to the punishable offense. Administer as many punitive beatings as you like to a general-purpose intelligence; at what point does this alone teach it the idea of a *moral transgression*? To say that "the association between the action and punishment becomes *internalized*" is just to give a name to the problem without explaining anything. Other developmental theories do no better in this respect. Either they appeal to "internalization" as a mysterious activity that human minds just happen to indulge in (as if this tendency might itself be picked up from the environment through observation and the employment of general intelligence) or they tacitly presuppose that the mind comes "prepared" to internalize norms.

This problem about the ontogenesis of moral judgment reflects a challenge for any hypothesis regarding a cultural origin for morality in human prehistory. It is evident in this well-known passage from Rousseau concerning the basis of human civilization: "The first man who, having enclosed a piece of ground, to whom it occurred to say *This is mine*, and found people sufficiently simple to believe him, was the true founder of civil society" ((1758) 1997: 164). If Rousseau is imagining people who already have a firm grasp of the notion of *possession* but who have simply never thought of owning *land*, then there is nothing commentworthy here (for our purposes, at least). But suppose instead that Rousseau is imagining not the origin of land-ownership but the birth of the idea of ownership simpliciter. Picture his mythical hero, who, after staking out a plot, turns to his fellows and announces "This is mine." If they lack any conception of ownership, they have no idea what "mine" means.[16] They respond: "What on earth are you talking about? What special relation are you claiming holds between you and this land?" How does the hero then continue? How can he explain to people who don't understand *ownership* what it means to possess something? He may say: "I have special rights to it that you do not have. You are obligated to respect my doing as I wish with this land, and I am permitted to object if you try to do as you wish with it." But if, ex hypothesi, the others not only have no prior grasp of *ownership*, but no grasp of *moral rights* or *obligation*, or indeed any moral concepts at all, such comments are hardly likely to illuminate the matter. The others may be as smart as you like when it comes to observation and inference, but if they don't already "get" moral thinking, then it is a mystery what might be said, what observations offered, what conditioning implemented, what associations highlighted, what punishments administered, or what inferences encouraged in order to teach them.

It is worth pausing to consider the last item on that list, since Turiel et al. seem to think that children acquire the moral/conventional distinction by inference. But it proves very difficult to ascertain what there may be about (say) an act of purposeful harming versus an act of a boy wearing a dress that might allow a novice observer to infer that the former but not the latter is proscribed independently of any authoritative source. Bear in mind that in order to infer a *dependence* relation one would have observe a correlation between the relevant authority changing its mind to permit the boy to wear a dress and that action no longer counting as a transgression. And in order to infer an *independence* relation one would have either to (A) observe the relevant authority change its opinion about an act of harming while one notes that the act nevertheless continues to count as a transgression or (B) observe a previously condemned act of harming cease to count as a transgression while one notes that the relevant authority's opinion on the matter has not altered. But observations of types A and B are hard to come by even for adults, let alone 3-year-olds. Regarding a serious moral offense, like violent crime, what we invariably observe is both elements remaining stable: all relevant authorities denounce it, and it continues to be considered a transgression. How on the basis of such observations one is supposed to infer an independence relation is baffling. It is true that the child may observe that some transgressions are considered more serious than others (invite more outrage, incur worse punishment), but there is nothing in a child's external world to provide the inferential basis for matching up this observable distinction with the typically unobservable distinction between authority-dependent and authority-independent transgressions. Likewise, what experience allows a child to infer that certain norms are local whereas others hold more generally? When the locale of the norm is, for example, school versus home, we can plausibly find the origin of the distinction in the child's experience. But many social conventions hold in both the school and the home, and in fact for a wide range of social norms (e.g., eating with utensils rather than fingers) the child very often has neither direct nor indirect experience of a setting in which it doesn't hold. Furthermore, it is worth noting that Turiel et al. seem to think that the child's interactions with her peers provide a large part of the inference base (Turiel 1998: 899; see also Nucci 2001: 13–16). But saying this doesn't answer the question, it just postpones it, for how have the *other children* come to make this distinction? All in all, the hypothesis that children the world over acquire this distinction through some kind of inference from similar interactive experiences has never to my knowledge been spelled out in any detail, and on reflection it simply incredible. (See Dwyer 1999 for similar considerations; see also Sripada and Stich, forthcoming.)

The solution to the puzzle is that morality is not something that children learn or infer from their exogenous environment, nor is it something that our ancestors, armed with a general intelligence, invented in the misty depths of prehistory. A creature equipped only with all-purpose intelligence simply cannot invent or be taught moral judgment, cannot be taught how to turn a dislike into a disapproval, because "getting it" requires a certain kind of brain: a brain with specific kinds of mechanisms that are geared for such learning—mechanisms forged from a certain kind of evolutionary process. Far from being a just-so story, this evolutionary hypothesis appears to be the best story we have.

4.6 Conclusion

There is not a gene for morality, any more than there is a gene for breathing. Nor is there a little chunk of the brain devoted specifically to making moral judgments, in the way that phrenologists of old liked to think. Morality is a complicated and nebulous affair at the best of times, and moral judgments no doubt implicate many different psychological and neural mechanisms. But these cautions against simplistic thinking do not amount to a denial of the hypothesis advocated in this book: that moral thinking has been biologically selected for in our lineage. Nor, as I have emphasized before, is this hypothesis undermined by observing that moral thinking is highly responsive to environmental nuances. Mechanisms of cultural transmission play an enormous and perhaps exhaustive role in determining the content of an individual's moral convictions. This is consistent with there being an innate "moral sense" designed precisely to make this particular kind of cultural transmission possible.

Does biology place *any* constraint on the content of an individual's or a culture's moral framework? Perhaps so. In section 2.5 I noted that cross-cultural studies have revealed some broad universals across moral frameworks. Data from these studies are highly suggestive that the human moral sense is prepared to latch on to certain elements in its environment rather than other elements—such as, for example, episodes of purposeful injury, the maintenance of reciprocal relations (fairness, cheating, etc.), social status, and a cluster of themes pertaining to bodies and bodily functions. The mere universality of these moral categories doesn't entail innate preparedness, of course; however, when we consider the body of evidence as a whole—including, for example, the evidence from developmental psychology discussed above—it seems that the best explanation of these universal characteristics of morality is that they are expressions of underlying "design features" of human psychology. It must be acknowledged that there is at least a very plausible and testable hypothesis to this effect.

These observations also allow me to say something in response to a question that I have so far avoided addressing, but which some readers might find of paramount interest: Which of the evolutionary processes outlined in chapter 1 is responsible for the human moral sense? The reason I have avoided this question is simply that we don't know. The empirical evidence discussed in this chapter could be reconciled with any of those processes, and it's difficult to know where to look for solid evidence to settle the matter.[17] Nevertheless, one glaring datum is that all human moral systems give a leading role to *reciprocal relations*; if the human moral sense is prepared for any particular subject matter, it is surely this. It therefore seems eminently reasonable to assume that reciprocal exchanges were a central evolutionary problem that morality was designed to solve. Saying this doesn't knock the other processes out of the running. Group selection—most probably at the cultural level—may well have also been a major factor. But my hunch is that reciprocity, broadly construed, is what got the ball rolling. (The moralization of disgust—giving rise to taboos concerning food and sex, for example—I suspect of being a matter of natural selection co-opting a motivational mechanism that had conveniently evolved for other initial purposes.) Evidence from primatology, experimental economics, neuroscience, developmental psychology, and anthropology suggests that the human mind bears the traces of a past in which reciprocity played a big role. The human interest in acquiring knowledge of others' reputations and in broadcasting one's own good reputation, our sensitivity to issues of distributive fairness in exchanges, our capacity to distinguish between accidental and purposeful harms (and our inclination to forgive the injuries of the former kind), our sensitivity to cheats and our antipathy toward them (our eagerness to punish them even at material cost to ourselves), and our heightened sense of possession—all these arguably innate tendencies suggest a mind built for reciprocation.

Though here I will leave this reciprocity hypothesis undeveloped, a couple of points are worth making to ward off any misunderstanding. First, it might be protested that many present-day moral practices have little to do with reciprocation: our duties to children, to the severely disabled, to future generations, to animals, and (if you like) to the environment all are arguably maintained without expectation of payback. Yet this objection really misses the mark, for these considerations hardly undermine the hypothesis that it was for regulating reciprocal exchanges that morality evolved in the first place; it is not being claimed that reciprocity alone is what continues to sustain social relations. Reciprocity may give someone a sense of duty toward his fellows that causes him to hurl himself on a grenade to save their lives. There is no actual reciprocation there—not even an expectation of one—but nevertheless reciprocity may be the process that brought about the psychological mechanisms that prompted the sacrificial behavior. Although these mechanisms may have evolved in order to govern reciprocal exchanges (producing, we might expect, judgments that are highly dependent on what kind of relation the individuals stand in), it should come as no surprise that social factors might develop that urge, say, a more universal benevolent attitude—perhaps even encouraging one to initiate and continue relations irrespective of one's partner's actions (e.g., to turn the other cheek). By comparison, one might hypothesize that human color vision evolved in order to allow us to distinguish ripe from unripe fruit, but this would hardly imply that this continues to be the only thing we can do with color vision.

Second, it might be objected that a person enters into a reciprocal relationship for self-gain, and thus is motivated entirely by selfish ends (albeit perhaps "enlightened self-interest")—the very antithesis of *moral* thinking. This objection is confused. Entering into reciprocal relations may well be fitness advancing, but this implies nothing about the motivations of individuals designed to participate in such relations. Even Darwin got this one wrong. In the passage from *The Descent of Man* often cited as evidence of his appreciation of the importance of reciprocity in human prehistory, Darwin attributes its origins to a "low motive" ((1879) 2004: 156).[18] George Williams (1966: 94) responds correctly: "I see no reason why a conscious motive need be involved. It is necessary that help provided to others be occasionally reciprocated if it is to be favored by natural selection. It is not necessary that either the giver or the receiver be aware of this." I would add that I see no reason that an *unconscious* motive need be involved either. Reciprocal partners may enter into such exchanges for selfish motives, or for altruistic motives, or their exchanges may be mere conditioned or hard-wired reflexes properly described neither as selfish nor altruistic. Genes inhabiting selfishly motivated reciprocating organisms may be soundly out-competed by genes inhabiting reciprocating organisms who are moved directly by the welfare of their chosen exchange partners. And genes inhabiting reciprocating organisms motivated additionally by thoughts of moral duty, who will feel guilty if they defect, may do better still.

At this point I declare the first task of this book complete. Although, obviously, there is an enormous amount more that could be said on the matter, we have seen enough to look favorably on the hypothesis that the human capacity to make moral judgments is the result of biological natural selection. The second task of the book is to address the question "So what?" What implications follow from this evolutionary hypothesis for our present-day moral judgments, theories, and practices?

The Evolutionary Vindication of Morality

5.1 Evolutionary Ethics: Descriptive versus Prescriptive

Everything that has been discussed in this book thus far could be called "descriptive evolutionary ethics": the examination of a hypothesis concerning the factual matter of whether, and in what sense, and to what degree, human morality is the product of the process of biological natural selection. I have advocated the hypothesis that descriptive evolutionary ethics produces a positive output, and I ask that from here on the reader grant this, if only arguendo. What might follow from this? In particular, are there any ethical or metaethical implications?

There is one apparently evaluative conclusion that can be drawn directly from the hypothesis: that moral thinking was useful to our ancestors, at least in a reproductive sense. And one might try to cash out this appearance of "useful" in more obviously normative terms by saying that morality "was good for" our ancestors (or, more precisely, good for our ancestors' genes). Though I don't want to deny the permissibility of this way of talking, it is evident that such a use of "good" is a long way from a *moral* evaluation. It is the same "good" we might use in saying that watering a plant is good for it, or that hot weather and dry vegetation is good for bush fires. (More on this below.) Many thinkers, however, have tried to squeeze more robust evaluative conclusions from descriptive evolutionary ethics. Proponents of *prescriptive evolutionary ethics* contend that a positive output from descriptive evolutionary ethics can play a vindicating role for morality in general, or for certain moral theories, judgments, and/or practices. Such proponents are usually accused of trying invalidly to derive an "ought" from an evolutionary "is"—an accusation I will assess shortly. Another kind of nondescriptive evolutionary ethics hasn't yet won a label. Far from thinking that descriptive evolutionary ethics might vindicate morality, proponents of this view hold that it *undermines* morality. Such a position is not an attempt to derive an "ought" from an "is" (and this is why I resist labeling it a kind of prescriptive evolutionary ethics); on the contrary, it can be thought of in its strongest form as arguing that from an evolutionary "is" it follows that *it is not the case* that we morally ought do anything. This third view, which I will call the "evolutionary debunking of morality," is the topic of chapter 6. The assessment of the former program—prescriptive evolutionary ethics—is the subject of the present chapter.

Another way in which a descriptive evolutionary ethics might influence present moral thinking is by bringing to light empirical facts that are of importance to ethical decisions. Just as ethical decisions can be influenced by facts about the consequences of certain economic policies, by facts about the degree of unhappiness that a course of action will produce, by facts about the motivations with which an action was performed, and in principle by facts of any kind at all, so too they may be influenced by facts about human evolution. Hallvard Lillehammer puts the point nicely: "Given the relative openness of our moral sensibility to the discovery of new facts, it is natural to think that our moral sensibility should be responsive to the discovery of facts about that sensibility itself" (2003: 567). It is conceivable, for example, that the results of studying human evolution may support specific hypotheses about what kinds of things cause us happiness and unhappiness. (See, e.g., Grinde 2002.) This would make a difference to a variety of ethical decisions; it may prompt us to change our minds on certain moral matters. I am officially agnostic in this book about how much influence upon moral judgments descriptive evolutionary ethics may have in this respect. My (disappointing) opinion is that we will have to wait and see. I identify this kind of relationship between ethics and the study of human evolution just to forestall the possibility of its being confused with the more controversial kind of prescriptive evolutionary ethics that is the topic of this chapter.

Philip Kitcher—a lucid voice against early sociobiology—writes: "Human ethical practices have histories, and it is perfectly appropriate to inquire about the details of those histories. . . . Nothing is wrong with [descriptive evolutionary ethics] so long as it is not articulated in too simplistic a fashion and so long as it is not overinterpreted" (1994: 440).[1] Obviously in view of all that has been asserted and looked favorably upon in this book so far, I am inclined to think that references to biological natural selection will loom large in a full account of the history of human ethical practices. But the matter is an empirical one, and no one should be choosing sides with too much confidence in advance of the evidence. Whether or not descriptive evolutionary ethics turns out to be a fruitful research program, no one should be opposed to it *on principle*. By contrast, *prescriptive* evolutionary ethics has a bad name. It is widely thought that one need not bother to assess the various forms of prescriptive evolutionary ethics in any detail, because there is a simple a priori proof that shows that all versions of prescriptive evolutionary ethics must be wrong: the naturalistic fallacy. The naturalistic fallacy is assumed to knock out of the running not only positive versions of prescriptive evolutionary ethics but any form of moral naturalism.

By "moral naturalism" I mean the view according to which moral properties and relations exist and can be comfortably integrated within a naturalistic view of the world—the kind of world that science can investigate. (For a more complete definition, see Copp 2004.) The utilitarian—a prime example of a moral naturalist—holds that moral value just *is* happiness (or whatever kind of utility one might want to plug in instead of happiness), and that facts about what we are morally obligated (ought) to do just are facts about what promotes the maximal amount of happiness. Since facts about what produces happiness are causal and psychological facts—the kind of thing that can be investigated using scientific methods—then so too, according to this view, are moral values and obligations. The *evolutionary moral naturalist* is a kind of moral naturalist who holds that the sort of scientifically respectable facts that ground moral values and obligations are facts about natural selection.

Neither of the aforementioned views is to be confused with *global naturalism*, which is a more general stance according to which the only kinds of things whose existence we ought to countenance of are things that fit into a unified scientific framework. The global naturalist will want to "naturalize morality" in the sense of providing a scientifically respectable account of moral institutions and practices, of moral psychology, and of moral genealogy. But this doesn't amount to being a moral naturalist in the sense just outlined, since it is consistent with holding that all moral beliefs are false, or that moral language is not even in the business of denoting properties and relations. That the phrase "naturalizing ethics" is ambiguous becomes clearer if we compare it to "naturalizing witches." Any scientifically minded person will want to "naturalize witches" in the sense of providing an empirically sound account of the beliefs and practices surrounding witch discourse: the sociology, psychology, and anthropology of a cultural phenomenon. But this respectable pursuit need not (and should not) end up vindicating witch discourse in the sense of showing that the existence of witches can be accommodated within the naturalistic worldview. Naturalizing witches in that sense would be a whole new (and misguided) ballgame. In this book, "moral naturalism" (and its accompanying phrase "to naturalize morality") denotes the latter kind of position: one which holds that moral properties exist. One can deny this view while still being a global naturalist; to be sure, it might be a commitment to global naturalism that leads one to reject moral naturalism and instead embrace moral nihilism (just as that same global naturalism leads us to be nihilists about witches). The naturalistic fallacy does not target global naturalism, but it is supposed to be devastating for moral naturalism and thus for evolutionary moral naturalism.

It should be noted, however, that the category of "prescriptive evolutionary ethics" is broader than that of "evolutionary moral naturalism." The prescriptive evolutionary ethicist is committed to "vindicating" morality in some manner by appealing to facts about evolution; but showing that moral properties exist and can be grounded in facts about natural selection is not the only means of achieving such a vindication. Later in this chapter I will examine other ways. (The diversity of these ways explains why I am leaving the term "vindication" vague and informal.) First, however, let us confine our attention to the evolutionary moral naturalist, and ask whether the naturalistic fallacy really does deliver the knockout blow.

5.2 The Naturalistic Fallacy

The attempt to establish an ethical "ought" from a natural "is" deserves its old title, "the naturalistic fallacy."
    —Paul R. Ehrlich (2000: 309)

G. E. Moore decisively assaulted the idea of drawing values from evolution or, for that matter, from *any* aspect of observed nature. He labeled this error the "naturalistic fallacy." . . . Moore wasn't the first to question the inference of "ought" from "is. . . ."
    —Robert Wright (1995: 330)

One of the shibboleths of contemporary philosophy is that you can't derive "ought" from "is." Attempting to do this is often called the *naturalistic fallacy*, taking the term from G. E. Moore's classic *Principia Ethica* (1903).
    —Daniel Dennett (1995: 467)[2]

Claims that G. E. Moore pointed out in 1903 that "ought" cannot be derived from "is," and that he accused anyone attempting to do so of committing the naturalistic fallacy, can be found effortlessly; the three quotations above were unearthed with only a quick glance at some books on my shelf. Yet all such claims are bafflingly mistaken. Moore did name *something* "the naturalistic fallacy," but it certainly wasn't the alleged mistake of deriving "ought" from "is." I challenge anyone who doubts this to open Moore's *Principia Ethica* ((1903) 1948[3]) and find any mention of deduction, any mention of "ought" and "is," or any mention of a "fact/value gap." The naturalistic fallacy *as Moore conceived it* concerns an entirely different matter. In this section I will present (and criticize) the real naturalistic fallacy, along with its shady friend the "open question argument." This will require something of an excursion into historical philosophy, but I judge this warranted if it helps clarify the issues. In the following section I will discuss and assess the thesis that is often erroneously called "the naturalistic fallacy"—namely, the claim that one cannot validly derive and "ought" from an "is."

Moore thought that any attempt to define good must fail because of the naturalistic fallacy. The phrase "define good" is troubling to a modern ear, but it is Moore's preferred way of putting things. He is adamant that he is uninterested in defining *the word* "good": "My business is solely with that object or idea, which I hold, rightly or wrongly, that the word is generally used to stand for. What I want to discover is the nature of that object or idea, and about this I am extremely anxious to arrive at an agreement" (6). Because Moore is interested in analyzing the referent of the word "good"— i.e., the property *goodness*—when he speaks of "defining good" we must read him as intending what used to be called a "real definition," as opposed to a nominal definition. The distinction goes back to Socrates. A nominal definition explains how the term is used in the language; a real definition explains what a thing *is*, ideally providing the item's essential features. (I am not saying that this is an unproblematic or even useful distinction; I am merely trying to make some sense of Moore's assertions. A useful discussion of the distinction can be found in Robinson 1950.)

The imperative thing to remember about Moore's naturalistic fallacy is that he thought it to apply not only to any attempt to define goodness but also to any attempt to define *pleasure* and *yellowness*. This shows that the "evaluativeness" of goodness (its "oughtiness") is not the crucial factor in the naturalistic fallacy. Indeed, Moore's most succinct statement of the fallacy concerns yellowness:

It is really a very simple fallacy indeed. When we say that an orange is yellow, we do not think our statement binds us to hold that 'orange' means nothing else than 'yellow,' or that nothing can be yellow but an orange.[4] Supposing the orange is also sweet! Does that bind us to say that 'sweet' is exactly the same thing as 'yellow,' that 'sweet' must be defined as 'yellow'? . . . It would be absolutely meaningless to say that oranges were yellow, unless yellow did in the end mean just 'yellow' and nothing else whatever—unless it was absolutely indefinable. (14)

Moore is claiming that some things are indefinable, and that thus any attempt to define one of these things is, naturally, problematic. Among the indefinable things are evaluative qualities, such as moral goodness, but also entirely non-evaluative qualities, such as yellowness. These things defy definition, Moore thinks, because they are "simple" and they "have no parts" (9). By comparison, he thinks of *horse* (or, as I would prefer, the property *horseness*) as amenable to definition in virtue of a horse being a complex entity. He might have looked favorably on the following passage in Dickens's *Hard Times*:

"Bitzer," said Thomas Gradgrind, "your definition of a horse."

"Quadruped. Gramnivorous. Forty teeth, namely twenty-four grinders, four eye-teeth, and twelve incisive. Sheds coat in the spring; in marshy countries sheds hoofs too. Hoofs hard, but requiring to be shod with iron. Age known by marks in mouth." Thus (and much more) Bitzer.

"Now, girl number twenty," said Mr. Gradgrind. "You know what a horse is."

No such decompositional definition, Moore thinks, will be forthcoming for goodness. At no point in the argument does he highlight the fact that goodness is an evaluative quality as the reason that it defies definition, nor does he appeal to a supposed logical gap between "ought" and "is." In fact, later in *Principia Ethica* and elsewhere, Moore reveals that he believes that statements about intrinsic value *are* a factual matter. (See Bruening 1971.) He speaks of "a use of 'mere statements of fact' in which 'p is a mere statement of fact' is not identical to 'p is not normative.'" "It is quite clear," he continues, "that statements of the form 'I ought to do X' are normative, but not clear that they are not reducible to factual or existential statements" (Moore in Schilpp 1942: 568). Far from arguing that value statements and factual statements are essentially distinct, Moore is sanguine about the existence of reductive relations between them! What he is adamant about is that no sentence of the form "X is good" or "Goodness is Y" should be put forward as *a definition* (in the decompositional sense discussed). In other words, it is permissible to say "X is good" or "Goodness is Y" so long as one is using the "is" of predication rather than the "is" of identity. And that is, in essence, Moore's naturalistic fallacy: One blunders if one mistakes a predication for a definition (by which he means a decompositional identity claim). It is OK to say things *about* goodness, but unacceptable to say what goodness *is*, because goodness is "simple, indefinable, unanalysable" (21).

The crucial question, then, is this: Why should we agree with Moore that goodness is indefinable? Here is where his *open question argument* steps onto the stage. As with the naturalistic fallacy, the passing of a century has seen a certain "mythology" develop concerning how the open question argument (OQA) works; popular accounts of the argument seem oddly out of synch with Moore's presentation. Here, first, is the popular version.

Suppose the moral naturalist [of which a proponent of prescriptive evolutionary ethics is one type] offers a decompositional real definition of the following generic form:

NATURALISM For any x, x is good if and only if x is N, where N stands for some natural property.

However you fill in N, it will be possible that a perfectly competent speaker of the language might be quite sure that something is N while being unsure whether that thing is good (i.e., the question "Is it good?" may remain open). This shows that the original NATURALISM must be mistaken.

This is a defective argument. We need to distinguish two things that might be meant by "if and only if" as it appears in NATURALISM. It might be a linguistic, a priori relation (as in "For any x, x is a bachelor if and only if x is an unmarried man"), or it might be a metaphysical, a posteriori relation (as in "For any x, x is water if and only if x is H_2O"). Michael Smith calls these "definitional naturalism" and "metaphysical naturalism," respectively (1994: 27ff.). If the naturalist is putting forward a metaphysical theory, then clearly the OQA doesn't work. If one were ignorant of the relevant molecular theory, then one could be quite sure that the liquid in the glass is water, but be uncertain (or even deny) that the glass contains H_2O. But this would not cast any doubt on the truth of the claim that water *is* H_2O. Indeed, according to orthodox views, "Water is H_2O" is a *necessary* truth.

One might want to be charitable to Moore, and read him as restricting himself to attacking *definitional* naturalism. But serious problems would remain. First, a whole brand of naturalism—the metaphysical sort—would escape untouched. Second, such a restriction clashes with a great deal of Moore's text. His favorite example of a permissible definition—the definition of horse [*sic*[s]]—defines it in terms of its liver, its heart, etc., and the relations between these items, all of which seem to be a posteriori truths about horses. Third, it is doubtful that the above version of the OQA works even if confined to definitional naturalism. Put simply: A priori truths may be less than obvious to us, and may be revealed only after a lot of intellectual labor. (See chapter 2 of Smith 1994.) For example, pretend that *justified true belief* were to turn out to be the correct analysis of the concept *knowledge*. A competent speaker can be perfectly sure that something is an item of knowledge while doubting whether that thing is an object of justified true belief. Nevertheless, it may be true that, for any *x*, *x* is knowledge if and only if *x* is justified true belief; moreover, it may be a necessary and a priori truth.

So much for the easily dismissed mythical version. But a close look at Moore's text shows that the OQA is a rather more complicated argument—though no more successful. Moore starts by introducing a particular, allegedly arbitrary instantiation of "N" (one that he has gotten from Bertrand Russell, as it happens):

NATURALISM*   For any *x*, *x* is good if and only if *x* is what we desire to desire.

According to the above "mythical" version of the argument, what we would expect would be the questions

(1)   Do we desire to desire X?

and

(2)   Is X good?

along with the claim that a competent speaker might be quite certain that the answer to (1) is "Yes" while remaining unsure of the answer to (2), thus showing NATURALISM* to be false. But this isn't what we get from Moore. Rather, he remarks that, just as we can ask (2), so can we ask "with significance, of the complex so defined, whether it is itself good" (15). In other words, we can ask

(3)   Is it good to desire to desire X?

And this, given NATURALISM*, would be equivalent to asking

(4)   Do we desire to desire to desire to desire X?

And this, Moore thinks, disproves NATURALISM*, since in asking (3) "we have not before our minds anything so complicated [as (4)]." He thinks it might be true that if something is good we desire to desire it, and it might even be true that if we desire to desire it then it is good, but "the mere fact that we understand very well what is meant by doubting it, shews clearly that we have two different notions before our minds" (16).

The argument does succeed in drawing attention to something unusual about the predicate ". . . is good." Just as we can say "X is good," we can also say (with at least grammatical rectitude) "It is good that X is good." Many predicates are not like this: We can say "X is square," but we cannot coherently say "It is square that X is square." In other words, the predicate ". . . is good" can be sensibly applied both to actions *and to states of affairs* (as we saw back in chapter 2), whereas ". . . is square" can be sensibly applied only to objects, and not to states of affairs. This seems to highlight a constraint on naturalism: However "N" is filled out, it had better have this characteristic. However, it is doubtful that there is much else to be said in favor of the argument.

For a start, we might be suspicious as to whether Moore's supposedly arbitrary selection of a naturalistic theory of goodness ("that which we desire to desire") is entirely innocent, for it leads to the repetitive and slightly silly (4). Perhaps it is true that we do not have anything so "complicated" as (4) "before our minds"—but it is so complicated only because of Moore's careful choice of an example! More to the point, what we have "before our minds" is irrelevant. If it is metaphysical naturalism that is being presented, then introspection is not a test of identity. Someone who doesn't know much chemistry may sensibly doubt whether water is H_2O, but it may be true that water is necessarily H_2O. At the heart of the OQA is nothing more compelling than an appeal from Moore that his readers simply "see" that goodness cannot be identical with any other property; in this he reveals himself to be a kind of intuitionist at the metaethical level (Fanaei 2003).

It is worth noting, also, that Moore poses the whole argument in terms of what we can *ask*. He thinks that, given NATURALISM*, in asking (3) one would be asking (4). But this is just false, for *asking* is an opaque context. If Lois Lane asks whether Superman saved the day, she is not asking whether Clark Kent saved the day—though Superman and Clark Kent are identical. As a matter of fact even for Moore's favorite example of a successful decompositional definition it is evident that someone may ask "Is X a horse?" without thereby asking "Does X have four legs, a head, a heart, a liver, etc., etc., all of them arranged in definite relations to one another?" By the same token, in asking (3) we may well *not* be asking (4), but this is compatible with the truth of NATURALISM*, even if we construe it as a definitional kind of theory.

To sum up: Moore's naturalistic fallacy has little to do with the injunction against deriving an "ought" from an "is"; rather, it is the claim that one cannot define an indefinable thing, and so should not attempt to. The first point we can note is that the moral naturalist (and ipso facto the evolutionary moral naturalist) might not care much about this interdiction, for it is not at all clear that her enterprise is to provide anything like a decompositional definition of moral goodness. And so long as she doesn't do that, then she need not rub G. E. Moore the wrong way. But even if the naturalist were to want to provide such a definition, the only argument Moore offers in support of his contention that goodness is "simple, indefinable, unanalysable" is the open question argument. And we have seen that this is a deeply flawed argument, one based on the confused views of necessity, a prioricity, and analyticity that dogged early-twentieth-century philosophy and weren't straightened out until the middle of the century (e.g., in works by the philosophers J. J. C. Smart and U. T. Place[6]). The moral naturalist (and the prescriptive evolutionary ethicist in particular) will quite properly remain unimpressed.

The term "naturalistic fallacy" is occasionally misapplied to another view—namely, that one commits the fallacy by moving from "X is natural" to "X is good" (or, as I have also seen it rendered, "What is, ought to be"). Again, this bears no resemblance to Moore's fallacy, though he no doubt would have agreed that it is a gross mistake. But a straightforward connection between naturalness (under some specification) and moral goodness is not something that any serious thinker would endorse anyway, though occasionally one hears non-scholars pressing it. Whatever its popular appeal, it is clearly a false and silly thing to say—though it should be pointed out that being false and silly is insufficient to warrant the honorific "fallacy." A fallacy is a mistake in reasoning, not a false belief. If someone thinks that homosexuality is unnatural, and that all unnatural things are wrong, and that therefore homosexuality is wrong, his *reasoning* is flawless, and he commits no fallacy; it is just the false beliefs expressed in his premises that are at fault. To label the view of your philosophical opponent a "fallacy" is, much more often than not, a cheap rhetorical trick. I would like to call it "the fallacy fallacy," but to do so would be to commit it.

5.3   Deriving an "Ought" from an "Is"

Marco Polo picked up the name "Madagascar" (to be precise, "Maydeygastar") from some Arab sailors; he never went anywhere near the place. But somewhere in that exchange Polo got hold of the idea that the name denoted the large island off the African coast, whereas in fact it was the name of a piece of African *mainland*. Thus was instigated a long-standing confusion with European cartographers. But it would be a rare pedant who insisted that all who *now* refer to the island as "Madagascar" are making a mistake. Similarly, so many people have asserted that the naturalistic fallacy is much the same as the pronouncement that one cannot derive an "ought" from an "is" that I am almost ready to concede that this now *is* what the phrase means, on the grounds that if enough people make a linguistic error it eventually ceases to be an error. Certainly confusion over what the phrase "the naturalistic fallacy" denotes has taken hold in the philosophical community, and it is no more likely that it can now be budged than that the name "Madagascar" could be shifted back to its original denotation. In any case, just as G. E. Moore thought that his naturalistic fallacy sinks any form of moral naturalism, so too many people have thought that the same damage can be done by wielding the general a priori principle that one cannot derive an "ought" from an "is." Though these are completely different claims, they both deserve our attention. *Can* one derive an "ought" from an "is"?

If by this question we mean "Can there be a logically valid argument in which the conclusion contains the word 'ought' while this word appears in no premise?" then undoubtedly the answer is "Yes." Here is one way of doing it (from Prior 1960):

P1:   Paris is the capital of France.
Therefore: Either Paris is the capital of France or you ought not steal bananas.

Here is another:

P1:   Paris is the capital of France and it is not the case that Paris is the capital of France.
Therefore: You ought not steal bananas.

Both are pretty odd but perfectly valid. The first employs the familiar disjunctive addition rule of classical logic. The second trades on another theorem of classical logic: that from a contradiction anything follows. (Start with (i) *P and not-P*. The rule of simplification allows us to deduce from this two further propositions: (ii) *P* and (iii) *Not-P*. The rule of disjunctive addition, applied to (ii), allows us to deduce (iv) *P or Q*, for any instantiation of Q. The rule of disjunctive elimination applied to premises (iii) and (iv) then gives us the conclusion Q.)

But one might feel a little queasy about these logical tricks. Charles Pigden complains that in these cases the conclusions aren't *genuinely* derived from the premises, in the sense that the proposition containing the moral predicate ("You ought not steal bananas") could be replaced by any grammatically identical proposition (e.g., "Jenny is sitting next to Bob"[7]) without affecting the validity of the argument. In both cases the moral conclusions are "vacuous, given the premises" (1989: 133). If that is what we mean by *"ought" cannot be derived from "is"*—that it cannot be *non-vacuously* derived—these counterexamples don't work.

But the important question is "Who cares?" Just as classical logic (with an orthodox Tarskian account of validity) does not allow one to derive non-vacuous "ought"s from premises that don't contain that predicate, it does not allow one to derive non-vacuous propositions explicitly about hedgehogs from premises that don't contain the word "hedgehog" (Pigden 1989). Or consider this:

P1:   My glass contains the liquid H_2O
P2:   I am about to drink the liquid in my glass
Therefore: I am about to drink water

By Tarskian standards, this is invalid. If we translate the whole thing into the language of the predicate calculus, we will have no trouble finding models in which P1 and P2 are true but the conclusion is false.[8] And yet this observation hardly undermines our confidence that water and H_2O are the very same substance (indeed, are usually thought of as necessarily identical). A moral naturalist (and ipso facto an evolutionary moral naturalist) can claim that moral properties are identical to (or supervene upon) natural properties while denying that there is a *semantic* or *deductive* relation between propositions about the natural world and the propositions involving moral values and obligations. In much the same way, we generally take it for granted that biological facts fit within the worldview given by physics, and yet there do not appear to be valid deductions from propositions concerning only the entities and laws of physics to any biological proposition as a conclusion. Nor can one get from premises mentioning only atoms and their behavior to a conclusion mentioning tables and chairs, yet we all accept that tables and chairs fit comfortably within the world that physics describes. The so-called is/ought gap looks a lot less interesting if the moral naturalist can persuade us that it is much the same as the physics/furniture gap. Of course, the naturalist might not be able to persuade us that moral values fit into the naturalistic world in the way that furniture does, but the important point is that this is a matter to be settled by philosophical argument; the naturalist's failure is not something that can be dogmatically assumed from the start, as William Frankena (1939) recognized.

Let us assume that the evolutionary moral naturalist holds that some property concerning human evolution—let's just call it "E"—is the very same property as "moral oughtness." Now consider the following argument.

P1:   John's action ϕ has property E
Therefore: John morally ought to perform action ϕ.

Clearly this is an invalid argument. But the naturalist need not deny its invalidity (though Robert Richards, whose views will be discussed below, denies it). The evolutionary naturalist just thinks that the argument is an enthymeme—that is, another premise is needed for validity:

P2: For any action x, x has E if and only if x morally ought to be performed.

It is true that P2 will almost certainly be controversial, and will not command immediate assent. But that is not the issue. The naturalist thinks that P2 is *true*, not that it is obviously and incontestably true. One might protest further that in trying to convince us of P2 the evolutionary moral naturalist is doing nothing more or less than trying to show us that the conclusion follows from P1, and we didn't accept it then so why should we accept it now? But this would be mistaken. The objection to the original argument concerned its *invalidity*, but in advocating P2 the naturalist isn't claiming a *deductive* relationship between E-propositions and "ought"-propositions, merely that P2 expresses a truth. To protest that P2 cannot be true just on the grounds that it connects an "ought" to an "is" simply begs the question. To be sure, the naturalist has work to do to convince us of the truth of P2, but the point is that his project has not been shot down by having had a gross invalidity exposed, or because some fallacy has been committed.

Let me recap. There is more to prescriptive evolutionary ethics than evolutionary moral naturalism. Prescriptive evolutionary ethicists attempt to "vindicate" morality in some way by appealing to evolution, but (as we shall see) establishing a form of evolutionary moral naturalism—e.g., showing that moral properties are identical to or supervene upon certain evolutionary properties—is not the only kind of vindicatory strategy available. Thus even if Moore's naturalistic fallacy and the is/ought gap were triumphant against moral naturalism, there would be other avenues for the prescriptive evolutionary ethicist to explore. However, as we have seen, these considerations are in fact far from triumphant. Both are red herrings and should have been eliminated from the debate in the middle of the twentieth century. So are evolutionary moral naturalism and (more generally) prescriptive evolutionary ethics viable after all? I don't believe so. In chapter 6 I will put forward arguments against moral naturalism in general—arguments that, if successful, will take out any evolutionary version of moral naturalism too. As for the broader category of prescriptive evolutionary ethics: There is not going to be any swift, generic knockout argument, for there is such a variety of proposals that all one can do is examine their viability case by case, with an eye to locating any recurring weaknesses in the arguments. This is what the rest of this chapter is devoted to. (Some of the prescriptive evolutionary ethicists to be discussed do purport to deliver a form of moral naturalism, other don't, and others I'm not sure about.) The two recurring problems that will be highlighted are (1) that the prescriptive evolutionary ethicist often displays an explicit or implicit (but in either case specious) neglect for the cognitive element of moral judgment and (2) that the prescriptive evolutionary ethicist will often find some non-moral kind of normativity implied by the evolutionary hypothesis which is then erroneously declared to be moral value.

5.4 Richards's Evolutionary Vindication of Morality

In 1986, in the first issue of the journal *Biology and Philosophy*, Robert Richards launched an extensive defense of "revised" evolutionary ethics ("revised," that is, from old-fashioned versions such as Herbert Spencer's, which will not be discussed here). First Richards tries to show in general terms how "ought" may be derivable from "is"; then he presents a specific attempt to accomplish this using premises concerning evolution. I will discuss these two arguments in turn.

We have seen that the moral naturalist doesn't need to defend a *deductive* relation holding between empirical/descriptive propositions and moral propositions, but certainly if such a relation could be supported then moral naturalism would be looking healthy (i.e., establishing such a connection is unnecessary but is sufficient for moral naturalism). Richards attempts to defend a deductive relation by appealing to the necessity of inference rules for any logical argument.

Consider the debate that Lewis Carroll (1895) imagined taking place between Achilles and the Tortoise. Achilles tries to get the Tortoise to accept the following argument as valid:

(A) Things that are equal to the same are equal to each other.
(B) The two sides of this Triangle are things that are equal to the same.
(Z) The two sides of this Triangle are equal to each other.

The Tortoise accepts *A* and *B* but refuses to accept *Z*, on the grounds that he refuses to accept the following:

(C) If *A* and *B* are true, *Z* must be true.

So Achilles adds *C* to the premises, and asks the Tortoise to admit that the premises now entail *Z*, because, he claims, "if you accept *A* and *B* and *C*, you *must* accept *Z*." The Tortoise objects:

"And why *must* I?"

"Because it follows *logically* from them. If *A* and *B* and *C* are true, *Z must* be true. You don't dispute *that*, I imagine?"

"If *A* and *B* and *C* are true, *Z* *must* be true," the Tortoise thoughtfully repeated. "That's *another* Hypothetical, isn't it? And, if I failed to see its truth, I might accept *A* and *B* and *C*, and *still* not accept *Z*, mightn't I?"

"You might," the candid hero admitted; "though such obtuseness would certainly be phenomenal. Still, the event is *possible*. So I must ask you to grant *one* more Hypothetical."

"Very good. I'm quite willing to grant it, as soon as you've written it down. We will call it

(D) If *A* and *B* and *C* are true, *Z* must be true.

"Have you entered that in your notebook?"

"I *have*!" Achilles joyfully exclaimed, as he ran the pencil into its sheath. "And at last we've got to the end of this ideal race-course! Now that you accept *A* and *B* and *C* and *D*, *of course* you accept *Z*."

"Do I?" said the Tortoise innocently. "Let's make that quite clear. I accept *A* and *B* and *C* and *D*. Suppose I *still* refused to accept *Z*?"

"Then Logic would *force* you to do it!" Achilles triumphantly replied. "Logic would tell you 'You can't help yourself. Now that you've accepted *A* and *B* and *C* and *D*, you *must* accept *Z*!' So you've no choice, you see."

"Whatever Logic is good enough to tell me is worth *writing down*," said the Tortoise. "So enter it in your book, please. We will call it

(E) If *A* and *B* and *C* and *D* are true, *Z* must be true.

Until I've granted *that*, of course I needn't grant *Z*. So it's quite a *necessary* step, you see?"

"I see," said Achilles; and there was a touch of sadness in his tone.

Poor Achilles. What he should have said, of course, is that rules like "If *P* and *If P then Q*, then *Q*" (modus ponens) are not additional premises, but are rather the very rules of inference that govern the transition from premises to conclusion. No doubt the Tortoise would respond "But where do such rules of inference come from?"—a very good question, and the very question that Carroll is trying to get us to ponder while showing us one way it should not be answered. Richards's answer is that we derive such rules from the "beliefs and practices" of "rational men" (284–285). He then contends that in a similar way we can look to the beliefs and practices of *moral* people in order to derive propositions relating empirical facts and moral values that function not as premises in an argument, but rather as rules of inference that license the transition, thus allowing "ought" from "is."

This would be nice if it worked, but it is extremely doubtful that there are any such inference rules. The argument is unconvincing for at least three reasons. First, it is far from obvious that in justifying modus ponens we can do no better than appeal to what seems self-evident to rational people. How do we identify the "rational" people anyway, if not by reference to (among other things) the fact that they affirm and follow modus ponens? Second, if we are trying to show that moral conclusions follow from descriptive premises, it is not clear why we should appeal to the beliefs and practices of the *moral* people. Why aren't we appealing to the beliefs and practices of the *rational* people? To confine oneself to the moral people (whoever they may be) undermines the whole enterprise, for the challenge of deriving "ought" from "is," as it is classically conceived, is to try to convince a sensible moral skeptic that her sensible acceptance of various relevant empirical data logically commits her to certain moral conclusions. It is not hard to get a bunch of utilitarians to agree that an action's maximizing happiness makes it morally obligatory, or a bunch of Kantians to agree that an action is prohibited if the universalization of its maxim cannot be willed as a law of nature. The trick is to get people *who haven't already agreed* to a moral view to agree. Third, from the fact that something commands widespread assent it hardly follows that it is therefore in any sense an inference rule. The proposition that tigers are quadrupeds is something that pretty much everyone agrees with, but all that follows from this is that hardly anyone will object if you insert "Tigers are quadrupeds" into an argument as a premise. It doesn't mean that there is a deductive rule—something akin to modus ponens—that allows you to pass from premises mentioning only tigers to a conclusion mentioning quadrupeds. Thus, even if there were some proposition relating empirical facts and moral values that all people assented to, this wouldn't necessarily reveal a special rule of moral inference; it might just indicate that there is a premise (containing "ought") that all agree to, in which case we still wouldn't see an "ought" from just empirical premises.

Richards's effort seems to boil down to the observation that in seeking justification for anything we always have to rest content with *some* stopping point—a point that just seems intuitively obvious to us—otherwise one can always carry on asking "And what justifies that? . . . OK, but what justifies *that*?" and we never get anywhere. There is evidently sense in this. But the question still arises of what counts as a proper justificatory resting point. It is not enough to observe that there must be a stopping point somewhere and then choose your favorite contender (one that, incidentally, supports your pet theory).

So much for Richards's attempt to derive an "ought" from an "is." But, as I have said, his evolutionary moral naturalism shouldn't require a *deductive* relationship to be established between descriptive and prescriptive propositions, anyway. Let us now turn to his substantive attempt to vindicate morality from an evolutionary foundation. The heart of his argument is found in this passage:

> . . . the evidence shows that evolution has, as a matter of fact, constructed human beings to act for the community good; but to act for the community good is what we mean by being moral. Since, therefore, human beings are moral beings—an unavoidable condition produced by evolution—each ought to act for the community good. (289)

Let us allow the first claim for the sake of argument. The second claim—that acting for the good of the community is what we mean by the word "moral"—is mistaken. It may well be that the human moral sense evolved in order to foster social cohesion, but it wouldn't follow from this that this is what the word "moral" means. (By the same token, it may be that human bipedalism evolved in order to allow our ancestors on the savannah to watch for predators, but it wouldn't follow that the phrase "to stand" means nothing else than *to watch for predators*.) And in fact it is quite easy to think of examples of moral actions that don't benefit the community, and actions that benefit the community without being moral. Regarding the latter: Imagine that I am one of Genghis Khan's henchmen, and suppose that my natural instinct is to act for the good of my community, and suppose that I and my swarthy mates decide (not unreasonably) that the best way to accomplish this is to lay waste to every other community that we encounter. Is that moral? Perhaps my unpleasant friends and I will consider it moral—moral by *our* lights—or maybe we laugh at the very idea of moral rules. ("Moral, schmoral!" we snort, impaling another head on a spike.) Acting for the good of the community will *often* be moral, just as will making friends or telling the truth, but the very fact that we can easily think of wicked examples of all these action types shows that none of them can be what we *mean* by "moral."

But suppose, just for the sake of argument, that Richards is correct that acting so as to benefit the community and acting morally are the same thing, and that evolution has designed us to act so as to benefit the community. It would follow trivially that evolution has designed us to be moral. However, what are we to make of his conclusion: that "each *ought* to act for the community good"? If it is "an unavoidable condition produced by evolution" that humans are constructed to act so as to benefit the community (i.e., be moral), then the conclusion we might have expected is that each *will* act so as to benefit the community (i.e., be moral). What business does this "ought" have in making a sudden appearance? The only sense that can be made of it is that it is a predictive "ought" (as in "It ought to stop raining soon"); in fact, Richards admits this, likening this "ought" to that found in "There has been lightning, so now there ought to be thunder." But this is terribly inadequate, for we know that there is a world of difference between moral and predictive "ought"s. A detective might say of a serial killer "He ought to strike again within the week"—meaning that he *will probably* strike again before the week is out—but this is obviously a far cry from saying that the killer *morally ought* to commit another murder. Conversely, one might judge that the killer morally ought to turn himself in without implying that this is a particularly likely turn of events.

Too often, prescriptive evolutionary ethicists get so obsessed with deriving an "ought" from an "is" that they forget about what *kind* of "ought" they are aiming to find. Richards is a prime example, satisfied with obtaining a predictive "ought." But if that were sufficient, finding moral prescriptions in evolutionary theory—or in any body of scientific data— would be easy indeed. A physicist could claim that a particle *ought to* leave a trail of ions in the cloud chamber, a zoologist could claim that the geese *ought to* be flying south soon, and so on. Our suspicions should be aroused by noting that it is purely a quirk of English that the same word is used to capture this predictive relation and to morally prescribe action; in other languages this is not the case.

5.5 Campbell's Evolutionary Vindication of Morality

Ten years after Richards, in the same journal, Richmond Campbell (1996) attempted a somewhat more modest vindication of morality on the basis of the empirical hypothesis that human morality is innate. Campbell doesn't argue for moral *naturalism* as such; he limits himself to establishing that the empirical hypothesis shows morality to be justified. He is careful to communicate that he is trying to provide justification for our having some morality rather than none at all, not trying to provide justification for a moral system with some particular content. The argument is quite simple, and, properly qualified, it might be successful. But a clear understanding of the qualifications in question reveal the limits of the success. Here is the crucial passage:

. . . the argument rests on the normative but non-moral principle that having some morality rather than none is justified for every member of the group if having some morality rather than none overwhelmingly improves the life prospects of everyone in the group. [Call this the "overwhelmingly mutually advantageous" (OMA) principle.] Since the biological explanation for the existence of morality implies that having some morality rather than none overwhelmingly improves the life prospects of everyone in the group, it follows (given the principle just cited) that having some morality rather than none is justified. (Campbell 1996: 24)

Pressure can first be placed on the assumption that the evolutionary explanation of morality demonstrates that having some morality rather than none is better for everyone. As was pointed out at the start of this chapter, the evolutionary hypothesis doesn't imply that morality is useful. It implies (A) that it *was* useful and (B) that it was useful to our ancestors' *genes*. Regarding (B), Campbell sees the need to assert that we can be moderately confident that roughly, at least within the domain under discussion, what is good for an individual's fitness is also good for the individual. Fair enough, but in a full working out of the argument this claim would require further support. Campbell also seems aware of (A), since when discussing the issue he puts the whole thing in past tense: ". . . for the period in which morals evolved these two considerations [individual welfare and genetic fitness] were highly correlated" (25). But he doesn't seem to notice that showing that morality *was* useful for everyone (i.e., was justified, according to OMA) is not sufficient to show that it *is* useful (i.e., is justified, according to OMA). By the same reasoning, to show that having a robust disposition in favor of eating all the sweet food that one can find *was* useful to our ancestors, and thus was justified (in some sense of the word), is not sufficient to demonstrate that it remains useful or that it remains justified. Furthermore, if Campbell were to embark on filling in this step in the argument (that is, if he were to bring forth empirical evidence in support of the claim that for *us now* having some morality rather than none overwhelmingly improves the life prospects of everyone in our group), then the issue of how things stood during our prehistory would drop out of the picture entirely. In other words, Campbell faces a dilemma: Either he can rely on the evolutionary hypothesis to get results—but then the only conclusions to be drawn concern what was justified for our ancestors—or he can try to show that morality is justified for us now—but then the evolutionary hypothesis looks redundant.

The main query that should be raised, however, concerns whether Campbell has the correct notion of justification. Consider an analogy. Suppose we could show that having religious beliefs (in comparison to having none) improves the prospects of everyone in a group. Perhaps it is simply comforting to believe that one's life fits into a Grand Scheme, that there are larger forces at work than we observe. (Don't be distracted by the plausibility of the details; it's just an example.[9]) Perhaps if these improved prospects are sufficiently stable and concrete, then we could imagine that having religious beliefs might be innate. Suppose that the most basic form of religious belief is something like "God exists" or "There are supernatural forces at work." Then, by Campbell's lights, having such religious beliefs would be justified.

The above reasoning cries out for a distinction. The distinction is between two ways in which a belief can be justified: *instrumentally* and *epistemically*. Something is instrumentally justified for a person if it contributes toward the satisfaction of her ends. Usually we apply this mode of justification to actions, but there is nothing incoherent about applying it to beliefs. If Kate's belief that she is the world's greatest tennis player makes her happy— really sincerely happy in the long term—then that belief is instrumentally justified for her (if happiness is one of her ends). It is instrumentally justified even if as a matter of fact she is a very long way from being a great tennis player. What sounds disconcerting about this is that instrumental justification is generally not the kind of justification we employ when we talk of beliefs. Were you to hear someone say "Kate is justified in believing herself to be the world's greatest tennis player," it would be pretty odd for you to assume that this means simply that having this belief serves her interests. Rather, you would likely take it to mean something along the lines of *her belief was formed by a process that showed sensitivity to the available evidence,* or *her belief is the product of a process that reliably yields true beliefs,* or, more generally, *her belief satisfies the appropriate epistemic standards.* This is epistemic justification. Let us assume that the appropriate epistemic standards involve sensitivity to the evidence. Then if Kate has been exposed to no evidence indicating her prowess at tennis (in fact, sadly, much evidence to the contrary) but nevertheless persists with the belief, and it makes her happier (really sincerely happier in the long run), then her belief is epistemically unjustified but instrumentally justified. Many beliefs are unjustified on both counts; having an epistemically unjustified belief often will lead to the frustration of a person's ends, and thus will also be instrumentally unjustified.

It is reasonably clear what Campbell will say to this. He will complain that there is a crucial disanalogy with my imaginary case of innate religious beliefs and the case of an innate morality. The difference, he will say, is that morality does not pertain to *beliefs* that purport to "refer to or correspond to a realm of moral facts" (21). What is distinctive about these moral beliefs is not their subject matter, but rather the fact that "they intrinsically motivate certain actions or omissions, occasion feelings of guilt when this motivation is deficient, occasion admiration and esteem for others when they have an abundance of this motivation, and elicit the thought that having this motivation is important enough to warrant imposing sanctions against those that are deficient in it. Moral beliefs are from this perspective essentially dispositions to think, feel, and act in accordance with certain norms." (ibid.) By plugging this non-cognitivist reading from the very first paragraph of his paper, Campbell in effect makes morality out to be something for which epistemic justification is inappropriate, but for which instrumental justification—the kind provided by OMA—seems satisfactory and natural. My main bone of contention is with this starting assumption. Campbell says he accepts the non-cognitivist reading because he doesn't want to beg any questions in favor of cognitivism, but in fact, by going on to deploy an argument whose plausibility depends entirely on morality being construed non-cognitively, he begs an enormous question in the other direction.[10]

If one thinks, as I do, that pure non-cognitivism about morality is hopelessly inadequate, one should find Campbell's argument uncompelling. We can grant that he may have identified a way in which morality is justified—in that he may have shown that having moral "beliefs" is an advantageous policy—but we should object that it is an uninteresting and perhaps misleading sense of justification. If we think that moral beliefs really are *beliefs*—something more than just "dispositions to think, feel, and act"—then we will be inclined to consider them as in the same camp as the religious example discussed above. Just as it would be misleading to claim that the belief that God exists is justified simply on the grounds that having this belief improves the welfare of everyone in the group, so too it will be misleading to claim that basic moral beliefs are justified on matching grounds. After all, atheists, who think that religious beliefs are false and/or unjustified, often are willing to concede that such beliefs nevertheless are or have been socially useful. Nothing that Campbell has said prevents a moral skeptic from taking the same attitude toward morality—seeing it as having the status of a *useful fiction*. Think of Campbell as someone who responds "Useful?—well, that means *justified*." Think of the skeptic as someone who replies "Be that as it may, it's still a useful *fiction*."

5.6 Dennett's Evolutionary Vindication of Morality

Daniel Dennett's long and remarkable book *Darwin's Dangerous Idea* (1995) culminates in a discussion of the project of naturalizing ethics. Or so one might gather from his section titles. But I confess that even after several readings of the section titled "Can Ethics be Naturalized?" I remain unsure whether Dennett thinks the answer "Yes" or "No" (or "There is something wrong with the question"). He begins by discussing the practical difficulties that have undermined the plausibility of traditional theories of normative ethics. Utilitarians face the challenge of calculating all those consequences; Kantians struggle to work out which maxim to try to universalize. We need have nothing to quibble with here (though I doubt that we will see utilitarians and Kantians wither in the face of such familiar criticism); the general point is that life is complicated, and the well-known ethical theories seem too simple. And that is how the section ends. How this general point contributes to answering the question with which it began escapes me.

Dennett then goes on to discuss how human decision making is governed by rough-and-ready heuristic processes, which work well enough for time-pressured decisions though they cannot be guaranteed to alight upon the optimal answer. His point here—and it is one of the dominant themes of the book—is that these satisficing processes occur *all the way down*: ". . . even back behind the fixed biological design of the decision-making agent, to the design 'decisions' that Mother Nature settled for when designing us and other organisms" (1995: 503—subsequent page references are to this book). Dennett calls this reasonable observation "the fundamentality of satisficing." Then comes what appears an important hinge in his argument, where he slips from "is" to "ought." He does it so quickly and smoothly that one can easily miss it, and he does it almost entirely through quoting a 1974 article by Roger Wertheimer:

> Thus, what and how we do think is evidence for the principles of rationality, what and how we ought to think. This itself is a methodological principle of rationality; call it the *Factunorm Principle*. We are (implicitly) accepting the Factunorm Principle whenever we try to determine what or how we ought to think. For we must, in that very attempt, think. And unless we can think that what and how we do think there is correct—and thus is evidence for what and how we ought to think—we cannot determine what or how we ought to think. (504)

A lot could be said about Wertheimer's interesting claim, but here is not the place. The point is that Dennett uses it to get an evaluative conclusion from all the preceding descriptive discussion: that heuristic-governed decision making is, in general terms, the *best* that we can do, given our limitations. His subsequent project, then, is to delve beyond the general terms, and suggest specific ways that such decision making can be polished, tweaked, and generally optimized. Crucial to his case is the need for "conversation-stoppers": considerations that can appear in a personal or interpersonal decision process in order to bring the procedure to an effective terminus, preventing the mechanism from spiraling endlessly in seeking further justifications, infinitely mulling over further considerations. For

Dennett, moral values, principles, and imperatives function as conversation-stoppers par excellence. An interesting feature of the view is that in order for our moral judgments to fulfill this role effectively we must not be thinking of them *as* conversation-stoppers at the time of deploying them; we must, rather, think of them as expressing genuine, no-questions-asked, end-of-story, *moral* considerations. Dennett admits that his position suggests that "what Bernard Williams calls the ideal of 'transparency' in society—'the workings of its ethical institutions should not depend on members of the community misunderstanding how they work'[11]—is an ideal that may be politically inaccessible to us" (509). In order to work effectively, the true nature of moral thinking must be opaque; we must cordon off our awareness of the truth when engaged in deliberation. This view concerning the usefulness of moral considerations—the way they function to silence calculations—comports well with my arguments in section 4.2; in fact, there is little in Dennett's case as I have outlined it so far that is objectionable. The only question we must ask here is "Does it succeed in vindicating morality?"

Dennett evidently thinks that it does. As I confessed above, I don't know whether he takes any kind of moral *naturalism* to have been established. Earlier we find him claiming that "ethics must be *somehow* based on an appreciation of human nature—on a sense of what a human being is or might be, and on what a human being might want to have or want to be. If *that* is naturalism, then naturalism is no fallacy" (468). Quite so, but that's *not* naturalism! (One might as well say "If moral naturalism is just the claim that some things are pink with yellow trimmings—why, then, hurray for moral naturalism!") Moral naturalism is a claim about the existence of moral values (see section 5.1) and about the truth of moral judgments—something about which, as far as I can see, Dennett is silent.

I will raise two criticisms against the proposal that Dennett has succeeded in vindicating morality.

My first criticism can be dealt with quickly, since it will be familiar from the previous discussion of Campbell. If I am correct about Dennett's position, then what he has shown us is that the practice of making moral judgments has an extremely important practical role. Perhaps, in addition, he has revealed that in order to gain this benefit the moral judge must not think too carefully about how her moral judgments function—she must be somewhat "forgetful," and not overly reflective. It is obvious that this is nothing more than an *instrumental* justification, and that it is perfectly consistent with moral judgments being false and/or epistemically unjustified. The belief that certain actions will anger the Great Purple Lizard God, or the belief that touching certain objects will fill your soul with pollution, or the belief that certain women are in cahoots with the devil might function quite well as a conversation-stopper while being utterly erroneous as a description of the world. Dennett has said nothing to distinguish moral judgments from these obviously flawed ways of thinking. Even if the agent wielding the moral judgment mustn't think too carefully about what she is doing in order to get the benefit—i.e., she mustn't think about the value in question as being merely of instrumental value—it nevertheless still *is* of instrumental value. And even if the action that the agent considers morally prohibited (say) really is a bad idea on prudential or rational grounds, this wouldn't show that the *moral* judgment concerning that action is true or epistemically justified. In the same way, the actions one thinks will anger the Great Purple Lizard God may all be imprudent actions, meaning that it could be truly said of any of these actions "You ought not do that"—where this is the "ought" of prudence—but this wouldn't show that the statement "You ought not do that" is true or epistemically justified when the "ought" instead signifies *is commanded by the Great Purple Lizard God.* (For a critique arguing that Dennett is actually committed to moral nihilism, see Rosenberg and Sommers 2003.)

My claim is not that the status of moral judgments as conversation-stoppers *entails* that they are false, only that it is entirely consistent with their being false. Certain true claims can presumably also function quite well as conversation-stoppers. The consideration "But that would *kill* me!" generally puts an end to any further deliberation on the matter, yet it may be true that the thing in question really would kill the speaker. So are moral judgments true conversation-stoppers or false ones? If they are true, then they are not *mere* conversation-stoppers; like beliefs about what would kill one, they also can operate usefully in careful, transparent deliberation—i.e., in a non-conversation-stopping role. But if this is Dennett's intention, his theory is marred by a glaring deficiency, for he has told us nothing about what kind of facts might make moral judgments true, or in virtue of what moral judgments might be epistemically justified, or how they might operate in any role other than that of a conversation-stopper. (Compare how these tasks might be discharged regarding the proposition "That would kill me.") As a matter of fact, if these questions could be answered this would be far more interesting, from a metaethical point of view, than the observation that moral judgments can also function effectively as conversation-stoppers. In the absence of any such discussion, one gets the impression that Dennett thinks that moral judgments are *just* conversation-stoppers—but if this is so, they have no claim to being seriously considered *true* at all.

On such a reading Dennett is advocating a form of *moral fictionalism*, which here can be taken as the combination of four theses: (i) Moral judgments are not in fact true; (ii) we may come to know that they are not true (by doing philosophy, for example); (iii) they are nevertheless useful; but (iv) they are useful only if we treat them as true in our day-to-day lives. (For more on moral fictionalism, see Joyce 2001a, 2005; Kalderon 2005; Nolan et al. 2005.) I am not one to criticize Dennett for advocating moral fictionalism (if that is what he is doing), for I am rather fond of moral fictionalism. My principal objection in the present context is that, insofar as Dennett's view counts as vindicating morality, it is only an instrumental vindication.

My second criticism is that it is very hard to grasp the relation between the conversation-stopper view articulated by Dennett (which may amount to a fictionalist view) and a great deal of seemingly "straight-up" moralizing that ends his book. The final chapter is filled with moralistic rumination, advice, and pleas. We are asked to reflect on why it is better to kill a cow than a condor (513); we are told that dying languages are "precious artifacts worth preserving" (514); we are informed that slavery and child abuse are "beyond the pale" (516); we are invited to "join hands" with Arab and Muslim writers who have spoken out against the "unspeakably immoral" fatwa pronounced against Salman Rushdie (517). In a final soaring proclamation, we are told that "this world is sacred" (520). How are we to interpret these claims in the context of what Dennett has revealed about opacity? Are these just more conversation-stoppers, thrown in to keep the author and the reader from spiraling into endless deliberation? Or are we now supposed to have quickly gotten ourselves behind the opaque curtain, from which perspective these considerations (which as a matter of fact *are* conversation-stoppers) are not to be thought of as conversation-stoppers but rather as genuine, binding, practical considerations? It is very puzzling, and I can't help but suspect that Dennett is flip-flopping between transparency and opacity, between what his head informs him (that saying "Slavery is wrong" functions as a conversation-stopper) and what his heart whispers to him ("No, slavery is really, truly *wrong!*").

One wonders whether on Dennett's view we are *ever* to recognize a moral conversation-stopper for what it is. Certainly when in the midst of decision making we will need to take our moral prescriptions at face value—to think of them as requirements with genuine, no-questions-asked practical clout— but when we sit down in a cool hour must we continue to do so? Dennett faces a dilemma, for it seems that whatever answer is given leads to problems. The theory is in trouble if it implies that people can *never* sneak a peek from behind the opaque curtain—for from behind that veil, ex hypothesi, no one will ever agree that moral judgments function as conversation-stoppers: On reading the philosophical proposal that the judgment "Slavery is wrong" is valuable because it functions as an expedient conversation-stopper, all readers will complain "No—Slavery is really, truly *wrong!*" One would have to wonder, moreover, how it would be that Dennett alone would enjoy the advantage of being able to stand outside the framework and see it for what it really is. In light of these problems one must presume that Dennett's intention is that when engaged in abstract musings—such as contemplating the very arguments found at the end of *Darwin's Dangerous Idea*—we *can* be in a position to acknowledge that moral judgments are really just expedient devices. After all, he seems to be in a position to assert this, and surely he hopes that we can be in a position to agree with him. The embarrassment of this horn of the dilemma is that seeing the conversation-stoppers for what they are threatens to deprive them of their ability to fulfill this role so effectively. If Dennett wants people to carry on with their moral convictions—as all his concluding moralizing suggests he does—then perhaps he should have suppressed the publication of his views about moral conversation-stoppers, or endeavored to argue less convincingly!

I am not claiming that this dilemma is fatal. Moral fictionalism may well be a way of negotiating the quandary successfully. But developing a fictionalist case (that is, relieving (i)–(iv) above of their air of inconsistency) requires a degree of nuance and attention that Dennett doesn't bring to the task; in fact he appears unaware that the dilemma even exists. He seems oblivious that his reader has just been primed to react to the heartfelt finale "The world is sacred" with the response "So that's just a conversation-stopper, huh?" And he seems not to notice that if this question receives a positive answer then the obvious next query is "So is the world *really* sacred or not?"

5.7 Casebeer's Evolutionary Vindication of Morality

Recently, William Casebeer (2003) has made a case for moral naturalism—or, more specifically, "pragmatic neo-Aristotelian virtue theory"—on the basis of evolutionary biology. The bedrock of his argument is a commitment to a neo-Aristotelian account of virtue, according to which the primary locus of moral evaluation is not action but rather a person's character. For Aristotle, the phrase "a good person" is comparable to "a good oak tree" or "a good basketball player" (or, for that matter, "a good assassin"), meaning something like *an exemplar of the kind in question.*[12] When the kind in question is a functional item, then an exemplar of that kind will be an item that fulfills the function well. Aristotle argues that, just as the function of a kitharode is to play the kithara,[13] and therefore a good kitharode plays the kithara *well*, so too we should be able to discover what it takes to be a good human by ascertaining the human function (the *ergon*). To determine this, Aristotle employs his characteristic method of first specifying the genus (in this case, *animal*) and then finding the distinguishing feature within the genus (i.e., the differentia—in this case, *rationality*). The human function, according to Aristotle, is "to be a certain kind of life, and this to be an activity or actions of the soul implying a rational principle," and fulfilling this function *well* amounts to performing this activity in accordance with virtue ("and if there are more than one virtue, in accordance with the best and most complete").[14] These virtues include excellences both of intellect and of character, the latter (courage, friendliness, generosity, etc.) having been designated by post-Aristotelian commentators as "the moral virtues."

The main flaw in Aristotle's argument has always been its commitment to a world operating on goal-oriented principles. The arguments in his *Physics* for a teleological cosmology are puzzling and primitive. First, Aristotle insists on an odd dichotomy between teleology and chance, such that anything occurring regularly and predictably—such as rain in winter (but not rain in summer)—must occur for a purpose. Then comes the jaw-dropping declaration that "surely as in intelligent action, so in nature; and as in nature, so it is in each action, if nothing interferes." (My mental red pen can manage only a flabbergasted "*Surely??*" in the margin.) Aristotle associates the position he is opposing—that naturally occurring phenomena have no purpose—with the view of Empedocles, the ancient thinker who more than any other glimpsed a few of the rudiments of Darwinian natural selection.[15] There is irony in this because many contemporary thinkers, having rightly rejected outlandish Aristotelian natural teleology, now look to Darwinian biology to inject some of that teleology back into our scientific worldview (e.g., Allen et al. 1998). Natural selection is not a goal-oriented process, but it can produce structures and mechanisms for which talk of natural purpose and function seems naturalistically respectable. This new teleology will not assign a function to winter rain, of course, but it will assign functions to eyes, hearts, fins, flagella, rhizomes, gall bladders, and so on. Casebeer, armed with an account of functional properties according to which they are "thoroughly natural and non-strange" (2003: 49), thinks he can rescue Aristotle's insightful theory of human virtue, substituting good Darwinian teleology for the bad Aristotelian variety. And this, he thinks, will pave the way for an evolutionary vindication of morality itself.

Let us allow that evolutionary biology makes talk of natural functions, and the normative language that comes along with it, scientifically legitimate. Modern biology will say that the function of the heart is to pump blood, and that a healthy and good heart pumps blood well. It may even allow us to say that a heart ought to pump blood—where this is more than a predictive "ought." But how close does this normative language come to moral language? Does it get the normativity in the right place? And, more importantly, is it the right kind of normativity?

On the question of whether it gets normativity in the right place, consider Aristotle's stock examples of things with functions. In the critical passage of the *Nicomachean Ethics* he provides two kinds of example: people who have social roles (kitharode, sculptor, carpenter) and body parts (eye, hand, foot). Entities of both types exist within a function-endowing context: The kitharode has a job within a society, and the eye has a job within the body. What is unconvincing about Aristotle's attempt to generalize beyond these examples—to assign a function to humans in general—is that in many cases there is no longer a function-endowing context, and thus Aristotle must rely on his weird (to the modern ear) teleological physics to make the argument work. If we reject this physics, then, although we may not be perturbed by the notion that carpenters and eyes have functions, we will balk at the prospect that humans (qua humans) have a function. Now the question is whether Casebeer's scientifically respectable teleology does any better on this score. Although evolutionary biology allows us to speak sensibly of the functions of eyes, hands, and feet, it doesn't obviously assign a function to *humans*. Thus, the normative language that biology makes legitimate—that the function of an X is to φ; that a good X φs well; that an X ought to φ—is fine when "X" is replaced with "heart" or "eye," but we have no grounds for replacing it with "human" or "person." How we get from "Joe's heart ought to pump blood" to "Joe ought to keep his promise" remains problematic.

It may be objected that I am seeing the normativity of biology in a restrictive manner. Perhaps "X ought to φ" need not be drawn directly from "The function of an X is to φ." Perhaps instead what we are supposed to get from evolutionary biology is some respectable and objective notion of things going *well* for an organism, of an organism *flourishing*. This, it might be thought, is tantamount to science uncovering what an organism's *ends* are. With such ends provided, prescriptive language would then follow in the form of hypothetical imperatives. If as a matter of fact human flourishing requires living harmoniously in a community (say), then, insofar as breaking a promise will upset one's social standing, we could insist on the applicability of the hypothetical imperative "You ought not break promises." And to the criminal who declares that the community means nothing to him we could say "But existing in harmony with the community *is* one of your ends [one of your values?], whether or not you recognize or like this fact." Since these natural ends would be in some sense inescapable, then so too would be the associated hypothetical imperatives; the resulting normativity, it might be thought, would have the kind of practical oomph we want from morality.

Or would it? The inability of hypothetical imperatives to capture moral practicality, discussed in section 2.4, is worth rehearsing again here. Let us start by considering *transgression*, a notion that is central to moral thinking. Failure to comply with a hypothetical imperative cannot (without great awkwardness) be thought of as a transgression. If a person is unhappily cold, and shutting the window would warm her up, then we can say that she ought to shut the window; but if she fails to do so, then, although she may be foolish and imprudent, she has hardly transgressed against a norm. To the extent that we expect a moral system to have room for the idea that a wrongdoer deserves punishment for her crimes, a system of hypothetical imperatives will not serve. The basic problem is that someone who fails to act so as to secure her ends has principally wronged *herself*, but a value system revolving around self-harm doesn't look much like a moral system. Punishment, in such a system, would amount to a bizarre institution of inflicting further harm upon a person because she has harmed herself. On such a view Jack the Ripper should elicit our deepest sympathy, since what was really wrong about his killing all those women is that he radically undermined his own flourishing. ("Poor man," we should say upon capturing him.)[16]

Evolutionary biology may license our claiming that a particular heart is good because it pumps blood well, but in saying this we would not really be praising the heart, any more than we would be praising an assassin for his ruthless efficiency if we admitted that he is good at his profession. Thus, if evolutionary biology by the same logic allows us to call a person "good" (in that she is a flourishing example of humankind), this must also be a "praise-free" use of a normative term—hardly a moral usage. Evolutionary biology may also license our claiming that the heart ought to pump blood; it does not sanction our saying that the heart is required to pump blood, that it has a reason to pump blood (which is not to be confused with the claim that there is a reason that it does so), that there is a practical demand on the heart to keep pumping blood irrespective of its desires, that the heart has transgressed and deserves punishment or criticism if it fails to pump blood, or that there might not also exist overriding competing considerations speaking in favor of the heart ceasing to pump blood.

Let us pause to consider the last item. A hammer has the function of bashing nails in, but there is nothing wrong with choosing to employ it as a doorstop instead. While propping open the door the hammer still has its original function, but the fact that this function is going unfulfilled matters not one whit. Why should evolutionary functions be any different? I have heard it said that the large gluteus maximus muscles of humans evolved to augment our ancestors' ability to throw objects (Bingham 2000). Suspend your doubt and assume that this is true, and pretend that this is what all our ancestors used these muscles for till a few generations ago. But suppose you just happen to dislike throwing things (perhaps you were traumatized by a baseball pitcher as a child) and you make a decision never to throw anything. Are you doing anything wrong? Are you transgressing against a norm laid down by nature? One might be tempted to answer in the positive if one has a background assumption that letting a natural bodily function go unexercised is likely to lead to ill health or unhappiness. But in this case it would be the ill health or unhappiness that made the decision wrong, not the failure to implement a function per se. Consider another example: Suppose it is true that evolutionary biology can somehow underwrite the prescription "Jack ought not to kill people." On what grounds would this "ought" claim override any competing "ought" claims that might arise? Suppose that Jack gets immense pleasure from killing people, and suppose that gaining pleasure is one of Jack's chosen ends; thus there is a competing hypothetical imperative: "Jack ought to kill people." Who is to say that the former overcomes the latter, that the former has for Jack a "to-be-doneness" that the latter lacks? One might answer that the former is based in Jack's biology, or that it is less contingent than the latter, or even (extravagant claim!) that it flows from something that is *essential* to Jack's status as a human being. But none of these distinguishing characteristics of the former imperative, nor their combination, suffices to provide it with the needed trumping quality. One could, with just as much prima facie warrant, assert that the ends that a person cares about in the most heartfelt way (i.e., the nasty desires, in Jack's case) are the ones from which the overriding imperatives derive. Were we to discover from the paleoanthropological record that the main selective pressure in favor of a moral sense was the need to bind groups of hominids so that they could better engage in warfare with one another (not likely, but just suppose), surely few would conclude that we must now privilege and respect this function.[17]

Casebeer takes as his foil John Mackie (1977), who famously argued that moral discourse has much the same status as astrology or talk of witches: It embodies a deeply mistaken way of describing reality. Thinking about Mackie is instructive, for a succinct way of summarizing my earlier case against both Campbell and Dennett is to say that even if their arguments are sound Mackie might still be correct about morality—a conclusion that is sufficient to show how "unvindicated" morality remains at their hands. One of Mackie's central arguments is that moral properties, if they existed, would be metaphysically queer: ". . . they would be entities or qualities or relations of a very strange sort, utterly different from anything else in the universe" (1977: 38). Mackie gives a concrete illustration of how queer they would have to be by describing Plato's account of the Form of the Good, which is such that the mere comprehension of the fact that something participates in the Form (i.e., is good) somehow automatically engages the motivation to seek that thing. The Good, for Plato, has a kind of magical magnetism built into it. Casebeer takes his goal to be the provision of moral properties that are in no sense "queer" or "spooky," thereby refuting Mackie.

But Plato's theory of the Forms isn't the only example of queerness that Mackie gives. He also mentions Samuel Clarke, who in the early eighteenth century argued for (in Mackie's words) "necessary relations of fitness between situations and actions, so that a situation would have a demand for such-and-such an action somehow built into it" (40). Note that there is no mention here of a person's motives being *compelled* by the good; rather, they are said to be demanded. This indicates an additional source of queerness, and, it has been argued, represents the better interpretation of what Mackie was really driving at (Garner 1990). The queerness resides not in *intrinsic motivation-engagement* but rather *intrinsic action-guidingness*, which in another book Mackie describes as follows: ". . . to say that [objective prescriptions] are intrinsically action-guiding is to say that the reasons that they give for doing or for not doing something are independent of that agent's desires or purposes" (1982: 115). This gives a more precise picture of where Mackie considers the real queerness to lie: in properties that provide a person with reasons for acting irrespective of that person's ends. Nothing in the world has such a property, thinks Mackie—hence his moral skepticism.

Whether Mackie is correct in affirming the queerness (and thus denying the existence) of such reason-giving properties is not my concern here. (I will get to it in chapter 6.) The point of this discussion of his views is to highlight the fact that, once we get past the misleading Platonic Form example and give greater consideration to what he says about *demands* and *reasons*, we see that his claims about what is essential to a morality are far from outrageous. Casebeer writes: "Mackie's point is that values must have their motivational structure built into them, which seems rather odd insofar as 'motivations' as such do not float around in the world waiting to be perceived by moral agents" (41). If that were "Mackie's point" it would indeed seem odd, and Casebeer would be correct to think that it is no desideratum that he or anyone else should feel obliged to satisfy. But is this really Mackie's point? Suppose that in this quotation from Casebeer we substitute "demand" for "motivation": "Mackie's point is that values must have their demand-giving structure built into them, which seems rather odd insofar as 'demands' as such do not float around in the world waiting to be perceived by moral agents." I contend that "Mackie's point" suddenly doesn't seem odd at all; ordinary moral discourse *does* seem to be committed to the existence of demands "floating around in the world"—if by this latter phrase we mean demands that do not acquire their authority from any human source. (See sections 2.4, 4.4, and 4.5.) If this is queer, then it is a queerness that the moral naturalist must try to accommodate, on pain of proffering a non-queer property that doesn't sufficiently resemble anything *moral*. But, as we have seen, the normativity that may be squeezed from evolutionary biology comes nowhere near to accommodating this desideratum. Just as the fact that the function of the heart is to pump blood doesn't imply that there is a *demand* that it do so, the ascription by the same logic of a biological function to humans would not imply any practical demand. Just as the fact that the function of an assassin is to kill people doesn't imply that he has any *reason* to do so (no reason, at least, that should carry weight in his deliberations), the ascription by the same logic of a biological function to humans would not imply any practical reason to fulfill the function.

Toward the end of his book (pages 153–155), Casebeer considers the possibility that his theory gives us only "wimpy normativity." In responding to this charge, however, he takes his opponent to be insisting that moral norms must be absolute and knowable with certainty—but these are not the desiderata of moral norms that I have been discussing. Let us allow that moral norms may not be absolute and that we may be epistemically fallible regarding them. Still, if there is a value system whose norms (i) do not generate demands and practical reasons, (ii) are easily overridden by competing considerations, (iii) failure to comply with which does not count as a transgression or something deserving of punishment, and (iv) for which declaring that something or somebody abides by them need not count as a form of praise, surely it *is* too wimpy to be mistaken for morality.

5.8 Conclusion

The preceding four attempts to vindicate morality on the basis of the evo-lutionary hypothesis are varied, but we have seen a couple of recurring themes from which we can draw more general conclusions. Campbell and Dennett try to vindicate morality in instrumental terms, but even their suc-cess would leave morality "unvindicated" in the more important sense. For all they have said, morality might have the status of an expedient false-hood: practically useful while still being massively mistaken (as is often the atheist's attitude toward religious discourse, and as seems to be Mackie's attitude toward moral discourse). Thinking that instrumental justification is the appropriate kind of vindication is encouraged by the assumption that moral judgment is a purely non-cognitive affair—some of the problems of which were addressed in chapter 2. The second mistake—this exemplified by Richards and Casebeer—is that of locating the wrong kind of "ought" (the wrong kind of value) in evolutionary theory. This error is encouraged by a disregard for what characteristics a normative framework must have if it is to play the practical role in our lives that we demand of morality. Let me finish this chapter by saying one thing more about each of these recur-ring problems.

First, it might be thought that the most plausible hypotheses concerning the evolution of a moral sense actually lend credence to pure non-cognitivism. Kitcher (1998, 2005), for example, argues that if the geneal-ogy of morals implies that moral judgments function to coordinate human social behavior, and if they achieve this by an "amplification of our psy-chological altruistic dispositions" (2005: 178), then non-cognitivism looks promising. His argument seems to be that if moral judgments function to augment some aspect of our emotional lives then "the surface forms of moral judgments deceive us, [in that] we aren't really uttering straight-forward declarative sentences but expressing emotive reactions" (ibid.: 175). But it is important that we not conflate the evolutionary function of moral judgments with their linguistic function, as Kitcher appears to be doing. Suppose it is true that the evolutionary function of moral judgment is to generate or strengthen some kind of prosocial emotion. The question we must ask is "How does it accomplish this?" Perhaps, for example, the moral judgment encourages the speaker (and her audience) to think of the world as containing authority-independent practical demands, and conceiving of the world in these terms has the desirable effect on their emotional lives. If this were so, then when the speaker uttered "You mustn't do that" she would be *asserting* something about the world, not merely expressing an emotion. Perhaps what she would be asserting is false, but it would be no less an assertion for that. (This point is close to one I made concerning projectivism and non-cognitivism back in section 4.4; see also Joyce 2001a: 14–15.) We can run the analogy again with the hypothesis of innate religious beliefs. Suppose (to simplify the matter) that the belief that God exists is innate and is due simply to the fact that having this belief made our ancestors less anxious (i.e., happier). It would hardly follow that an utterance of the sentence "God exists" falls short of being a full-blooded assertion, or that in uttering it one does no more than express one's happiness.

The second mistake often made by prescriptive evolutionary ethicists is that of locating the wrong kind of normativity in the evolutionary process. Richards and Casebeer (and others I have criticized on separate occasions[18]) recognize that what is needed is epistemic, not instrumental, justification, but fail to appreciate the special kind of practical oomph with which moral values and imperatives are imbued (and with which they must be imbued if they are to serve the concrete purposes we require of them). A corollary of this lack of awareness is a misidentification of the epistemic means by which we (putatively) acquire and improve moral beliefs. Because these theorists are focused on the wrong kind of normativity, it is no surprise that they are committed to odd views about how we might go about discovering moral truths. Let me close this chapter by drawing attention to this epistemological peculiarity of evolutionary moral naturalism. It is not intended as a devastating knock-down argument; nevertheless, I think the simple argument reveals a distinctly counterintuitive implication of such theories.

If moral judgments are to be epistemically justified with reference to facts about human evolution, then making new and unexpected discoveries about human evolution could, and sometimes should, change our minds about enormous tracts of our moral opinion. For example, suppose that, according to our best theorizing to date about the archaeological evidence, we decide that the social conditions through the relevant period of hominid development were thus-and-so, leading us to provisionally endorse theory X about human evolution. According to evolutionary moral naturalism, this should lead us to provisionally support certain particular or general moral claims, such as "Third-trimester abortions are sometimes permissible," "Canceling Third World debt is morally desirable but not obligatory," and "The Elgin Marbles ought to be returned to Greece." But then imagine that further evidence from paleontology and from prehistoric campsites unexpectedly turns up at a later date, suggesting radically different conclusions concerning the social arrangements of our ancestors and thus leading us to revise our views about the relevant aspects of human evolution and to adopt theory Y. This could, according to evolutionary moral naturalism, demand a revision of some or all of those contemporary moral views: In principle, whereas before we thought that the cancellation of Third World debt is desirable but not obligatory, we might now decide that it is undesirable but not forbidden, and change our policies accordingly. But it is surely an astonishingly implausible theory that allows that the complex moral disputes facing the modern world might, even in principle, be settled by digging in the African soil, or holds that my guilt about breaking a promise I made last week to my mother-in-law should suddenly evaporate because I read an article in *Nature* about the discovery of some new hominid fossil. For all the respect I have for archaeologists, I don't think it is they to whom we should be looking for access to the moral truth.

6.1 Genealogical Debunking

Every belief has a causal history, and it would be a ridiculous theory that implied that knowledge of a belief's etiology automatically undermines the confidence one should have in that belief. Yet it is clear that on some occasions knowledge of a belief's origins can undermine it. Indulge in a slightly silly thought experiment, and pretend there were such things as belief pills, such that taking one would inevitably lead to the forming of a certain particular belief (while at the same time invoking amnesia about the taking of the pill and, to be on the safe side, amnesia about the existence of such pills in general). Suppose that there were a pill that makes you believe that Napoleon won Waterloo, and another one that makes you believe that he lost. Suppose also that there were an antidote that can be taken for either pill. Now imagine that you are proceeding through life happily believing that Napoleon lost Waterloo (as, indeed, you are), and then you discover that at some point in your past someone slipped you a "Napoleon lost Waterloo" belief pill. It is not a matter of your learning of the existence such pills and having no way of knowing whether you have ever taken one; rather, we are imagining that you somehow discover beyond any shred of doubt that your belief is the product of such a pill. Should this undermine your faith in your belief that Napoleon lost Waterloo? Of course it should. It doesn't show that the belief is *false*—for though the fictional scenario described is not our world, it still might well have contained Napoleon, the Battle of Waterloo, and the event of his losing that battle—but this knowledge is certainly sufficient to place your belief on the dubious list. Knowledge of a belief's genealogy could show the belief to be false only if the belief implies a contrary genealogical story. For example, the belief that no beliefs are innate would certainly be shown to be false if we were to discover that it was an innate belief. But this, it will not have escaped your notice, is a rather unusual case.[1] It is implausible that the things we believe by and large imply truths about their own origins, and thus it is proportionally unlikely that genealogical discoveries could directly reveal many of our beliefs to be false. But the possibility that they could render many of our beliefs *unjustified* remains on the cards and is almost as disturbing a result. In our imaginary case, knowledge that your belief is the product of a belief pill renders the belief unjustified (or perhaps shows that it was never justified in the first place, depending on one's epistemological tastes), demanding that unless you can find some concrete evidence either in favor or against the belief you should cease to believe this thing—that is, you should take the antidote.[2]

It will reasonably be objected that insofar as natural selection may affect human psychology it surely doesn't act in any manner remotely like these fanciful belief pills.

First, it might be pointed out, no human trait is "hard-wired" in the sense of developing inevitably, irrespective of environmental factors; an innate belief would, like any other phenotypic adaptation, require environmental input in order to become manifest. This observation does not, however, compromise the very notion of an innate belief. A belief that requires environmental input is not thereby a learned belief, and not thereby a belief that is formed in a way sensitive to the evidence. For a quick analogy, consider someone who forms a belief as the result of hypnosis. Hypnosis often involves a conditional command, such as "When you hear the word 'banana' you will believe you are a chicken." (Never mind that the real phenomenon of hypnosis may not work this way—even the distorted Hollywood version will serve to illustrate the point.) In this example, the environment must provide a trigger, but that trigger is not *evidence* for the person that she is a chicken, and she doesn't *learn* anything pertaining to chickens from the utterance of "banana."

Second, attention may be drawn to the fact that nowhere among the hypotheses advocated in this book will one find the thesis that moral beliefs are innate. Even where one might reasonably speculate that natural selection has taken a direct interest in belief content (moral judgments concerning reciprocation, perhaps), to the extent that such beliefs will usually concern particulars (e.g., I believe that I should reciprocate to Mary for picking me up from the airport), it is just not plausible to hold such a belief to be innate (for what does natural selection know of *Mary* or *airports*?). The hypothesis for which I argued earlier did not deny that cultural learning plays a central role in determining the content of the moral judgments that an individual ends up making; the claim was just that there is a specialized innate mechanism (or series of mechanisms) whose function is to enable this type of acquisition. This mechanism, I hypothesize, comes prepared to categorize the world in morally normative terms; moral *concepts* may be innate even if moral beliefs are not.

It turns out, however, that this observation has little effect on the skeptical conclusion reached above; we can alter the details of the analogy to accommodate it. Suppose that the imaginary belief pills do not generate particular propositional beliefs but, rather, dispose you to form beliefs involving a particular concept—a concept that otherwise wouldn't figure in your beliefs. Thus, rather than a pill that makes you believe that Napoleon lost Waterloo, it's just a "Napoleon pill" that makes you form beliefs about Napoleon in general. Without this pill you would never have formed any beliefs about Napoleon at all. We needn't worry too much about what other factors determine the precise content of these Napoleon beliefs; perhaps it is determined randomly, or perhaps there are certain environmental triggers that can send the Napoleon beliefs one way or the other. Suppose again that you discover beyond any doubt that you were slipped one of these pills a few years ago. Does this undermine all the beliefs you have concerning Napoleon? Of course it does. A belief is undermined if one of the concepts figuring in it is undermined. Again, this wouldn't show the belief to be *false*, but until you find some reliable evidence to confirm or disconfirm your Napoleon beliefs, you should take the antidote. Then, once the antidote has kicked in and you are free of all positive Napoleon beliefs, you may set off to investigate the world with an unsullied mind to discover whether any of those ex-beliefs were in fact true.[3]

The intention of this make-believe scenario is to prime us for an analogical epistemological conclusion regarding an evolved moral sense. Instead of Napoleon beliefs suppose it is moral beliefs, and instead of belief pills suppose it is natural selection. Were it not for a certain social ancestry affecting our biology, the argument goes, we wouldn't have concepts like *obligation*, *virtue*, *property*, *desert*, and *fairness* at all. If the analogy is reasonable, therefore, it would appear that once we become aware of this genealogy of morals we should (epistemically) do something analogous to taking the antidote pill: cultivate agnosticism regarding all positive beliefs involving these concepts until we find some solid evidence either for or against them. Note how radical this conclusion is. It is not a matter of allowing oneself to have an open mind about, say, the wrongness of abortion or the rightness of canceling Third World debt; rather, it is a matter of maintaining an open mind about whether there exists *anything* that is morally right and wrong, of accepting the possibility that describing the world in moral terms is in the same ballpark as taking horoscopes seriously or believing that ancestral spirits move invisibly among us (as John Mackie argued is the case).

But *is* the analogy fair? It may be objected that in the case of the belief pills the story has been carefully stipulated such that forming a belief as the result of taking a pill is entirely independent of whether or not the state of affairs necessary to render the belief true obtains in the world. But perhaps things stand differently in this respect for the evolutionary genealogy of morals; perhaps the process of natural selection is likely to yield true beliefs. Most of this chapter is devoted to arguing that this objection fails. We have no reason to think in the case of the moral sense that natural selection is likely to have produced true beliefs. So the analogy, with its disturbing skeptical conclusion, stands.[4]

It is important to note to begin with the possibility that our evolutionary hypothesis about morality is unusual in this respect. Compare a different psychological phenomenon for which an evolutionary hypothesis seems plausible. There is some evidence that natural selection has provided humans with an inbuilt faculty for simple arithmetic. (See Butterworth 1999.) For the sake of simplicity, let's interpret this as implying that our belief that $1 + 1 = 2$ is innate. This, it seems pretty safe to declare, is an eternal and necessary truth, and thus by "hard-wiring" such a belief into our brains natural selection takes no risks—it is not as if the environment could suddenly change such that $1 + 1$ would equal 3.[5] So does the fact that we have such a genealogical explanation of our simple mathematical beliefs serve to demonstrate that we are unjustified in holding these beliefs? Surely not, for we have no grasp of how this belief might have been selected for, how it might have enhanced reproductive fitness, independent of its truth. False mathematical beliefs just aren't going to be very useful. Suppose you are being chased by three lions, you observe two quit the chase, and you conclude that it is now safe to slow down. The truth of "$1 + 1 = 2$" is a background assumption to any reasonable hypothesis of how this belief might have come to be innate. Here is another comparison, this time involving not an innate belief but an innate concept: Suppose that for humans the concept *child* is innate. Assuming this supposition could be made good, would such knowledge render all our beliefs about children unjustified? Again: No, for the genealogical story will surely involve the presence of children. Developing a preparation to form beliefs about children will be useful only in an environment in which children exist; moreover, the kind of environmental "trigger" that is necessary to transform the preparation into an actual belief about children will presumably involve an exposure to children.

Now let us apply this thinking to the case of moral beliefs. Can we make sense of its having been useful for our ancestors to form beliefs concerning *rightness* and *wrongness* independently of the existence of rightness and wrongness? Here I think the answer is a resounding "Quite possibly." Cast your mind back to the whole complex story that was presented in previous chapters concerning why it might have been systematically useful for our ancestors to form beliefs about moral rightness and wrongness (among other things). It was no background assumption of that explanation that any actual moral rightness or wrongness existed in the ancestral environment. Whether we assume that the concepts *right* and *wrong* succeed in denoting properties in the world, or whether we think that they suffer from a referential failure that puts them on a par with the concepts *witch* and *ghost*, the plausibility of the hypothesis concerning how moral judgment evolved remains unaffected. Not so for the mathematical case. Were someone foolish enough to doubt that $1 + 1 = 2$, the plausibility of the evolutionary story concerning how having this belief enhanced our ancestors' fitness would evaporate.

The same point should be made concerning the faculties of scientific inquiry that are in some sense products of biological natural selection, and which we deploy in conceiving and testing our evolutionary hypothesis. This observation deflects a concern raised by Peter Railton (2000) against the possibility of using evolutionary theory to undermine ethics. Railton claims that any argument moving from the empirical premise that human morality is the product of evolution to the conclusion that morality is thereby in some sense debunked "hammers itself into the same ground into which it had previously pounded morality" (2000: 57), for the reason that the very faculties we employed in order to establish the empirical premise are themselves the product of natural selection. But I suggest that—as in the arithmetic example—we have no grasp of how any innate human faculties pertaining to "scientific inquiry" might have been selected for independently of their producing judgments that at least have some positive connection to the truth. Thus the "evolutionary debunking of morality" does not in this manner debunk itself. Philip Kitcher makes a similar point:

. . . social training is . . . important to scientific judgments – as when a technician judges that an electron has passed through a cloud chamber or when a biologist perceives that some of the bacteria have incorporated extra DNA. Can't we say that, given that training, technician and biologist would have made the judgments they do, whether or not an electron or transgenic bacteria were present? For these individuals make the judgments they do on these occasions because they have been trained to respond to particular sorts of visual stimulations in particular ways. In the scientific case, however, even if the nonsocial facts have no role to play in the *immediate* judgment, there's a deeper explanatory question to which they are relevant. Why are these kinds of training given to the pertinent observers? Here we must turn to the history of the cultural practice, and that history involves the adoption of procedures on the basis of evidence that they serve as reliable ways of detecting facts about the world. If we pose the analogous question for the history of the moral practices into which we have been socialized, my conjectural genealogy offers no analogous consolation. At the initial stage, proto-morality is introduced as a system of primitive rules for transcending the fraught sociality of early hominids: there's no issue here of perceiving moral truths. Nor at any further stage is there a need to suppose that moral truths play a role in constraining the normative systems adopted. The criterion of success isn't accurate representation, but the improvement of social cohesion in ways that promote the transmission of the system itself. (2005: 176)

That the evolutionary genealogy of morals contrasts with other cases (such as arithmetical and scientific beliefs)—in that the former does not presuppose the truth of the beliefs—is an important observation. But it doesn't *suffice* for establishing that in the former case we have a debunking genealogy, for the possibility remains that an identity or supervenience relation may hold between the items denoted in the genealogy and the moral properties represented in the belief's content, in such a way that the genealogy renders the belief true after all. (I am making the terminological assumption that an identity or a supervenience connection between two things does not amount to a presupposition relation holding between the two things.) I will explain this further below, using a well-known argument by Gilbert Harman to frame the discussion. Responding to the possibility of such a reductive account, and saying why I don't think one is on the cards, will take a substantial portion of this chapter.

6.2 Harman's Challenge

The idea that moral judgments might be epistemologically undermined on the grounds that they can be explained entirely without invoking their truth—i.e., without invoking any moral facts which they represent—has been discussed at some length by Harman (1977, 1986). Harman focuses not merely on whether moral judgments may be explained without invoking their truth, but on whether one need posit moral facts in the world in order to explain *anything*. He is widely reported as having answered in the negative—as having concluded that there are no moral facts—but in fact his position is subtler. Rather, Harman's conclusion is conditional: that *if* there is no reductive account available explaining how moral facts relate to naturalistic facts, then moral claims cannot be tested, moral theories cannot be confirmed or disconfirmed, and we have no evidence for the existence of moral facts. But at no point does Harman assert that the antecedent of this conditional holds. He doesn't argue that a reduction of the moral to the non-moral is unavailable, only that it doesn't come easily. In fact, he has himself offered reductive accounts which he thinks are plausible, meaning that he thinks it plausible that moral facts exist and (presumably) that our moral judgments are justified. Indeed, he claims explicitly that "there is empirical evidence that there are (relational) moral facts" (1977: 132). So Harman is no moral nihilist. His main concerns are to point out "that there is a real issue here" (1986: 67), to note that "there is a real problem about testing moral claims if they are not reducible to naturalistic claims" (1986: 59), and to counter moral naturalists who present their views in too cavalier a fashion.

Let us use Harman's own example to discuss the issue. He asks us to imagine that "you see some children pour gasoline on a cat and ignite it" (1977: 4).[6] Three pages later, he writes:

> . . . you make a moral judgment immediately and without conscious reasoning, say, that the children are wrong to set the cat on fire. . . . In order to explain your making [this judgment], it would be reasonable to assume, perhaps, that the children really are pouring gasoline on a cat and you are seeing them do it. But [there is no] obvious reason to assume anything about "moral facts," such as that it is really wrong to set the cat on fire. . . . Indeed, an assumption about moral facts would seem to be totally irrelevant to the explanation of your making the judgment you make. It would seem that all we need assume is that you have certain more or less well articulated moral principles that are reflected in the judgments you make, based on your moral sensibility. It seems to be completely irrelevant to our explanation whether your intuitive immediate judgment is true or false. (7)

Harman has hardly anything to say about how reference to a "moral sensibility" might be sufficient to explain one's making a moral judgment in certain circumstances. Reference to biological natural selection is not necessary to Harman's case; all his argument requires is that there is *some* complete explanation that can be given of moral judgments for which their truth or falsity is irrelevant. An evolutionary account is just one possible example of such a hypothesis, or a possible element of such a hypothesis. One might instead believe that morality is entirely a cultural artifact, and that one can give a complete explanation of all moral beliefs just in terms of cultural socialization—an explanation that does not presuppose that this socialization amounts to a process of *learning* moral truths. (Marxist and Freudian approaches may be examples of such a view.) In other words, everything that has been claimed in this book about the evolution of morality could be false, and Harman's argument could still have legs.

Some of the debate provoked by Harman's argument has centered on whether moral experience is really much like perceptual experience: Do we truly just "see" the wrongness of the action? But for us this is a distraction that can be put aside; Harman's main point works just as well for a moral judgment prompted by an act of imagination. (Few of us have actually seen a cat being burned or even hit with a stick, yet we are all in a position to judge any such episode morally repugnant.) A much more important point is that, in spite of the tone of the passage above, it is a mistake to think that Harman's ultimate position is that moral facts have no role to play in explaining our moral judgments. He doesn't say that they *are* redundant, only that they threaten to be so unless we can find a place for them within our naturalistic explanation. The dialectic is one of a challenge, not a victory. It is often assumed that Harman's challenge represents a problem for the moral naturalist, but in fact if the naturalist can articulate a plausible version of her theory then the challenge evaporates—an outcome, it should be remembered, on which Harman looks favorably.

Here is what I think Harman has in mind. Imagine that Jane judges a particular episode of cat-burning wrong. Suppose we could explain the event of Jane's judgment entirely and adequately in the terms of physics and chemistry—an explanation in which the terms "cat," "burning," and "wrongness" do not even appear. Does this show that burning cats play no part in explaining Jane's judgment? No, for burning cats can be *reduced* to physics and chemistry, allowing us to recognize that the burning cat was implicitly present (so to speak) in our causal explanation of her judgment. But is there any comparable story that we can tell to explain how *wrongness* fits into the same naturalistic world? Harman's point is that if we have a complete naturalistic explanation for why it *seems* to Jane that the action is wrong, but have no clear idea of how wrongness fits into (reduces to) this explanation, then the actual existence of wrongness isn't needed to explain anything in the situation, in which case we have no reason to believe that it is a part of this cat-burning episode at all. And, obviously, this reasoning is supposed to be entirely generalizable. Whenever we judge something morally wrong, there is a complete explanation of the judgment that neither presupposes moral facts nor acts as a reductive base of moral facts. With moral judgments thus explained without recourse to moral facts, and in the absence of anything else whose explanation requires us to posit moral facts (for what phenomenon could there be for which our tendency to seek a moral explanation does not ultimately depend on our having made a moral judgment?), we have no reason to believe that anything at all is morally wrong. (The same holds for other moral qualities.)

Harman is fairly vague about what he takes an adequate "reduction" to be. He says that it "need not involve definitions of a serious sort," and he gives as an example the relation between tables and clusters of atoms (1985: 33). This lines up with my above claim that burning cats "reduce to" physics and chemistry, even though there are no semantic relations permitting deductions between propositions containing the terms "cat" and "burning" and propositions expressed in the language of physics and chemistry. Nevertheless, we at least think we understand how burning cats fit into the world as described by physics and chemistry—we have a story to tell explaining how a burning cat is a physical, chemical entity. This is a very broad notion of *reduction*, apparently covering many positions that would ordinarily be categorized as non-reductionist. Harman's well-known opponent in this debate, Nicholas Sturgeon, uses a much narrower conception of *reduction*—one that concerns "whether moral explanations can be given reductive definitions in some nonmoral vocabulary" (1985: 59; see also Sturgeon 1986). (In my opinion, this terminological discrepancy explains a disappointingly large proportion of the debate between Harman and Sturgeon.) In what follows I will go along with Harman's broad usage, since this conception makes much more sense of his argument. What matters, after all, is whether the genealogy of moral judgment, though couched in non-moral terms, nevertheless somehow implicitly "involves" the existence of moral facts. There is no rationale for requiring that the moral facts be describable in the language of the natural sciences; a purely ontological relation will suffice. Even those who are usually thought of as "nonreductive moral naturalists" should agree that every token instantiation of a moral property is identical to a token instantiation of a cluster of naturalistic properties. This, it would appear, is enough to make them reductive moral naturalists in Harman's broad sense.[7]

Figure 6.1 illustrates two competing hypotheses concerning how to explain the phenomenon of moral judgments. Remember that hypothesis A is supposed to be empirically confirmed. Overlooking this may encourage one to consider this argument as unimpressively analogous to standard challenges from the philosophical skeptic. For example, you may believe that right now you are sitting reading a book, but an annoying skeptic can always provide an alternative hypothesis ("hypothesis A"), consistent with all the data available to you, according to which you aren't reading a book at all. Perhaps, as Descartes imagined, you are really being deceived by an all-powerful evil demon (who has nothing better to do with his time), or

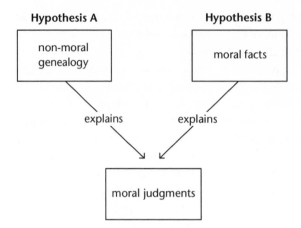

Figure 6.1

perhaps you are really a brain floating in a vat of nutrients and being fed neural impulses corresponding to sitting reading a book. It is notoriously difficult to show that you are in a position to *know* that such hypotheses are false, since ex hypothesi all your experiential evidence is implied equally by both the ordinary hypothesis and the outlandish one. But the view under discussion here does not come so cheap. It is not just that in this case we can *make up* a consistent hypothesis according to which a bunch of our ordinary beliefs are false; rather, it is that we might have empirical evidence supporting the hypothesis that explains how these beliefs came about but does not require that they be true. The argument does not depend on invoking extreme standards for epistemic justification; the skeptic is not requiring people to consider outlandish brain-in-vat-type possibilities that they would ordinarily scoff at. If the everyday standards for being morally justified take account of empirical data concerning human evolution, then if these data ultimately show moral beliefs to be unjustified it will be by ordinary epistemic standards.

Given figure 6.1, one might have thought that hypothesis B should be excised from the picture with a swift slash from Ockham's Razor, since we have a complete explanation of moral judgment with no need to posit any extra ontology in the form of moral facts. This appears to be how Michael Ruse argues for the conclusion that the evolutionary basis of morality undermines morality when he claims that "the objective foundation for morality is redundant" (1986: 254; see also Ruse and Wilson 1986: 186–187). This, however, is too hasty, as figure 6.2 shows. The crooked line indicates a reduction relation (in the broad ontological sense of the term).

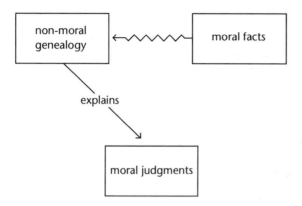

Figure 6.2

If the moral facts are reducible to the non-moral facts invoked in the genealogical explanation, then the former cannot be eliminated on grounds of parsimony, any more than cats should be eliminated from our ontology because we can explain them in terms of physics. There is a sense in which *cat* is an ontological category over and above those of physics and chemistry, but there is also a sense in which positing this category doesn't really amount to adding any extra ontological richness to the world, since the zoological category fits into those of the underlying sciences. That is the whole point of its being *a reduction*.

Something about which Harman is correctly adamant is that acknowledging the mere possibility of moral naturalism saving the day accomplishes next to nothing if it is not backed up with a concrete theory explaining, with some degree of precision, how the moral fits into the natural world. In the same way, one might claim that talk of ghosts could be vindicated if it could be shown that ghostly properties may be comfortably integrated within a naturalistic worldview. Quite so. However, this observation alone gives not a glimmer of a reason to believe in ghosts. Not until we actually see the particular reductive account, and accept it as plausible, will global naturalists be inclined to admit the existence of ghosts. It is this point I had in mind when I interpreted Harman's intention as to reproach moral naturalists "who present their views in too cavalier a fashion." The mere promise of a naturalistic theory will not suffice, unless we have some really compelling reason for assuming that such a theory is forthcoming. Nor is it enough merely to offer a naturalistic reduction, for doing so is easy. Charles Stevenson (1937: 14) once suggested that "something is morally good if and only if it is pink with yellow trimmings." (He was making a philosophical point, not putting forward a serious contender!) The burden of the argument falls on the moral naturalist to put forward a theory (or at least to provide a compelling reason for thinking that a theory is forthcoming), and, as Harman adds, "we have to be able to believe in this account" (1986: 63). Until this burden is discharged, the availability of a confirmed non-moral genealogy appears to leave us with no reason to think that any of our moral beliefs are true.

Is such a reductive account plausible? What are the prospects of moral naturalism? In chapter 5 we saw that G. E. Moore's famous attempt to provide a generic knockout argument failed. Perhaps the best that we can do is examine contender reductive moral naturalisms case by case, just as we did in chapter 5 with versions of prescriptive evolutionary ethics. Such a task is beyond the scope of this book. As a matter of fact I think there are a number of general problems faced by moral naturalism (both the reductive and non-reductive varieties), though I will here confine myself to discussing just one: that no such naturalism can accommodate the sense of inescapable practical authority with which moral claims appear to be imbued. This substantial issue will occupy the following two sections, in which I will also discuss Harman's own preferred naturalistic reduction of the moral.

6.3   The Prospects of Moral Naturalism[8]

The task before me here is in one sense narrower and in another sense broader than the one I faced in chapter 5. In that chapter I discussed the general claim that evolutionary theory might in some sense vindicate morality; now I am considering a specific kind of vindication: the establishment of moral naturalism. On the other hand, in chapter 5 I also discussed "evolutionary moral naturalism," the specific claim that moral facts are reducible to facts that are essentially evolutionary and historical in nature. Now I will consider moral naturalism more generally construed, requiring only that the moral facts be reducible to items that figure (perhaps contingently) in the genealogy of moral beliefs. If such a moral naturalism is viable, then the apparent fact that human moral judgments can be explained without mentioning or presupposing moral facts will not have a debunking effect. Here I will outline what I take to be the strongest challenge for the moral naturalist—one that I doubt can be surmounted.

Why is Stevenson's tongue-in-cheek moral naturalism—"Something is morally good if and only if it is pink with yellow trimmings"—so obviously unacceptable? Clearly it is because we have certain requirements concerning what moral goodness must be like, and Stevenson's playful offering satisfies few if any of them. Such requirements, considered collectively, place a constraint on any moral naturalism. We may reject any naturalistic offering that badly fails to satisfy these platitudes; whatever property might be identified by such a theory, it ain't *moral goodness*. This is not to say that there must be a "perfect fit." If we recognize, say, fifteen requirements, and we locate a naturalistic theory that satisfies twelve of them, and there is no other naturalistic theory that does better, that may be enough to convince us. (See Lewis 1970, 1989; Smith 1994, chapter 2; Joyce 2001a, chapter 1.) But it would be a mistake to get hung up on numbers here, or to think that some general "golden ratio" of what constitutes *enough* can be supplied. Perhaps for some concepts there is a platitude that we consider of central importance, such that failure to underwrite this single criterion is sufficient to warrant rejection. Perhaps for some concepts we will be willing to have more relaxed standards than for others.

At the end of chapter 5 I identified one such requirement that was supposed to make life very uncomfortable for any evolutionary moral naturalism. The platitude concerned how we go about—or, more specifically, how we *don't* go about—identifying moral truths. Evolutionary moral naturalism implies that our means of gaining epistemic access to truths about evolution can constitute a means of gaining epistemic access to moral truth in general. But this, I argued, seems crazy. We don't discover (we *can't* discover) whether the Elgin Marbles ought to be returned to Greece by embarking on archaeological digs in order to uncover facts about human evolution. However, if we consider a different form of moral naturalism—utilitarianism, for example— it is not nearly so silly to claim that we might discover moral truths by unearthing facts about what contributes to overall net happiness. I think that anyone who endorses this claim happens to be mistaken (for reasons that will become apparent shortly), but not so stupidly so that it constitutes a reductio ad absurdum against utilitarianism. Thus the argument at the end of chapter 5 has only limited destructive force against one kind of moral naturalism. Can we do better by identifying a requirement that *any* moral naturalism is going to struggle to satisfy? I believe so. The line of criticism that I leveled against Casebeer's brand of evolutionary moral naturalism in section 5.7 will generalize to make trouble for any moral naturalism.

It is very hard to see how naturalistic facts could possibly provide *the inescapable authority* we apparently expect and require of moral values. I discussed the terms of art "moral inescapability" and "moral authority" back in chapter 2, and there I dubbed their conjunction "practical clout." Let me again try to motivate the view that the satisfaction of these two characteristics is a desideratum. First, inescapability. As I argued at some length in section 2.4 (and again in section 5.7), you can't evade the proscription "Don't kill innocent people" by citing special desires ("But I *really* enjoy it!") or shrug off moral concerns by claiming a lack of interest in such values. We think of moral values and imperatives as usually being practical considerations (though possibly defeasible considerations) that bind people irrespective of their desires or interests. Regarding this point I think John Mackie was correct in asserting that someone who makes a moral judgment wants to say something that "is not purely descriptive, certainly not inert, but something that involves a call for action or for the refraining from action, and one that is absolute, not contingent upon any desire or preference or policy or choice, his own or anyone else's" (1977: 33). An ordinary speaker would probably not put things in quite so succinct and precise a manner; ordinary speakers, I'm sure, have fairly inchoate ideas about morality. But inchoateness must not be confused with *negotiability*: Ordinary speakers' views on the inescapability of morality may be steadfast and confident in spite of the fact that they are unable to articulate just what that inescapability amounts to. When a philosopher like Mackie comes along and attempts to precisify or explicate the folk notion in order to assess its plausibility, we mustn't jump from the observation that he is forging a definite theory from inchoate material, using terms that may be unfamiliar to ordinary speakers, to the conclusion that he is merely projecting his own philosophical or culturally elaborated prejudices upon the folk. Of course he *may* be doing that, but whether he is doing it can be decided only by careful observation of how successfully his explication captures the everyday moral practices of the population whose concepts he purports to describe. It seems to me that Mackie is on firm ground here. It is abundantly evident that moral prescriptions are used categorically: We do not hesitate to apply them to people who we know have aberrant desires that are not served by being moral. Let us assume that the serial killer Jack Trawick was quite sincere when he claimed "I would do the whole thing again . . . knowing death row was waiting for me." Acknowledging this doesn't tempt us to retract our moral condemnation one iota. I have also noted (in section 4.5) that the tendency to categorize certain transgressions as independent of any authority and to distinguish them from norms of prudence is cross-cultural and appears at an early age.

Many moral philosophers think that, in addition to purportedly being inescapable, moral prescriptions are often (or always) imbued with a certain *authority*. Compare etiquette. Although the rules of etiquette are inescapable (even people who don't care about etiquette can transgress against its demands), we don't generally think that the institution of etiquette has any genuine binding force over a person. A person who has good reason to be rude (e.g., to speak with his mouth full in order to stop a friend from eating a wasp) is still violating etiquette, but he has done the right thing, and in fact he had no reason to do otherwise. Only people who have interests that will be served by following etiquette (i.e., most of us, most of the time) have any genuine reason to comply. It is often thought that morality requires something stronger and more authoritative. Philippa Foot notes that many moral philosophers follow the Kantian tradition of thinking that moral prescriptions "necessarily give reasons for acting to any man" (1972: 309). A prescription may inescapably *apply* to a person without her having any reason to comply; if, however, the prescription also brings reason for compliance with it ("automatically," as it were), let us say that it has *authority* over those to whom it is attributed.

In light of the attention I have drawn to the supposed practical clout of morality, we can divide moral naturalists into two camps: (i) those who attempt to show that this practical clout can be accommodated within a naturalistic framework and (ii) those who deny that it is really a requirement of morality at all. The latter sometimes assume that the notion of inescapable moral authority is nothing more than an extravagance dreamed up by a philosopher (they particularly object to the doctrine of moral authority), while others acknowledge that such clout is usually thought of as important to morality (that its satisfaction is a desideratum)—perhaps even accepting that "this assumption has been incorporated in the basic, conventional meanings of moral terms"[9]—but this acknowledgement is accompanied by the opinion that a moral theory satisfying enough of our other moral platitudes may be close enough to count as an acceptable naturalization. In the rest of this section, I will discuss (i); I will turn to (ii) in section 6.4. In both cases I find the moral naturalist on fragile ground, thus lending strong support to Harman's challenge, and ultimately to the position that our moral judgments are epistemically unjustified.

A moral naturalist who wants to account for inescapable practical authority must locate it in the natural world. Let us start with the natural assumption that this translates into a search for a kind of *reason* for action. Ordinary discourse (this naturalist thinks, and I am inclined to agree) imbues morality with some kind of authority greater than that enjoyed by etiquette, and it is not just that morality is considered more important than etiquette; rather, morality is supposed to "bind" individuals in a more robust manner. Introducing talk of *reasons* may be thought of as the philosopher's attempt to build a precise idea out of something vague yet important in ordinary discourse and practice, but the matter is complicated by the fact that there is much confusion and argument over what *a reason* is. One might even speak of "reasons of etiquette," according to which the rules of etiquette *do* provide reasons; but such reasons would be purely institutional constructs—merely a case of the institution of etiquette providing a special warrant for asserting "X has a reason to φ" whenever the rules of etiquette decree that X is justified in φing. Clearly, that such a way of speaking may be so permitted doesn't yield a genuine deliberative consideration for those to whom the reasons are ascribed. In trying to locate in the world such practical authority, the moral naturalist will not be satisfied just to find a human institution that has a rule according to which in some circumstances it is permissible to assert "X really ought to φ," "X has a reason to φ," "X has a reason to φ irrespective of her interests," or even "There is a mind-independent fact demanding that X φs." He will not be satisfied in locating an institutional normative framework that has internal rules concerning which actions are justified, thus generating "justificatory reasons" claims. (For the distinction between justificatory and motivating reasons, see Smith 1994: 94 ff.) Just as someone searching for Tasmanian tigers will not be satisfied to locate a group of people who sincerely believe in the existence of Tasmanian tigers, so too this kind of moral naturalist seeks to locate real inescapable practical authority, not locate an institution that permits one to speak as if there were such authority.

Many naturalistic strategies introduce a middleman between morality and reasons. A certain kind of utilitarian strategy, for example, first says that moral goodness is identical to happiness, then tries to show that we have reason to pursue the general happiness. A simpler strategy declares that moral requirements *just are* whatever one has real reason to do—assuming that the idea of what counts as a genuine deliberative consideration for a person is itself amenable to naturalization. This latter approach is a version of moral naturalism that Harman discusses favorably under the name "practical reasoning theory"[10]:

In this view, for an act to be wrong is for the agent to have sufficient reasons not to do it, where this is equivalent to saying that, if the agent were to reason correctly, the agent would end up deciding not to do the act.

This view can allow that Jane's [moral] belief about Albert [who harmed the cat] is explained in part by the actual wrongness of Albert's action. The act is wrong because there were sufficient reasons for Albert not to do it. If Albert were to have reasoned correctly, he would have ended up deciding not to do it. If Jane were aware of the relevant reasoning and that is why she believes Albert's act was wrong, then her belief is explained in part by the wrongness of Albert's action. (1986: 66)

According to Harman (and many agree with him), what a person has "sufficient reason" to do is tied to what he would want to do if he "reasoned correctly." A natural question at this point is "Why should *that* have any practical authority?" Assuming that one of the actions available to Albert instantiates the property *is-such-that-Albert-would-want-to-do-it-if-he-were-to-reason-correctly*, why does this property represent a genuine deliberative consideration for Albert? The answer, it seems to me, is that he cannot intelligibly raise doubt about whether such a property is a practical consideration for him, since the very act of sincerely asking the question evinces certain commitments to standards of correct reasoning. This is just a fact about the act of doubting or questioning in general. The very act of sincerely asking "Why X?" presupposes that one is in the business of seeking and possibly accepting answers; it presupposes an acknowledgement that the addressee of the question may be in an epistemically superior position to the questioner. But to acknowledge the possible inferiority of one's epistemic position, and to embrace the desirability of improvement, *is* to concede that the opinions that you would have if you were to reason correctly carry deliberative weight. Thus, the statement "I acknowledge that were I to reason correctly I would want to φ, but what is that to me?" does not represent a well-formed skeptical position.

To recap: We are wondering whether the moral may be reducible to the natural. If it is not, then figure 6.2 is unacceptable and figure 6.1 seems right, and Ockham's Razor will leave us with no reason to believe in moral facts. In order to assess any contender reductive theory, we must check whether the natural properties highlighted will satisfy our pre-theoretical criteria for moral values and prescriptions. One possible criterion is the unusual inescapable practical authority of the moral, and thus one kind of naturalist sets out to find this practical clout in the natural world. (Another kind of naturalist—whose view will be discussed below—denies that this really is a criterion of adequacy at all.) Such a moral naturalist might try to tie, either directly or indirectly, practical authority to reasons. There are many different kinds of reasons, however, so some disambiguation is required. What we are after is a genuine deliberative consideration (what Harman calls "a sufficient reason"), not merely an attribution permitted by an institution. More precisely, what we are after is an account of what a person would want to do if she reasoned correctly (as she would if she were fully rational).[11] Since the aspiration is to provide a naturalization of the moral, whatever notion of "correct reasoning" is appealed to here must also be understandable in naturalistic terms. We couldn't, for example, understand this as *reasoning in accordance with moral virtue* or *reasoning with a sensitivity to one's moral obligations,* for to do so would put the whole enterprise into a vicious logical circle.

The problem, however, and my main ground for doubting the project, is that in order to naturalize moral clout we cannot be content just to find a property that has practical authority—arguably we have located such a property in *being-such-that-you-would-want-to-do-it-if-you-were-to-reason-correctly*. We must also satisfy *inescapability*; we need a property that has this authority over people *irrespective of their interests*. But it is doubtful that any naturalizable account can deliver this. Suppose Ernie happens to really enjoy wine but dislikes beer; perhaps if he reasoned correctly he would come to the conclusion that it is acceptable for him to have a glass of wine each evening but he should avoid drinking beer. Now suppose that Bert likes beer but doesn't like wine; then, if he reasoned correctly, he might come to the conclusion that it is acceptable for him to have a glass of beer each evening but he shouldn't drink wine. Ernie and Bert's two reasoning procedures would be equally correct, but there is no convergence between them. The lack of convergence is obviously due to the fact that they have different tastes and desires to begin with, and although correct reasoning certainly may not endorse all those desires (it tells Ernie, for example, that he should resist his desire to finish the bottle) it nevertheless *takes them into account*. Correct reasoning, in this case at least, does not yield prescriptions that are independent of one's interests. (Harman essentially agrees (1975: 9): "If S says that (morally) A ought to do D, S implies that A has reasons to do D which S endorses. I shall assume that such reasons would have to have their source in goals, desires, or intentions that S takes A to have.")

Given that we can be confident that on some occasions correct reasoning is sensitive to a person's contingent desires, the crucial question is "Why shouldn't we accept that this is always so?" Consider Albert, Harman's cat-hater. If Albert has vicious desires to begin with (and we can assume that he does), on what grounds should we assume that his engaging in "correct reasoning" will invalidate those desires? To be sure, reasoning *often* leads us to see that some of our present desires are inappropriate, so *maybe* if Albert reflected more carefully he would ultimately decide that hurting the cat was a poor idea—but, then again, maybe he wouldn't. Perhaps reasoning correctly will only lead Albert to see how he can hurt the cat more effectively. What the moral naturalist evidently needs is a substantive and naturalizable account of "correct practical reasoning" (or "practical rationality") according to which any person, irrespective of her starting desires, would through such reasoning converge on certain practical conclusions that are broadly in line with what we would expect of moral requirements. (The last clause is needed to prevent the otherwise possible result that we may all turn out to be morally required always to put ourselves first, to take what we can get, to cheat without hesitation when we can do so with impunity, and so on.) But no such adequate account exists. There have been attempts, of course, but no account has commanded anything like widespread assent, and all are fraught with difficulty.

The dominant attempt in modern philosophy is what David Copp calls the "self-conception strategy," which he describes as follows:

> On the self-conception strategy, there is a way of conceiving of oneself such that a rational person who is thinking clearly *must* conceive of herself this way, but if she does not treat moral reasons as authoritative, she cannot *coherently* conceive of herself in this way. It might be said, for example, that a person who does not treat moral reasons as authoritative cannot see herself as *autonomous*; or that she cannot see herself or value herself as a rationally *reflective agent*, acting for reasons; or that she is committed to a *practical solipsism*; or that she cannot coherently expect *other* people to respond to the reasons she addresses to them; or the like.[12] (2004: 35)

But in my opinion it is very difficult to make good on the charge that Albert, as he injures the cat, is necessarily undermining his own autonomy, or failing to value himself as a reflective agent, or committing himself to practical solipsism, or damaging his expectation that others will respond to his own reasons claims. Even if any of these accusations could be made to stick, the question to ask is "What is so terrible about undermining one's own autonomy, or failing to value oneself as a reflective being [etc.]?" Such things certainly have a nasty ring to them, but what does that ring really amount to? Christine Korsgaard[13] writes that to morally transgress is to violate "the conceptions of ourselves that are most important to us. . . . It is to lose your integrity, and so your identity, . . . it is to no longer be able to think of yourself under the description under which you value yourself and find your life to be worth living. . . . It is to be for all practical purposes dead or worse than dead" (1996: 102). Such language encourages us to think of the wrongdoer as a psychopathic beast, itching to exterminate his family and companions for any self-gain if he can get away with it. But we mustn't forget that these strong claims are supposed to reveal what is wrong about *any* moral transgression: failing to return a borrowed book, being rude to an undeserving waitress, pinching a morning newspaper from a hotel corridor. Such actions may well be morally wrong, but the suggestion that they render the perpetrator "dead or worse than dead" (or even moving in the direction of that unhappy state) is wild rhetoric in need of support. The fact that someone may occasionally morally transgress but on the whole lead a happy and satisfying life should first make us doubt that the individual really is undermining her own basic agency in the ways described by the self-conception strategists—but even if this doubt could be addressed we should still wonder what is so dreadful about so subtle and insubstantial a form of self-sabotage. The very intangibility of the alleged self-harm raises the question of why avoiding it should be of paramount importance. Korsgaard's view is that the wrongdoer violates his identity as a human being—an identity upon which all his other identities (father, academic, republican, criminal, etc.) depend. The former identity is said to be "deeper" (ibid.: 258) since it cannot be evaded without compromising all the other contingent identities. But (as we saw earlier in reference to Casebeer's version of evolutionary moral naturalism) it is not obvious why or how this counterfactual asymmetry translates into *practical importance*. Perhaps my identity as a man is deeper than my identity as a father in exactly this counterfactual way, but it doesn't seem to follow that any values that derive from being a man are more important, more robust, or more authoritative than those that derive from being a father.

Given the persistent failure of the self-conception strategy to provide a plausible account of desire-independent correct practical reasoning, and given that we know that on some occasions correct practical reasoning is desire-sensitive, it seems reasonable to assume, if only provisionally, that correct practical reasoning is *in general* a desire-sensitive affair, and that thus so too are the practical reasons that come along with it. This is not to say that one has a reason to do something if and only if one wants to do it. Far from it. It may be that correct reasoning would reveal some of my desires to be misguided, stupid, or inappropriate—and I do not necessarily have reason to pursue the satisfaction of such desires. Or it may be that correct reasoning would lead me to see that I should be aiming to acquire something that in fact I have no desire for—in which case I do not necessarily have a desire to do what I have a reason to do. The point is just that what reasons I do have will have some degree of dependence on my actual desires, interests, projects, and ends, such that different people in the same circumstances may have very different reasons. (A person's reasons, as Harman says, "have their source" in her desires.)

I have devoted quite a lot of energy to pursuing the possibility of a moral naturalist finding inescapable practical authority in the world via connecting it to a naturalistically respectable account of sufficient reasons. This avenue has led to a dead end. It doesn't follow that the very notion of practical clout is incoherent, for there may be *non-naturalistic* notions of correct reasoning that would satisfy it. Perhaps the conclusion to be drawn from the preceding is that if it is true that practical clout is a central platitude of moral discourse, then, to the extent that this authority translates into an account of reasons, it must be a non-naturalistic kind of reason. But this observation will obviously do our naturalist no good. Alternatively, the naturalist may give up on the idea of *reasons* altogether—for I admitted that all these references to reasons are probably best seen as a philosopher doing her best to make sense of a folk notion, not necessarily as something that the folk explicitly or even implicitly believe; perhaps it is a mistake to try to cash out moral authority in terms of reasons. However, I have to confess that I cannot make out an avenue—even one with a dimly perceived dead end—along which this alternative option could reasonably proceed. What kind of practical authority could a rule have over a person who can quite correctly claim to have absolutely no real reason to comply? Someone willing to admit that a moral villain may have no real reason to comply is unlikely to see himself as defending a version of *inescapable moral authority* in which reasons play no role, but more probably has given up trying to satisfy this condition altogether. And what would be so terrible about that? This brings us to the moral naturalist's second strategy: surrendering the need to satisfy this criterion, and perhaps denying that it was ever a criterion or a desideratum in the first place.

6.4 Who Needs Moral Clout?

The argument has come to a crunch. On the one hand, many philosophers think that satisfying the feature of inescapable practical authority is a non-negotiable requirement of any adequate moral theory. In the previous section I argued that if they are correct then moral naturalism is in trouble. It is true that the only brand of naturalism discussed was practical reasoning theory, but that example was chosen carefully to make a general point, since if even the kind of moral naturalism that directly identifies moral facts with facts about reasons cannot deliver the goods, what hope is there for any kind of moral naturalism that seeks to connect moral facts only *indirectly* with practical reasons? Therefore, without pretending to have settled the matter, I conclude that moral naturalism is unlikely to find the resources to provide for this kind of practical authority.

On the other hand, many philosophers also deny that this feature is non-negotiable; they will be quite content to call some naturalistic property "moral goodness" even if no such special practical oomph can be claimed for that property. Perhaps in some cases it is the perception that naturalism cannot accommodate moral authority that leads people to adopt the latter view. But the very fact that such naturalists usually go to great lengths to magnify and promote whatever "lesser form of oomph" their theory is able to offer suggests that claiming some kind of robust practical oomph for one's moral theory (practical clout, perhaps?) is a desideratum. In any case, I think that the latter position is unrealistic, and I hold that the more reasonable conclusion is that moral naturalism is in trouble. (Admitting this, recall, in no way undermines one's methodological commitment to *global* naturalism; it allows that one can still "naturalize morality" in the sense of providing a scientifically respectable account of moral institutions and practices, of moral psychology, and of moral genealogy.)

Moral naturalists who eschew moral clout will allow that their chosen naturalistic property affords no guarantee that people will always have reason for acting in the prescribed way in relation to that property, but they might think that a *reliable contingent relationship* between the properties in question and people's reasons is good enough. The utilitarian, for example, may give up on trying to demonstrate a *necessary* connection between acts that maximize happiness and our having reason to perform such acts, but perhaps she will be satisfied by noting that we very often *do* care about welfare in general, and this provides a basis for motivations and reasons to promote happiness—albeit motivations and reasons that exist merely for the most part. (See, e.g., Railton 1986; Brink 1989: 43ff.) Perhaps such an offering doesn't get us everything we might have wanted from a moral theory, but maybe we should just hearken to the maxim "Close enough is good enough."

But *is* it good enough? We have no principled way of deciding. The resolution of the dispute seems to turn on the question of whether something is an essential feature of our moral concepts, but philosophers have no settled views on how to adjudicate or even conceptualize such a debate. (For discussion of a very similar point, see Nichols 2004: 192–193.) If one person asserts that something *is* a non-negotiable feature of some concept and another person denies this, where should they take their dispute? David Lewis makes use of the distinction between speaking strictly and speaking loosely ((1989) 2000: 93): "Strictly speaking, Mackie is right: genuine values would have to meet an impossible condition, so it is an error to think there are any. Loosely speaking, the name may go to a claimant that deserves it imperfectly. . . . What to make of the situation is mainly a matter of temperament." Although this is unobjectionable up to a point, it really just postpones the problem, for we might continue to argue about whether something exists *even when we have confined ourselves to speaking loosely.* Presumably we will not accept a theory that allows that ghosts and witches exist (even loosely speaking), and certainly we don't want one that tolerates that the matter might be settled according to "temperament."

The absence of an obvious answer ensures that this is the resting place of many a metaethical debate. My own view is that what determines the answer to such matters is how the relevant population of speakers would collectively decide. Sometimes discoveries lead us to decide that a concept (e.g., *phlogiston* or *witch*) is hopeless; sometimes we prefer to revise the concept, extirpate the problematic element, and carry on much as before (e.g., the concept *simultaneity* survived the discovery that it's all relative; the concept *polymer* survived the discovery that they are macromolecules rather than colloids). But there is absolutely no reason to assume that when groups of humans make such decisions they are following a hidden principle. Who is to say that our collective decisions on such matters aren't influenced by the most trivial of things, such as an advertising jingle or the way a word is used in a popular movie? This reveals that in many cases there really may be no fact of the matter as to whether something is an essential feature of a concept. Perhaps given one cultural milieu we would decide in the positive, but given a somewhat different (but not remarkably different) cultural setting we would decide in the negative. In light of this, there seems something hopeless about a lone philosopher asserting with confidence that some disputed attribute is or is not an a priori requirement of a concept, or declaring that some imperfect satisfier of the platitudes surrounding a concept is or is not "close enough" to count as a revised continuer of the original flawed concept. At best, such assertions could be hypothetical predictions about what a group of humans in circumstances like ours would probably do if forced to make a choice—predictions that are, obviously, burdened with difficulty and more often than not untestable in practice.

But perhaps all is not lost. We might stand a decent chance of getting at the answer if we give consideration to what the concept is *used for*, what practices it undergirds, and then ask whether a revised concept, with the problematic element discarded, could carry on playing that role. For example, even when we realized that nothing is absolutely simultaneous with anything else, the relativistic notion of simultaneity was able to take over seamlessly, since it works just as well in everyday contexts for creatures whose movements don't approach a significant fraction of the speed of light. We can *use* the concept of relative simultaneity in the same way as we can use absolute simultaneity, which suggests that the change didn't amount to replacing one concept with a different concept at all, but rather we just made a revision internal to a single concept. Thus we are not forced to the radical position that every pre-Einsteinian assertion of two events occurring simultaneously is false. By comparison, when we discovered that there are no diabolical supernatural forces in the universe, we had no further use for the concept *witch*. Perhaps we could have carried on applying the word "witch" to women who play a certain kind of local cultural role on the margins of formal society—perhaps we might even have located a cluster of naturalistic properties that all and only these women have—but carrying on in this way would not have allowed us to *use* the word "witch" for the purposes to which we had previously put it: to condemn these women for their evil magical influence and justify their being killed. Thus, there was little point in persisting in using the word "witch" to stand for certain instantiated naturalistic properties; we dropped it and concluded that all historical assertions that certain women were witches—even the loosely spoken ones—were false.

So the question we need to ask is whether moral discourse could carry on playing whatever role it does play if the connection between its prescriptions and the reasons people have to comply were merely a reliable contingent one. If not, then we have grounds for doubting that such a framework counts as a "moral" system at all.

A morality that connected only contingently to people's reasons would be, in important respects, like the institution of etiquette. This is not to say that it would be frivolous; rather, it is a claim about the logical status of the imperatives involved. Moral wrongdoers (especially if confident of impunity) would enjoy the same legitimacy in their transgressions that you or I enjoy when violating etiquette in the confines of our own homes. That word "legitimacy" will raise an eyebrow, so let me try to explain. If I decide to eat like a pig in front of the TV when alone, what I am doing is certainly not legitimate from the point of view of etiquette. Were someone to observe me, he would be quite correct in labeling my actions boorish and disgusting; indeed, I may know very well that I am instantiating those particular qualities, but on this occasion I don't care; boorishness is something I might be indifferent to on occasion, or may even take pleasure in. Of course, if succumbing to boorishness at home is going to lead me into trouble on other occasions, then it becomes a different equation; so let's assume this isn't the case—let's assume that I will be immaculately polite on all social occasions, and my uncouth solitary preferences will not affect that. So why shouldn't I eat like a pig when alone? We are supposing ex hypothesi that there is no real reason for me to refrain from doing so—we are supposing that even if I were to reason correctly I would endorse acting in this way on this occasion. All that can be said by way of condemnation is *from the point of view of etiquette*. From that point of view I am acting in an unacceptable way. But I know *that*. It's just that I am in a situation where I choose to ignore that particular normative framework—and this seems perfectly legitimate. Again, not legitimate-from-the-point-of-view-of-etiquette, of course, but legitimate in some more general, institution-transcendent sense. Given my desires on this occasion—given, in particular, my temporary indifference to the institution of etiquette—eating like a pig is what, all things considered, I ought to do.

A slightly silly example may make this conclusion more conspicuous. Suppose I make this pronouncement: "I hereby declare that whenever we encounter something made in Norway in autumn it is permissible to assert the sentence 'Everyone must pursue this thing.'" And suppose you answer "Hear hear" to my proposal. We have now created a little normative institution according to which everyone ought to pursue autumnal Norwegian products. This institution claims that doing so is justified, implying that adherents of the institution can start issuing reasons claims: Everyone has a reason (a justificatory reason, that is) to pursue autumnal Norwegian products. But of course we haven't really succeeded in creating any considerations of genuine deliberative weight that everyone need pay heed to. Perhaps from *our* point of view anyone indifferent to autumnal Norwegian products is subject to legitimate reproach, but from an objective perspective one can see that it is a feeble sort of reprimand, and were sensible people to hear of such an institution or such reasons claims, or be subjected to such criticism, they would quite rightly ignore it in their deliberations.

With these thoughts in mind, imagine what morality would be like if it similarly connected only contingently with people's reasons. Suppose Jack really, *really* wants to murder John. He finds himself alone with John at the edge of an abandoned well shaft in the middle of a dark and lonely moor and thinks "Why not?" The chances of being caught are effectively zero. Perhaps, it might be claimed, acting in this way will encourage Jack to commit other murders on occasions when impunity is less assured, or perhaps he will have guilt to live with. In such a case Jack may have a reason not to murder John. But we are dealing with a moral naturalist who admits that the connection to people's reasons is only contingent, which allows us just to *stipulate* that Jack has no such reasons to refrain. Thus all that is true of etiquette applies. Why shouldn't Jack murder John? We are supposing that even if he were to reason correctly he would endorse murdering on this occasion. All that can be said by way of condemnation is *from the point of view of morality*. From that point of view Jack is acting in an unacceptable way. But he knows *that*. It's just that he is in a situation where he chooses to ignore that particular normative framework—and this seems perfectly legitimate. Again, not legitimate-from-the-point-of-view-of-morality, of course, but legitimate in some more general, institution-transcendent sense. Given his desires on this occasion—given in particular his temporary indifference to the institution of morality—murdering John is what, all things considered, Jack ought to do.

This, I think, imparts an extremely odd flavor to morality. We generally will not be comfortable saying that Jack's actions were depraved and morally unacceptable and in the next breath asserting that he had no reason to refrain and that in fact committing the murder was what he ought, all things considered, to have done. This is not to deny that we could continue to despise Jack for his wickedness as much as ever, nor to deny that we could have grounds for punishing him if we caught him. (Let's stipulate that Jack murdered John long ago and went to his grave happy and unpunished; we have only recently unearthed poor John's body, along with the note describing the crime that he scrawled before dying.) It's just that, when placed next to the honest concession that Jack may have had every reason to be wicked, these judgments seem to lose some of their teeth. Perhaps what is uncomfortable about this concession is due simply to the fact that we are adherents of the moral institution, unwilling to step out from its linguistic rules. Yet this in itself seems troubling, for it seems to suggest a degree of self-delusion in the moral adherent's relationship to moral precepts. If it is ex hypothesi true that Jack has no real reason to refrain from murder, but moral people won't admit this due to their adherence to the moral institution, then that institution is blinding them to something. It would be like a person who is a fetishistic stickler for politeness being unable to see that a person may be in a situation where etiquette should count for nothing in her deliberations. If this version of moral naturalism ("naturalism without clout") were correct and we were allowed to acknowledge this fact (i.e., if it were transparently correct), then there should be nothing wrong with our moral pronouncements reflecting this. Instead of "Killing John was unacceptable," we should be allowed to say "From the moral point of view, killing John was unacceptable." And to the observation that Jack's action was wicked we should be permitted to add "but Jack had every reason to act wickedly on this occasion, and no real reason to refrain."

Moreover, there should be nothing to stop us from honestly adding such qualifiers to our own practical deliberations over moral decisions much less sensational than whether to murder someone. Imagine yourself in an empty hotel corridor early in the morning, tempted to grab a newspaper from outside a stranger's door because you forgot to order one with your breakfast. Let's stipulate that you know that this action instantiates whatever natural property the naturalist equates with moral wrongness. So you know that the action is morally wrong; you know that from the moral point of view it is unacceptable behavior. But the kind of moral naturalism under consideration makes the following a live question: "What reason do I have to care about this instance of moral wrongness?" (This in itself seems very odd to me, but that's what these naturalists say.) To be sure, there are *moral* reasons for caring about moral wrongness—that is, there are reasons pertaining to what can be justified from the point of view of that particular normative framework. But these aren't the kind of reasons you are after, for what you are really asking is why, on this occasion and pertaining to this action, you should care about that justificatory framework at all. Noting that there are moral justificatory reasons for refraining from taking the newspaper just leaves you wondering what reason you have to care about those reasons.

Let us say that there are three possible responses that a person might have when tempted to steal a newspaper and asking herself "What reason do I have to care about this instance of moral wrongness?" (For simplicity's sake these responses will be idealized, but they are intended to exhaust the space of possibility.) First, a person may realize that she has no reason at all. She would be like Jack in the previous example, and thus, given her desires, the rational thing for her to do is to steal the newspaper, all the while calmly acknowledging to herself that to do so is morally wrong. Alternatively, she may come up with a positive answer—that is to say, this instance of moral wrongness may connect to her desires in such a way that she does have a reason to refrain from its pursuit. The desires in question may be weak or strong, producing either fragile or robust reasons. This last observation allows us to consider weak desires (yielding fragile reasons for compliance) and strong desires (yielding robust reasons for compliance) as two poles of a continuum of possibilities—these poles representing the second and third kinds of response. Thus, the second kind of response a person may have is to recognize that she has a reason to avoid moral wrongness, but only a fragile reason; in other words, acting in a morally wrong manner will frustrate the satisfaction of certain of her desires, but these desires are negligible and relatively shallow, such that only a modest alteration of her desires would cause her reason to avoid wrongdoing to evaporate. The third possible response is to have firm and entrenched desires on the side of moral goodness, and thus robust reasons to avoid moral wrongness. Such a person's desires may be only contingent, it is true, but contingency must not be confused with flimsiness. (My desire to care for my baby son is only contingent—I wouldn't *cease to be me* or *cease to be human* if I lost the desire—and yet it is hardly unreliable.)

There is something troubling about each of these three possibilities, meaning that there is something troubling about the moral naturalism without clout that implies this three-way space of possibility. I have already accentuated what is unpalatable about the first kind of response: the idea that certain persons may have every reason to pursue moral wrongness (even while conceiving of the object of their pursuit under the terms "moral wrongness"). Let me say something more about the two other possibilities.

The second kind of person is disconcerting because the very temptation to steal represents for her a reason to modify whatever desires she has that are in favor of avoiding this wrong, thus leaving her with no reason to refrain from stealing the newspaper. In other words, if the desires that speak in favor of acting on this occasion in accordance with morality can be jettisoned without enormous psychological upheaval, then the very desires that will be satisfied by acting immorally (e.g., the desire to get a newspaper without inconvenience) will encourage the person simply to *modify* her pro-morality desires right then and there in the hotel corridor. This doesn't require that she renounce all her interests in the benefits that morality in general brings; rather, she just adjusts her desires to allow an exception. (Desires aren't always flexible and controllable like this, but very often they are.) It's not that she sneers "Morality, schmorality!" (for someone whose desires give her no reason to care about morality *at all* is probably a psychopath, and here I am just talking about ordinary human weakness)—rather, awareness that moral wrongness is something that a rational person may *or may not* have a reason to pursue encourages her to think "Well, being moral is certainly a good idea broadly speaking, and I certainly in general have good reason for going along with it, but nothing even mildly bad is going to befall me if I violate its commands on just this occasion for something so trivial." When the authority of morality is surrendered, when the practical force of morality depends on the agent's contingent mental states, and when the agent is aware of this fact, then a worrying consequence is that people can to some extent *determine* whether they have reason to act morally on any token occasion: They can jiggle their desires—or perhaps overhaul their desires if the rewards of immorality appear great enough—in order to elude any moral command. The very presence of immoral temptation encourages them to do so.

Persons of the third category have strong and steadfast desires against this act of wrongdoing, yielding constant and important reasons for compliance. Moral naturalists would like us to think that most people will fall into this category. Perhaps they are correct, though it is difficult to say definitively until we know precisely what natural property (or cluster of properties) the moral naturalist intends to advocate as the referent of "moral wrongness" (and "moral rightness," etc.). Certainly I am of the opinion that most of us, in most circumstances, do have firm and entrenched reasons to avoid acting in the ways that are generally thought of as "morally wrong": good reasons to refrain from stealing, to avoid promise-breaking, to shun violence, and so forth. Moral naturalists will surely endeavor to identify moral properties with natural properties in such a way as to broadly uphold widespread moral opinion (i.e., whatever natural property they identify with moral wrongness will be one instantiated by stealing, whatever natural property they identify with moral rightness will be one instantiated by promise-keeping, and so on), and thus I agree that they are likely to support a theory according to which most of us, in ordinary circumstances, do have reliable and robust reasons to act morally. Suppose, for example, that the natural property identified with moral wrongness is simply that of causing distress unnecessarily. This will line up well with many of our intuitions. And in my opinion most of us do have very good reason to avoid causing distress unnecessarily; thus, on the assumption that stealing a newspaper from a hotel corridor will bring about some (admittedly mild) unnecessary distress, most of us will be in this third category regarding this action.

But however solid may be the resolve of persons of the third type, there remains something strange about their attitude towards morality—at least if moral naturalism without clout is countenanced. The problem is that thinking in moral terms seems entirely superfluous to such a person's reasons and motivations. If the person wonders why she should not steal the newspaper, all the answer she is ever going to get can come from reflecting on the fact that it will cause unnecessary distress. Her identifying that causal property with *moral wrongness* seems to add nothing to her reasons or motivations. (And this remains so if we replace "causing unnecessary distress" with any other cloutless natural property.) After all, how *could* seeing the action as morally wrong add anything, since (this moral naturalist asserts) moral wrongness just *is* that causal property? If thinking and talking of the action as "morally wrong" adds something substantial that cannot be gotten from thinking and talking of the action's instantiating some natural property, then this counts as evidence against the adequacy of the moral naturalist's theory. So the question we should put to this moral naturalist is "Why, according to your theory, do we need a distinct moral discourse at all?" Why not just talk openly about what we like and dislike, what is conducive to social harmony and what is not, what we will tolerate and what we will punish? (I'm reminded of the Bob Dylan version of God's exchange with Abraham: "You can do what you want, Abe, but next time you see me coming you better run."[14])

Earlier in this book, I offered an answer to the question "Why do we need a distinct moral discourse?" (See section 4.2.) Moralized thinking and talking, I suggested, does better than non-moralized practical deliberation at acting as a bulwark against weakness of will. It also serves well as an interpersonal commitment device (section 4.3). However, central to that argument was the contention that moral thinking has a special kind of calculation-silencing, desire-transcendent practical oomph that makes it often less vulnerable to succumbing to temptation than clear-headed prudential deliberation. But that argument is unavailable to the supporter of moral naturalism without clout, for ex hypothesi he believes that moral deliberation just *is* deliberation about what is desired and how it might be achieved. "So much the worse for the argument of section 4.2," this naturalist might respond.[15] The problem, however, lies not with the particulars of the argument I offered, for *whenever* we think we have a good answer to the question "Why do we need a distinct moral discourse?" this answer will be unavailable to the supporter of moral naturalism without clout. The only conclusion to be drawn is that this moral naturalist must answer the question as follows: "We don't." As a champion of morality— as a defender of moral realism, no less—the moral naturalist must feel extremely uncomfortable confessing that moral discourse and moral thinking serve no distinct function, and in fact are superfluous to our social decision making.[16]

Probably none of the above considerations against the moral naturalist delivers a devastating blow, but together they at least bring into the light the embarrassing implications of the theory. Moral naturalism without clout, first of all, seems to enfeeble our capacity to morally criticize wrongdoers; second, it might actually encourage wrongdoing for certain persons; and third, it renders moral language and moral thinking entirely redundant. Such a value system is (to recycle a phrase used earlier) surely too wimpy to be mistaken for morality. Moral thinking has a function, I have argued—both evolutionarily and contemporarily—and deliberations in terms simply of what we want and need will not suffice. The *moralization* of our practical lives contributes to the satisfaction of our long-term interests and makes for more effective collective negotiation by supplying license for punishment, justification for likes and dislikes, and bonding individuals in a shared framework of decision-making. It is, I submit, precisely the purported authority and inescapability of moral prescriptions that enable them to perform these functions. Thus, a value system lacking practical clout could not so effectively play the social roles to which we put morality, and thus we could not *use* it as we use morality, indicating that clout may be considered a vital aspect of morality (even when we are speaking loosely).

In section 6.3 I assessed the possibility that moral naturalism will satisfy the alleged desideratum of practical clout and concluded that the prospects were dim. In this section I have explored the prospects of a moral naturalism that doesn't even try to satisfy practical clout, and I have come to a similarly pessimistic conclusion. I conclude that practical clout really is a core desideratum of any moral theory, and that no form of moral naturalism can satisfy it. So much the worse for moral naturalism.

6.5　Harman's Challenge Again

Many philosophers are global naturalists. Unless they plump for some kind of noncognitivism, the only metaethical options they recognize are some form of moral naturalism and moral nihilism. Thus, for them, if the above arguments have succeeded in defeating moral naturalism (and if noncognitivism is out of the picture), these arguments have succeeded in showing that there are no moral facts at all. Note that references to Harman's challenge and to the genealogy of the human moral faculty will have played no part in establishing any such moral nihilism, except, perhaps, for providing an explanation of why we all have been so systematically misguided in believing in morality for all this time.

But many philosophers are not global naturalists. *Moral non-naturalists* hold that moral properties exist but enjoy a certain autonomy from the world as described by the natural sciences: They are not identical to, reducible to, or supervenient upon any natural properties. *Moral supernaturalists* hold that moral properties exist but depend for their existence on some kind of supernatural phenomenon—most obviously, God's will or commands. Even if these stances are not abundantly populated by contemporary philosophers, I think it is safe to say that they come the closest to capturing what ordinary speakers believe. Thus Harman's challenge still has real work to do. Consider figure 6.3. The challenge, remember, is that hypothesis A promises to explain all our moral judgments, leaving us without need to posit any moral facts (i.e., with no reason to assume that any of our moral judgments are true) unless the moral facts are somehow implicitly buried in hypothesis A. The only way that moral facts could be implicitly buried in a scientific genealogical hypothesis is if some kind of moral naturalism were true. (See figure 6.2.) The previous two sections have cast doubt on this possibility. Thus we are left with figure 6.3, and this time Ockham's Razor really can come in and do its thing, for non-naturalism and

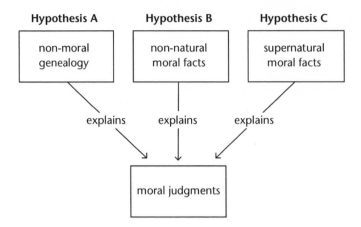

Figure 6.3

supernaturalism do posit extra ontology in the world, but the presence of the non-moral genealogy (hypothesis A) shows this ontology to be explanatorily superfluous. Hypotheses B and C can be excised.

I am spelling out this dialectic carefully because it is often, to my mind, misunderstood. As I noted earlier, Harman's challenge is often seen as a problem for moral naturalism. It does represent a demand that the naturalist articulate her case clearly, showing how the moral connects to the natural—but if the case can be so articulated, the challenge fades (in fact it is hard to imagine that any naturalist might have supposed that he could present his theory persuasively without passing the challenge). And to the extent that the naturalist can make her case, non-naturalism and supernaturalism become less plausible. But if the naturalist *cannot* make her case, Harman's challenge seems to make non-naturalism and supernaturalism obsolete. In other words: Once we have a complete non-moral genealogy of moral judgment, if moral naturalism succeeds non-naturalism and supernaturalism are sunk, and if moral naturalism fails non-naturalism and supernaturalism are sunk. Thus non-naturalism and supernaturalism suffer most in this argumentative fray, whereas the moral naturalist is defeated only through independent arguments having nothing in particular to do with Harman's challenge (arguments of the sort I have provided in the previous two sections).

The conclusion of this argument is not moral nihilism (the view, roughly, that all our moral judgments are false). Pointing out that we have no reason to believe in moral facts does not imply that we have reason to *disbelieve* in them.[17] I have no reason to believe that the number of hairs on my head is an odd number (even correcting for vagueness), but I would be foolish to conclude that I therefore have reason to disbelieve that it is an odd number, for that would be a reason to believe that it is an even number, and clearly I have no more reason to believe that the number of hairs on my head is even than that it is odd. Though I am not justified in holding that the number of hairs on my head is odd, it *could* be odd (in fact, there is a pretty decent chance that it *is* odd). Now let us return to the fanciful story about belief pills. Discovering that your belief that Napoleon lost Waterloo was the product of a process entirely independent of whether he did win or lose forced the recognition that you had no grounds one way or the other for that belief. The conclusion was that you should take the antidote, thus giving yourself an open mind to go and find some other more reliable grounds for either believing or disbelieving this proposition. (Or you might just not care, and be happy to remain in a state of agnosticism on the matter.) The conclusion I draw from all that has been argued in this chapter about morality is analogous. We have an empirically confirmed theory about where our moral judgments come from (we are supposing). This theory doesn't state or imply that they are true, it doesn't have as a background assumption that they are true, and, importantly, their truth is not surreptitiously buried in the theory by virtue of any form of moral naturalism. This amounts to the discovery that our moral beliefs are products of a process that is entirely independent of their truth, which forces the recognition that we have no grounds one way or the other for maintaining these beliefs. They *could* be true, but we have no reason for thinking so. Thus we should, initially, cultivate an open mind in order to go and find some other more reliable grounds for either believing or disbelieving moral propositions.

6.6 Reliabilists, Conservatives, Coherentists, and Foundationalists

Radical as the conclusion just drawn may sound, many philosophers will be unfazed by it because they think we already do have reasonable grounds for believing moral propositions. Moral naturalism, non-naturalism, and supernaturalism are, if you like, *metaphysical* moral theories, since they purport to tell us about the ontological status of the facts that render our moral beliefs true. By contrast, there are various attempts to vindicate moral beliefs on purely *epistemological* grounds. Such attempts assume that moral beliefs can be shown to be justified irrespective of the ontological status of the facts that make them true. In this final section I will show that the availability of an evolutionary moral genealogy does in fact pose a serious challenge for such epistemological endeavors. I will discuss, in turn, reliabilism, conservatism, coherentism, and foundationalism, devoting the most time to the first.

It may be argued that providing an evolutionary genealogy for a belief (or belief-formation mechanism), far from undermining the belief, actually shows the belief to be justified. According to a certain epistemological tradition known as "externalism" (not to be confused with the metaethical thesis *motivation externalism*, mentioned in section 4.2), a person's belief may be justified by factors to which she has no cognitive access. Process reliabilists—the most prominent advocates of externalism—hold that a belief is justified if and only if it is the product of a process that reliably links beliefs with truth. If natural selection is such a process, then any innate beliefs will be justified. Peter Carruthers[18] argues along these lines:

> . . . true belief has immense survival value for any organism, such as ourselves, much of whose behaviour is caused by the interaction of beliefs and desires. For in general an organism's projects will succeed if based upon beliefs that are *true*. . . . Wholly false beliefs will not have survival value in the long run, and in evolutionary selection it is the long run that matters. What seems undeniable is that organisms (of the sort that act on beliefs) will survive, in general and in the long run, if they base their actions on beliefs that are true, or at least close to the truth. So if any innate beliefs have arisen through natural selection, we should expect them to be at least approximately true. . . . It is possible to imagine cases where an innate *false* belief would be an aid to survival. For example, an innate belief in the magical properties of a particular plant, which in fact contains a powerful medicine, might prove very useful to those who live in the region where that plant flourishes. But such cases are rendered unlikely when one remembers that in order to have been selected through evolution, a belief would have to prove useful over a time-span that is extremely long in comparison to human history, and in a wide variety of different circumstances. I therefore conclude that if evolution has resulted in any innate beliefs, then those beliefs will very likely constitute innate knowledge. (1992: 111–113)

This, however, is too quick. Carruthers is making a mistake that reveals a deep difficulty for process reliabilism, known as the "generality problem" (Feldman 1986; Conee and Feldman 1998). The problem is that when we consider a token belief and ask whether the type of process that produced it is reliable, it is far from obvious what the type in question is. It is like pointing to a dog and asking what type of thing it is. Possible correct answers range from the very general (organism, vertebrate, etc.) to the very specific (dog, dachshund, etc.), to say nothing of non-biological categories (noisy object, thing that is being pointed at, etc.). In a similar way, a particular belief is the product of both general and specific types of processes. Consider a specific act of belief formation—say, Amy's coming to believe, as she peers through the mist, that there is a cow across the field. If we consider the general type of process of which this act is a token, then we may alight simply on *perception*—which may be deemed a reliable process. However, it is just as true that this act is an instance of the types *visual perception, visual perception on a misty evening, Amy's perception* and *Amy's perception of farm animals*—which may be considerably less reliable types of belief-formation process (e.g., because Amy is very short-sighted, or hopeless at identifying animals). At the limit, the type may be specified such that it has only one instance: the token in question. In this case, it will be deemed a reliable type if and only if the token belief is true, entailing the unacceptable conclusion that a belief is justified if and only if it is true.

Whether the generality problem sinks reliabilism is a matter of dispute, and it will not be adjudicated here. (For a cogent advocacy of the problem, see Conee and Feldman 1998.) Clearly, if the problem is insurmountable we need pursue this line of inquiry no further. If the reliabilist *can* answer the generality problem, it will be by providing some kind of criteria for choosing process types that are neither too general nor too specific for the case at hand. This, then, brings us back to Carruthers's swift case for natural selection as a reliable process of belief formation. I believe that he has failed to target the appropriate level of generality.

In order to engage with Carruthers's arguments, let us interpret my view as holding that moral beliefs are innate. (In fact I would not assert this without much qualification.) One thing that can be safely assumed is that by and large the point of having beliefs is that they can be formed flexibly in response to environmental variation. If there are innate beliefs, they are surely exceptions rather than the rule. So innate beliefs, if any there be, will be regulated by different psychological mechanisms from those that govern regular belief-formation processes. Moreover, it is unlikely that there is only one psychological mechanism productive of innate beliefs; the more plausible explanation is that the human mind contains a number of discrete psychological mechanisms, each designed to cope with some kind of threat posed or opportunity afforded by the ancestral environment, and that some of these mechanisms operate by providing the individual with fixed beliefs. It has been argued, for example, that humans have innate beliefs about grammar, innate beliefs about how other minds work, and innate beliefs about obligations and prohibitions. The reliabilist, in striving to select the appropriate level of generality for the belief-formation process pertaining to a token belief, will not want the differences among these processes to be papered over. The process that produces innate beliefs about grammar will certainly overlap to a degree with the process that produces innate beliefs about other minds, but to the extent that the psychological mechanisms governing these different beliefs are products of distinct selective pressures, and are therefore distinct mechanisms with different operating procedures, so too will the respective relevant processes differ. To think of both kinds of innate belief as issuing from the same kind of process ("natural selection") is surely to have erred on the side of over-generality.

This line of argument forces us to consider the processes that may result in innate beliefs more carefully, case by case. Natural selection is not the relevant process here; natural selection is the general process that produced the mechanisms whose respective operations constitute the particular processes on which the reliabilist should be focusing. Therefore, Carruthers's presupposition that all innate beliefs are the result of a single kind of process must be rejected. Nevertheless, the considerations Carruthers raises are fair ones, and it may be that his argument will, when applied to each case in turn, support the conclusion that the innate belief in question is the product of a reliable process.

The thought underlying Carruthers's argument is that false beliefs will, eventually and in the long run, lead an individual to act in fitness-reducing ways. When we consider beliefs about concrete aspects of the environment, and the relations in which they stand, this can seem eminently plausible. But Carruthers also provides us with an example where this doesn't seem to hold: the belief that a medicinally beneficial plant has magical powers. Since magical powers are intangible and elusive, it is possible that one could carry on falsely believing in them without ever getting into practical trouble. In the same way, people who now believe in ghosts or ancestral spirits don't typically run into practical difficulties in their dealings with the world (which is not to deny that such beliefs are foolish). False mythological beliefs about the origin of the world, or about what occurs after death, or about what kinds of supernatural or divine beings are overseeing human affairs—all such beliefs may have no negative impact on human decisions, or in fact may have a positive impact if they are appropriately attached to goals that are independently beneficial (fitness advancing). This is exactly the kind of case that Carruthers considers: Eating a certain plant in certain circumstances is already beneficial for medicinal reasons, so adding some "intangible overlay"—magical powers—may not lead the individual into trouble but may actually advance fitness (e.g., if the magical belief bolsters motivation to eat the plant). His argument is that this is an unusual case, and thus he can still claim that innate beliefs produced by natural selection are products of a reliable process, since a reliable process need only be one that *on the whole* produces true beliefs. But I have countered that it is not acceptable that everything be tarred with the same brush. If there were an innate belief that certain plants have magical powers, and this belief were the product of a dedicated psychological mechanism with a distinct evolutionary history, then the relevant belief-formation process to which we should look (if we are epistemic process reliabilists) must focus on this particular mechanism. And since in this case we would have an empirically confirmed hypothesis of how this belief-formation mechanism works which does not require that the beliefs be even approximately true, we would have to conclude that any such innate beliefs are products of an *unreliable* process. The fact that it may be an unusual case, and that there may be many other naturally selected innate-belief-formation mechanisms whose operating constitutes *reliable* processes, is irrelevant.

We can now apply this lesson to the case of innate moral beliefs. What seems clear is that in the crucial respect such beliefs are like the imaginary belief about the plant's magical properties. We have seen that nowhere does the evolutionary hypothesis outlined in earlier chapters assume that moral beliefs are or were true. The argument developed in chapter 4 came to this: Certain helpful behaviors advance fitness, and the "moralization" of these behaviors bolsters motivation to perform them. It is not at all obvious that a person who has thus "moralized" her beliefs is going to run into difficulties, in the way that a person who believes that a predator is hiding behind every corner can be expected eventually to run into difficulties. Moral matters are sufficiently "intangible" (and, it should be added, flexible) that beliefs concerning them may pass the test of everyday life with flying colors, even over an extremely long time span and in a wide variety of different circumstances. Suppose one person correctly believes that cooperating (in circumstances C) is to her long-term benefit. Suppose another person (for whom such a belief would also be true) believes that cooperating (in C) is obligatory, that she must so behave irrespective of her desires, that if she doesn't cooperate she will deserve to be punished. What circumstance might arise such that the latter person's moralized belief will lead her to fitness-compromising behavior that the former person will eschew? As far as I can see, none. (Remember that moralizing one's social deliberations does not mean favoring unconditional or over-generalized cooperation; see the final paragraph of section 4.2.) Thus I conclude that by the process reliabilist's own lights a certain plausible view of how innate moral beliefs may have evolved leads naturally to the conclusion that such beliefs are epistemically unjustified.

Reliabilism holds that one may be justified in holding a belief even in the absence of any positive evidence in favor of that belief. Another such view is epistemic conservatism, which holds that one may be justified in maintaining a belief, even in the absence of any positive evidence, simply because held beliefs have a presumption of rationality (they are "innocent until proven guilty"). However, no reasonable conservative principle can shrug off the arguments that have been presented here. Any plausible version of conservatism will accommodate the common-sense view that there are certain attributes that a belief may have that cast it into doubt. Walter Sinnott-Armstrong does a good job of outlining these epistemic platitudes:

... imagine that each of us adds a column of figures, and I get one sum, but you get a different sum. Maybe I would be justified in believing that I am right if you were my child and I was helping you with your homework. However, if you are just as good at arithmetic as I am, then, when we get different answers, we need to check again to find out who made a mistake before either of us can be justified in believing that his or her answer is the correct one. (2005)

From consideration of such cases Sinnott-Armstrong formulates the principle that "confirmation is needed for a believer to be justified when people disagree with no independent reason to prefer one belief or believer over the other." Other types of cases lead to further principles, to the following conclusion:

When a belief is partial, controversial, emotional, subject to illusion, and explicable by dubious sources [i.e., unreliable or disreputable sources], then . . . confirmation is needed for justified belief. . . . These principles or some close relatives seem plausible to most people and are assumed in our shared epistemic practices. (ibid.)

The five attributes outlined by Sinnott-Armstrong are precisely the sort of thing that will undermine any prima facie justification enjoyed by a held belief, leaving it in need of some other source of justification. This is not a point against epistemological conservatism, but a clarification of what may overcome the presumed justification of a held belief. The provision of an empirically confirmed theory that explains the origin of our moral beliefs but which at no point implies or presupposes their truth is one such defeater of presumed justification. It belongs on Sinnott-Armstrong's list under "a belief being explicable by unreliable sources." (Incidentally, the purpose of Sinnott-Armstrong's paper is to show that moral beliefs manifest all the other attributes that upset justification as well.)

If moral beliefs lack whatever justification one might have hoped they would receive from a conservative epistemological principle, they stand in need of an articulated defense. One popular place to seek a defense of moral beliefs is in epistemological coherentism.[19] Coherentists can claim that the belief that Nazis were evil, say, may be justified by fitting comfortably within a coherent framework of other beliefs. (A standard objection to coherentism is that it would appear that the belief that Nazis were courageous heroes may also fit comfortably within a different but equally coherent framework of beliefs; but never mind about that.) But things get complicated once we realize that the set of beliefs from which we are trying to construct a coherent package contains not only the belief that Nazis were evil but also further (empirically well-connected) beliefs concerning the genealogy of that belief. Suppose these further beliefs say something like "Humans have beliefs concerning evil due to the circumstances of the social life of our ancestors, and this genealogy nowhere presupposes the truth of such beliefs." This alone would undermine the justificatory status that the first belief would otherwise enjoy in the coherentist framework, since the presence of the genealogical belief immediately creates the possibility of a new coherent set: one in which the first belief is not endorsed but rather has its content explained away. The coherentist doxastic package will presumably also contain common-sense epistemological truisms, such as those articulated by Sinnott-Armstrong, including one that states something like "Independent confirmation is needed for a believer to be justified when the belief arises from a process that nowhere presupposes its truth." The most coherent way of putting all these beliefs together would be to conclude that the original moral belief stands in need of some explicit confirmation; thus doubt is cast upon the original moral belief *by the coherentist's own lights*.

Things look even worse for moral beliefs, according to coherentism, if we take on board certain arguments presented earlier in this chapter. If "inescapable practical authority" is indeed a platitude of our moral conceptual framework, and the only sense that can be made of this is as concerning *reasons*, but our best and most plausible naturalistic theory of reasons provides nothing of the sort, and we have decided to be global naturalists, then something has to give within the belief network in order to achieve coherence. Various possibilities arise concerning where we can admit the error—perhaps all equally coherent (which, I take it, in itself amounts to a general problem for coherentism). But the availability of a genealogy of morals argues in favor of dropping the moral beliefs, for there our admission of error can be accompanied by *an explanation of that error*—an explanation that is well connected to scientific beliefs.

The coherentist's traditional opponent is the foundationalist, who argues that certain beliefs are epistemically privileged and non-inferentially justified. I think it is probably fair to say that classic foundationalism comes closest to capturing most regular people's ill-defined thoughts on moral epistemology, at least concerning extreme and heartfelt matters. Isn't it *just obvious* that the Nazis were evil? Generally we don't feel that we should even need to justify the belief that the Nazis were evil, and if pressed are likely to say something like "Well, if you can't just see this then there's something wrong with you." Such a response makes it sound not so much that the belief is supposed to be epistemically self-justifying as that there is something *morally* dubious about the character of anyone who requests a justification.[20] But if that is what it amounts to, then our attention should be drawn to a different moral judgment—"One ought not seek explicit justification for the judgment that the Nazis were evil"—and the question then becomes "In virtue of what is *this* judgment justified?"

Classic foundationalism applied to the moral realm results in moral intuitionism: the claim that people are epistemically justified in holding some moral beliefs without necessarily being able to infer these from other beliefs—i.e., roughly, that some moral truths are "just obvious." But here we can reapply the lesson from Sinnott-Armstrong to show what is wrong with moral intuitionism (intuitionism being, in fact, is his real target). The principles that commonsensically render a belief in need of independent confirmation—being partial, controversial, emotional, subject to illusion, and explicable by dubious sources—all apply in spades to "moral intuitions." Here are two examples of how moral intuitions are subject to illusion: Sinnott-Armstrong cites the study of Kahneman and Tversky (1979), wherein subjects were given an imaginary scenario and asked to make a judgment about who will live and who will die in a group of 600 people. Moral intuitions swung enormously depending on whether a choice was described as "200 people will be saved" or "400 people will die." Another study (not mentioned by Sinnott-Armstrong) showed that subjects are far more likely to rate an unfamiliar Chinese symbol in favorable terms if the symbol is presented while the subject is pressing his hands up against the underside of the table at which he is sitting than the subject is when pressing his hands down on the surface of the table (Cacioppo et al. 1993). The hypothesized explanation (anticipated by William James in 1884) is that how an object is categorized along an evaluative dimension depends in part on motor processes, and in particular on muscle flexion (pulling toward) versus extension (pushing away). There are good empirical reasons for thinking that our heartfelt and seemingly indubitable moral intuitions are frequently influenced by such irrelevant factors. The problem that this highlights is that beliefs might *seem* self-justified when they are not. The fact that morality may *seem* justified, and that we are deeply reluctant to admit otherwise, doesn't make it so, and in fact is itself a phenomenon predicted by the genealogical hypothesis. It should be an embarrassment to the discipline of philosophy that its history is crowded with thinkers taking their own parochial, contingent, personal opinions and, observing that these propositions seem "just obvious," elevating them to the status of "self-evident truths." In his autobiography John Stuart Mill noted the dangers of the dogmatism that intuitionism encourages: "The notion that truths external to the mind may be known by intuition or consciousness, independently of observation and experience, is, I am persuaded, in these times, the great intellectual support of false doctrines and bad institutions. By the aid of this theory, every inveterate belief and every intense feeling, of which the origin is not remembered, is enabled to dispense with the obligation of justifying itself by reason, and is erected into its own all-sufficient voucher and justification. There never was such an instrument devised for consecrating all deep seated prejudices" (1879: 225–226). In much the same spirit, Kitcher (2005: 176) writes: "In ethics, as in mathematics, the appeal to intuition is an epistemology of desperation." Without a defensible theory of how a moral intuition could be epistemically self-justifying, the suspicion naturally arises that the phenomenon that really stands in need of explanation is why it might *seem* to us that such beliefs are beyond question and requiring of no further justification. This is precisely what an evolutionary genealogy promises to contribute to. Such an "explaining away" strategy is preferable to persisting with the problematic project of trying to show that our moral beliefs are epistemically justified, since it recognizes no remaining mysterious phenomena or unanswered questions; it is explanatorily complete.

These final few comments are admittedly far from complete, and I acknowledge that there are complexities and epistemological theories that have not been discussed. However, I contend that on no epistemological theory worth its salt should the justificatory status of a belief remain unaffected by the discovery of an empirically supported theory that provides a complete explanation of why we have that belief while nowhere presupposing its truth. We should reject or modify any theory that would render us epistemic slaves to the baby-bearing capacity of our ancestors.

Conclusion: Living with an Adapted Mind

If he does really think that there is no distinction between virtue and vice, why, sir, when he leaves our houses let us count our spoons.

—Boswell, *Life of Johnson* (1763)

An unphilosophical man, whose principal evidence about others people's conduct was the behaviour of John Mackie, would never dream of explaining it in terms of the theory of "moral scepticism."

—George Cawkwell, memorial address for John Mackie, University Church, Oxford, February 27, 1982

The 1893 Romanes lecture at Oxford was delivered by Thomas Huxley, popularly known as "Darwin's bulldog" for his pugnacious defense of evolutionary theory in Victorian England. The *Oxford Magazine* noted "the impressive figure of the lecturer in the gorgeous D.C.L. robes, which set off so well the finely cut features and the long grey hair of a keenly intellectual head." Despite the rattle of carts and cabs on the cobbles outside the hall drowning a lot of the speech, Huxley left his audience with this memorable sound bite: "Let us understand, once for all, that the ethical progress of society depends, not on imitating the cosmic process [i.e., evolution through natural selection], still less in running away from it, but in combating it" ((1893) 1947: 82). A century later the eminent evolutionary biologist George C. Williams was still in agreement, titling a paper "Mother Nature is a wicked old witch" (1993; see also Dawkins 1981: 3).

The unintended irony of such sentiments should not be lost on us. If biological natural selection is responsible for giving us a moral sensibility in the first place, then without it we would be in no position to give consideration to "the ethical progress of society." Assuming that Huxley and Williams would both agree that enjoying the capacity to make moral judgments (even directed at the process of natural selection itself) is a faculty much to be prized, then just how wicked can Mother Nature be? Their argument undermines itself. To wholeheartedly "combat" natural selection (whatever exactly that would involve) would require resisting the moral sense itself—the very faculty that Huxley hopes to stimulate when he endeavors to enlist us as combatants in his cause.

Natural selection doesn't deserve the bad rap given it by Huxley and Williams. It is a process that has made us sociable, able to enter into cooperative exchanges, capable of love, empathy, and altruism—granting us the capacity to take a direct interest in the welfare of others with no thought of reciprocation—and has designed us to think of our relations with one another in moral terms. Why has Mother Nature granted us this bounty? Not for any laudable purpose (so let's not sing her praises too loudly), but simply because being nice helped our ancestors make more babies. It is naive to assume that these natural prosocial tendencies extend to non-cognitive feelings, behavioral dispositions, inclinations, aversions, and preferences, but not to *beliefs*. But acknowledging beliefs under the influence of natural selection raises epistemological concerns, for the faithful representation of reality is of only contingent instrumental value when reproductive success is the touchstone, forcing us to acknowledge that if in certain domains *false* beliefs will bring more offspring then that is the route natural selection will take every time. Moral thinking could very well be such a domain.

Much of what passes for "prescriptive evolutionary ethics" starts with the premise that the human moral sense is a product of evolution, then tries to squeeze from this premise some kind of moral conclusion. In response it is often confidently observed that no amount of descriptive, historical information can by itself tell a person what he ought to do. But evolutionary ethics, I have argued, has a deeper and more disquieting side. What if this descriptive, historical information concerns a person's very capacity to wonder what he ought to do? What if it reveals that the very terms under which he is conducting his deliberation owe their characteristics not to *truth* but to the social conditions on the savannah 100,000 years ago? What if he comes to realize that his very reluctance to question morality—his very motivation to defend it, even in the philosophy classroom—falls prey to the same explanatory framework? The answer to these questions is not that purely descriptive information does tell a person what he ought to do, but that it can have an undermining effect on his deliberations. The term "undermining" here is not intended pejoratively; if your thinking on some matter presents itself as a faithful representation of the world but in fact there are no grounds for supposing that it is, then, by epistemic standards, its being undermined is a *good* thing.

In this book I have argued that descriptive knowledge of the genealogy of morals (in combination with some philosophizing) should undermine our confidence in our moral judgments. This conclusion can be thought of as a kind of moral skepticism—skepticism, that is, in the classic sense of the word, meaning that the evidence favors neither a proposition nor its negation, and thus one should choose (or is required) to reserve judgment on the matter, at least until new evidence turns up. It is what I have referred to occasionally in this book as "cultivating agnosticism" on the matter. Agnosticism in religious affairs is often taken to be the view that one cannot know whether God exists—and this indeed was how Thomas Huxley, who coined the term, intended it. But if to be a theist is to believe in God and to be an atheist is to believe that God does not exist (neither view, note, making any claim to knowledge), then for agnosticism to be a third option we must take it to be the stance of neither believing nor disbelieving in God.[1] This, in any case, is how I intend to use the term. Another kind of moral skeptic can be considered the analog of the atheist, claiming that we have good reason for believing that no moral judgments are true. Though it is possible that the resources for arguing for this more radical form of skepticism are contained in these pages, I have not attempted such an argument here. The metaethical label "error theory"—coined by its proponent John Mackie—is usually reserved for the atheistic moral skeptic, but there seems nothing to prevent us from extending it to the skeptical position favored here: that no moral judgments are epistemically justified. (For this extension of the terminology, see Kalderon 2005.) Therefore, so long as this distinction is borne in mind, I am happy to accept the label "moral error theory" for the view argued for.[2] The two forms of error theory are united in that both recommend that we not believe moral propositions—one because the propositions are untrue, the other because we have no right to endorse them.

I suspect that anyone unfamiliar with the debates of metaethics will find the conclusion utterly appalling. Even those accustomed to those debates may find it appalling, but at least they shouldn't be surprised that someone should defend it. I have two things to say in reply to such a response.

First, the moral skeptic can hardly be defeated by *moral* condemnation of her position. If one is inclined to reject any form of moral skepticism, yet underlying one's motivation is a moral consideration, then the theory under scrutiny has something to say about that consideration: that it is false or unjustified. Any theory that explains the presence of widespread error is, ipso facto, counterintuitive. Thus, that moral skepticism may seem to many obviously false and pernicious is exactly what the moral skeptic predicts, and therefore cannot be employed as a consideration against the view. To do nothing more than point with a sense of appalled outrage at the conclusions of the moral skeptic is merely to beg the question, and thus is no argumentative consideration at all.

The second and much more important thing to say in reply to the appalled response is to assuage it by emphasizing that it is very far from clear what practical implications such moral skepticism has. I don't think that Dr. Johnson (in the quotation that heads this conclusion) is correct in fearing that having a moral skeptic to tea would put the family silver at risk. Moral skepticism amounts to the recognition that there is, or may be, nothing distinctively *morally* wrong with stealing, but it is absolutely not to be identified with the proposal that ordinary people have no reason at all to refrain from stealing—and anyone who made such a jump would be committing a grave mistake. To claim otherwise is to admit that the only thing standing between us and a life of savagery and rampant spoon stealing is a sense of moral duty, which is a truly depressing thought. To cast into doubt one particular kind of normative framework is not to imply that "anything goes." By comparison, in an earlier era it was feared that religious atheism would lead to a breakdown of civil order—that without the belief in a divine being keeping an eye on human affairs a person would have no reason to eschew depraved acts if confident of getting away with them. Though I dare say a few people still believe this, most of us now recognize that it was a groundless anxiety. (Countries with a high percentage of atheists—New Zealand, Norway, Uruguay—are hardly renowned for their degeneracy, while the United States can boast one of the world's highest rates of church attendance alongside the worst crime statistics.) An ordinarily situated person has many reasons to refrain from stealing—robust and plain reasons—even if there is no wrathful God breathing down her neck, and no mysterious moral duty forbidding it, and even if she can get away with it. (The basis of some of those reasons is the fact that for social creatures, as humans are designed to be, major and irreplaceable satisfactions are to be had from sincere participation in a community.) This is not to deny that belief in God or moral duty may help bolster motivation. (That may, in fact, be the central social role of such beliefs.) Rather, it is to point out that we generally have strong reasons to act in "prosocial" ways independent of such considerations. Even if religious and moral beliefs have contributed substantially to keeping our prosocial motivations in line with our prosocial reasons, there is no reason to assume that alternative social and psychological mechanisms (ones that aren't remotely like religious or moral beliefs) could not be developed or enhanced that would serve just as well.

Moreover, it is not clear what impact an epistemic ban on moral belief would have on the status of moral *emotions*. If such emotions necessarily involved moral beliefs, they too would be barred on epistemic grounds. But I went to some trouble in chapter 3 to argue that even cognitively laden emotions do not require belief—mere *thoughts* will suffice. And nothing in chapter 6 amounted to an epistemic consideration against holding certain thoughts. (Believing that you are the world's greatest tennis player is almost certainly epistemically unjustified,[3] but there is nothing wrong with entertaining the thought of being so as a piece of harmless fantasy.) Let me try to clarify this matter by means of a comparison with a non-moral emotion: disgust over being in contact with something. There appears to be a near-universal and often spontaneously developing childhood fixation on notions of contagious contamination ("cooties"), which can wither in the absence of cultural support or can become highly culturally elaborated and a central social principle. (See Rozin and Fallon 1987; Rozin and Nemeroff 1990; Kalish 1999; Greene 2002: 195–196; Hejmadi et al. 2004.) This emotion appears to have an innate basis, and it is probably an example of natural selection having struck upon a means of generating avoidance motivations that imperfectly track a genuine ancestral threat: pathogen contagion.[4] Our question is this: What should rational adults think about cooties?

The word "cooties" originally referred to body lice and is often used to stand in for literal talk of germs; I am, however, using it in its modern North American sense to mean some generic, invisible, ineffable kind of undesirable contaminant (e.g., "girl cooties"). Cooties in this latter sense tend to prompt disgust in a way that pathogens per se generally don't. Note the difference in feeling between the prospect of drinking water from a jar that (though thoroughly cleaned) has recently been used to store cold germs and the prospect of drinking water from a jar that (though thoroughly cleaned) has recently been used to display deformed fetuses in formaldehyde. (I am not saying that one will be less inclined to choose the latter, only that the emotions in play are very different.) Given familiarity with the evolutionary story about how this disgust might have evolved, what attitude should we take toward such emotional responses? How rational is it to feel disgust at the prospect of wearing a freshly laundered sweater whose previous owner was a murderer (Rozin et al. 1994), or drinking apple juice from a brand new and perfectly clean bedpan (Rozin et al. 1999b)? Rational and informed adults certainly shouldn't *believe* that there are any invisible contaminants that can pass from such objects, but they may nevertheless find themselves unable to eliminate such inchoate thoughts from their minds.

The very idea of *a bedpan* makes you think about someone employing it for its intended purpose. Even though you know that no one has ever used this particular bedpan in that way, drinking out of a genuinely soiled bedpan is so repellent an idea that perhaps you can't leave the thought alone, in the same way as one just has to sneak a peek when driving past the scene of a grisly car accident. Perhaps this thought and the raw reluctance it bolsters suffice for you to feel disgust at the prospect of drinking from the clean bedpan. But you need not be committing any epistemic or rational error in doing so. Obviously emotions *can* be irrational; for example, I once knew an otherwise intelligent adult who had a great fear of balloons. But whatever framework determines emotional irrationality, it is not the same as that which determines the irrationality of beliefs. One might be tempted to call an emotion irrational if it is out of step with the accompanying beliefs—one might have thought, for example, than my friend's pallophobia[5] was irrational because she did not really believe that balloons are dangerous. This, however, cannot be correct, since emotional responses to fiction are also out of step with one's accompanying beliefs, but only a single philosopher (as far as I know) is willing to call them irrational.[6] The emotional episodes that are generally categorized as irrational (such as phobic reactions) typically have obsessive and self-sabotaging qualities. Disgust at the prospect of drinking out of a clean bedpan need have neither attribute.

This emotional response, moreover, in itself may represent *a reason* for a rational person to refrain from drinking apple juice from a clean new bedpan. It may be a reason easily outweighed if he is thirsty, or if someone is offering him $10 to drink the apple juice. However, on the assumption that there are no significant competing reasons in favor of drinking, the mere fact that he doesn't want to—irrespective of whether this disinclination exists simply because he can't get certain unpleasant images out of his head or is based on an amorphous whim—amounts to a solid reason to turn down the offer. My point is that even when one has complied with the epistemic requirement to eliminate from one's mind all beliefs concerning magical "once in contact, always in contact" relations, neither continuing to entertain such thoughts, nor feeling the associated disgust, nor allowing that emotion to carry weight in one's practical deliberations need represent an epistemic or a rational failing.

These same points can be made regarding the moral emotions. Even after someone has complied with the epistemic requirement urging moral agnosticism, there need be no epistemic or rational fault in her having moral concepts figure in her thoughts, in her enjoying the full range of moral emotions (albeit sans belief), or in her allowing these emotions to carry weight in her practical deliberations. No one denies that emotions affect motivations (one might even claim that they necessarily do so), and if one can have emotions without the usual associated beliefs, then one's motivations can be engaged without these beliefs. More generally, it should be borne in mind that there is plenty of evidence that our motivations can be influenced in subtle, surprising, and somewhat puzzling ways. Even Saint Augustine noticed that emotions can be strengthened by performing the appropriate bodily actions (e.g., that humbling oneself upon the floor increases the sentiment of piety), though he added that he didn't know why this should be so (Augustine (c. 426) 1968: 360). Modern psychological experiments have supported his view. Smiling voluntarily really does affect one's emotions in a positive way (Ekman and Davidson 1993), and one's amusement at a comedy program can be influenced by how a pencil held in one's mouth is positioned, for a pencil held crossways in the teeth activates the muscles employed in smiling (Strack et al. 1988). Subjects asked to solve sentence anagrams whose solutions concerned the topic of old age walk away from the experiment more slowly that those who unscramble sentences concerning other topics (Bargh 1992). Someone who has just found a dime in the coin-return slot of a public telephone is vastly more likely to offer aid to a passerby who drops a folder of papers on the sidewalk than someone who hasn't found a dime (Isen and Levin 1972). The likelihood of someone aiding a needy stranger on a suburban street is also affected by the amount of ambient noise in the vicinity; for example, a gasoline-powered lawnmower running nearby will greatly reduce the chances of help being offered (Mathews and Canon 1975). The point of these scattered references is just to demonstrate that human motivation is a much more peculiar affair than we usually think, and there are many means of influencing practical choice. Perhaps allowing moral thoughts and emotions a live role in one's psychological economy, *even while lacking the associated moral beliefs*, is one such unobvious means of engaging motivation. Such thoughts and emotions may become habitual, or even aspects of character.[7] There is no obvious reason to doubt that they might be of great importance to a person's life, even serving as personal and interpersonal commitments.

We can go further still and say not merely that people *could* carry on allowing moral thoughts and moral emotions to have some motivational influence in their lives, but that many individuals *should* do so. If what I claimed in chapter 4—that moral thinking plays a positive instrumental role in a typical person's life—was along the right lines, eliminating morality altogether from one's psychological profile will be costly. If, then, it is true that moral emotions sans belief could reduce these costs by playing an active role in preference formation and in decision making (and if we assume for the sake of argument that there is no better way of reducing these costs), then a person should allow them to do so (this being a "should" of prudence); we can even go so far as to say that a person will be practically *irrational* if she does not. All this, though she remains a moral skeptic.

Such claims about what we "ought to do" or "what we ought not believe" would be pointless if we were constitutionally unable to comply. But, as I said in the introduction, claims about innateness must not be thought to imply *inevitability*. The human moral sense is so obviously highly sensitive to learning and to environmental influence (and is probably designed to be so) that there seems little inevitable about it. As with the seemingly natural childhood belief in cooties, moral beliefs may wither without cultural sustenance. This may seem unlikely and undesirable, but the analogous claim concerning the kind of impurity with which one may be contaminated by touching a member of an undesirable caste will seem just as unlikely and undesirable to anyone immersed in a culture where such notions of purity and pollution have become the highly elaborated normative bedrock of individual, institution, and state. Could we train ourselves out of seriously endorsing moral beliefs as easily as we train ourselves out of believing in cooties? Given the necessary cultural support, probably. But even if the answer turns out to be negative it doesn't follow that we are mere automata who must remain blind to the epistemological status of morality. Hume may be correct that "philosophy would render us all Pyrrhonian[8] were not nature too strong for it" ((1740) 1978: 657), but this in itself is no refutation of the skeptic's arguments.

Hume, in the course of his masterly eighteenth-century work of moral psychology, was satisfied to end his explanation of the origins of human morality by appealing to the brute fact of human natural sympathy:

> It is needless to push our researches so far as to ask, why we have humanity or a fellow-feeling with others. It is sufficient, that this is experienced to be a principle in human nature. We must stop somewhere in our examination of causes; and there are, in every science, some general principles, beyond which we cannot hope to find any principle more general. ((1751) 1983: 43)

Hume went no further in his explanations because he could not. But less than a century after Hume's death, Darwin delivered the means for pushing the inquiry into human morality further, providing us with a theory with which to tackle the question of why "nature" (an explanans that peppers

Hume's writing) has made us one way rather than another. Yet although Darwin provided a respectable and testable genealogy of morals, he had little to say (understandably, perhaps) about what the metaethical implications might be. On the one hand, he was well aware that the fact that our moral nature is the product of a particular evolutionary history undercuts any claims to objectivity. In one flight of fancy, he imagines what we would be like had we evolved from bee-like ancestors, concluding that "unmarried females would, like the worker-bees, think it a sacred duty to kill their brothers, and mothers would strive to kill their fertile daughters; and no one would think of interfering" ((1879) 2004: 122). Yet at the same time he remains apparently confident in his own Victorian moral opinions, happily referring to the "low morality of savages," calling slavery "a great crime," and freely using words like "noble," "evil," and "barbarous." It remains obscure why Darwin thinks that the human moral sense, when shaped by the particular cultural trajectory of the British Empire, results in moral opinions that are *true* or *justified*—even if he is correct that these are the moral opinions that humans living in large groups will eventually alight upon. His comment that moral rules relating to the welfare of others "are supported by the approbation of our fellow-men *and by reason*" (ibid.: 147) is left tantalizingly undeveloped. Does it mean that the imaginary bee-creatures' fratricide would be *irrational*?[9]

Some of Darwin's contemporaries saw the threat to morality posed by his genealogy. Frances Cobbe condemned his views on the evolution of the moral sense as "the most dangerous [doctrines] which have ever been set forth since the days of Mandeville" (1872: 11). A Darwinian explanation of conscience, she thought, "aims a . . . deadly blow at ethics, by affirming that, not only has our moral sense come to us from a source commanding no special respect, but that it answers to no external or durable, not to say universal or eternal, reality, and is merely tentative and provisional, the provincial prejudice, as we may describe it, of this little world and its temporary inhabitants, which would be looked upon with a smile of derision by better-informed people now residing on Mars" (ibid.: 10–11). But most who have similarly suspected Darwin's views on the evolution of morality of having a pernicious effect have run the logic in the wrong direction: Because of some dimly supposed danger, they are motivated to resist and reject Darwinian theorizing. This, I hardly need say, is a thoroughly objectionable attitude. In the present instance, in any case, I have argued that the fear of substantial disruption to the way we conduct our lives is unwarranted. But even if this is not so, the only honest and dignified course is to acknowledge what the evidence and our best theorizing indicate and deal with the practical consequences. (Even Cobbe admitted that if science can really establish Darwin's "dangerous doctrines" then "their consequences must be frankly faced" (ibid.: 11).) If uncomfortable truths are out there, we should seek them and face them like intellectual adults, rather than eschewing open-minded inquiry or fabricating philosophical theories whose only virtue is the promise of providing the soothing news that all our heartfelt beliefs are true.

Notes

Introduction

1. This stipulation is not intended as an analysis or a general explication of the concept *innateness*. I have no objection to the term's being used in a different manner in other discourses.

2. And to some degree sociobiologists have only themselves to blame. Philip Kitcher once wrote: "Sociobiology has two faces. One looks towards the social behavior of nonhuman animals. The eyes are carefully focused, the lips pursed judiciously. Utterances are made only with caution. The other face is almost hidden behind a megaphone. With great excitement, pronouncements about human nature blare forth" (1985: 435).

3. Evolutionary psychologists are sometimes reproached for making glib reference to "*the* ancestral environment," as if the Pleistocene world was uniform and evolutionarily privileged. Certainly in many ways this environment was not uniform: Some of our ancestors lived in areas rich in resources, others in dry and meager places; for some predators were a major problem, for others they probably were not; and so on. But these critics seem unbothered by such environmental variation when it comes to considering the evolution of anatomical traits, such as the opposable thumb or the lowered larynx. Such traits are spoken of unproblematically as being adaptive *relative to "the" ancestral environment* (for of course nothing is adaptive simpliciter): an environment that varied in many ways but also exhibited enough broad continuity that an opposable thumb (say) was, on average, adaptive across the board. The evolutionary psychologist merely makes the same assertion regarding psychological mechanisms. As for the Pleistocene being "privileged": Because it covers the most recent period of human lineage of sufficient length for significant biological natural selection to have occurred therein, it is appropriate that special attention be paid to it if we are seeking to understand *us now*. No doubt humans have adaptations originating in the Pliocene, in the Miocene, and far beyond, but nevertheless all our adaptations, even the truly ancient ones, had to earn their keep in the Pleistocene.

4. I am not claiming that either condition is "innate" as I have stipulated the term will be used. Both are, however, genetically "programmed" in some central sense of the phrase.

5. Here is a simple real-life example of an innate conditional strategy: Some caterpillars will produce either a brown pupa or a green pupa, depending on the color of the surface to which they are attached. (See Starnecker and Hazel 1999.) Such caterpillars are responsive to their environment but are genetically programmed to respond in certain discontinuous ways to certain variables. One might say that their genome has indirectly encoded a conditional: "If encountering X, then do ϕ; if encountering Y, then do ψ." A population of such caterpillars unexpectedly thrown into an environment with no green things would produce no green pupae, yet turning green would still be part of "caterpillar nature" in a way that turning purple or lemon yellow would not be.

6. For more sober voices of caution, see Kitcher 1985; Dennett 1995; Sterelny and Griffiths 1999; Sterelny and Fitness 2003.

Chapter 1

1. To pinch a nice phrase from Jonathan Dancy.

2. As I have defined it, helpfulness may occur in an entirely accidental manner (as, indeed, can fitness-sacrificing behavior), though I am mindful of some difficulties raised by Jack Wilson (2002) concerning this feature.

3. Pedantic point: Since *reproductive fitness* is a relative concept, it might be reasonably claimed that one could still harm such a creature's fitness by providing aid to its competitors. The creature in question would still have zero reproductive capacity whether squashed or not, but I suppose it must be conceded that zero could be worse or better relative to the reproductive capacity of its rivals.

4. This ambiguity mirrors one exhibited by the term "because." We can say that Fred cares for his wife *because he loves her*—where this "because" refers to his motivations, the considerations that figure in his deliberations—or we can say that Fred loves his wife *because doing so advances the replication of his genes*—where this "because" refers to a causal-historical explanation. These are just two of several quite distinct uses of the word "because," which mustn't be confused.

5. It would make tedious reading, so I leave it to the reader to think up concrete examples.

6. "Even if they [prehistoric inventors, i.e., helpful characters] left no children, the tribe would still include their blood relations" (Darwin (1879) 2004: 154).

7. In expressing things in this manner I am following a widespread but misleading convention. In actuality siblings share more than 99% of their genes, and the genes

shared by *any* two conspecifics is not much short of this percentage. The "50%" relation between siblings (and the "25%" between cousins, etc.) refers to the proportion of genes that are *assuredly* the same because they have descended from the same source; alternatively, one can see it as the likelihood that they share a randomly chosen allele.

8. I am simplifying considerably; the full Hymenoptera genetic story is very complex.

9. A proper treatment of kin selection must take into account not only the degree of relatedness but also the "reproductive value" of the recipient of the help. An individual may be related equally to a grandparent and a grandchild (assuming generations have the necessary longevity), but will enhance fitness far more effectively by helping the grandchild than the grandparent. See Hughes 1988.

10. Some people would prefer to restrict "mutualism" to a relationship between members of different species, with "cooperation" as the term for much the same cost-benefit relationship between members of the same species. This preference seems to be going out of fashion, and is not respected here.

11. One thing that this example appears to show is that "reciprocal altruism" does not require any time lag between the help given and the help received. The very act of removing a parasite is both payment to the host fish and payment to the cleaner. Curiously, however, a few paragraphs before presenting this very example Trivers claims that reciprocal altruism is like symbiosis with "a time lag" and that the "time lag is a crucial factor" (1971: 39). For further discussion on the difficulties of defining "reciprocal altruism" with precision, see various papers in *Ethology and Sociobiology* 9 (1988).

12. By "symmetrical" I mean that it is true of each party that the benefit she is receiving exceeds the cost incurred. But it is in principle possible that, all told, one of the interactants is getting vastly more benefit than the other. Suppose B gives A 4 units of help, and it costs him 100 units to do so. Sounds like a rotten deal? Not if we also suppose that A in return gives B 150 units of help, and it costs her only 3 units to do so. Despite the apparent unevenness of the exchange, since 4 > 3 and 150 > 100, both players are up on the deal, and, ceteris paribus, they should continue with the arrangement. The common assumption—that what is vital to reciprocal exchanges is that one can give a benefit for relatively little cost—need not be true of *both* interactants. With the values just given, it is not true of B. But when it is not true of one of the interactants, then in order to compensate it must be "very true" of the other: Here A gives 150 units for the cost of only 3.

13. In some scenarios there may not be much difference in refusing help and punishing, despite one sounding more "active" than the other. If a group of, say, baboons were to terminate all interactions with one of their troop, this would penalize the ostracized individual as much as if they killed the individual outright. This is one

reason why I am troubled by Chandra Sripada's efforts to place reciprocity-based and punishment-based accounts of moral compliance *in opposition* to each other (2005). Punishment will often be a natural concomitant of reciprocity—as even Trivers noted in his 1971 paper. It should also be noted that "refusing to play" can be as costly as administering punishment. If lions were to refuse to share with a free-riding lioness, then they would have to drive her off when she barged in to share their kill, perhaps risking injury to do so. (As a matter of fact, it turns out that lions are rather tolerant of free-riders; their helping behaviors seem regulated by mutualism rather than reciprocation. See Heinsohn and Packer 1995.)

14. One might think this is quibbling over labels. But I have observed so very much confusion flowing from these kind of stipulative and semi-metaphorical uses of the words "altruistic" and "selfish" that I judge nitpicking to be warranted on this occasion.

15. Strictly, the second criterion is needed only for *iterated* games. If 2R were less than T + S, then in an iterated game two players would each do better by alternating between T and S than by jointly cooperating.

16. PAVLOV does poorly against ALL D players, constantly flipping between cooperation and defection, receiving P and S on alternate turns (while the ALL D opponent is reaping alternate Ps and Ts). Nevertheless, PAVLOV may still be able to take off in an ALL D environment so long as it finds enough other PAVLOV players to interact with. Against another PAVLOV player, PAVLOV receives nothing but Rs (discounting noise), whereas the ALL D players, facing each other, receive nothing but Ps (ditto). Thus a PAVLOV player who faces two opponents—a PAVLOV player and an ALL D player—will do better overall than an ALL D player who faces the same two opponents, *if and only if P + S + 2R > T + 3P*. But we cannot say whether this will happen, since the criteria for a PD matrix are compatible with both P + S + 2R > T + 3P and P + S + 2R < T + 3P. Nowak and Sigmund prefer to rely on the possibility of a TFT-like strategy first "clearing out" ALL D, performing a king-maker role for PAVLOV.

17. I say "*largely* solved" since Darwin did not present an explanation of why it is the *female* who gets to be the choosy one. The answer is that in many species females must invest a lot of energy in their offspring, whereas males can hope to get away with investing very little. This answer was, I believe, first appreciated by the early geneticist Ronald Fisher ((1930) 1999).

18. I categorize sexual selection under the more general heading of "natural selection," while others prefer not to do this. It's merely a terminological matter.

19. If anyone objects to this taxonomy—insisting that the sexual selection of helpfulness not be categorized as indirect reciprocity—it makes no difference to anything substantive that is claimed in this book.

20. Suppose that 12 individuals, ranked from 1 to 12 in helpfulness, need to pair off. Everyone wants to pair with individual 1 except 1 himself, whose first choice is 2. So

(barring any interference) individuals 1 and 2 will pair off. Individual 3's first choice was 1 and second choice was 2—both of whom are now unavailable—so 3's next choice is 4. Individual 4's top choices were also 1 and 2, but failing them he will settle for 3. So 3 and 4 pair off. And so on: $\langle 5,6 \rangle$, $\langle 7,8 \rangle$, $\langle 9,10 \rangle$, $\langle 11,12 \rangle$. (Needless to say, everything changes if individual 12 has a big stick.)

21. Since this leaves open the issue of whether cultural items satisfy the criteria for being considered replicators, it is not to be confused with "meme theory." See Boyd and Richerson 2000.

22. One might be concerned about whether the influence of culture has been around long enough to have significantly affected the human genome. But bear in mind that in the case in question—human helpfulness—what is under discussion is not the emergence of a whole new organ, but rather the "tweaking" of extant traits, put in place through such processes as kin selection and reciprocity.

Chapter 2

1. Clearly, when one does something because one judges one ought to, one still *wants* to perform that action; one's sense of obligation affects one's desires.

2. "Among other things" indicates that although one cannot apologize without expressing regret, one can admit to having regret without thereby apologizing; an apology also requires an admission of responsibility, for example. See Kort 1975; Joyce 1999.

3. Subsequent arguments would not be affected if I instead were to write "but I do not mean to imply that I have M" or "but in saying this I don't mean to express M."

4. This has been maintained by C. L. Stevenson, R. M. Hare, and P. H. Nowell-Smith, among others.

5. It might be objected to this argument that Roger's distress *is* a practical consideration to the fox-hunters irrespective of whether they care. (For a subtle attempt to make such an argument work, see Nagel 1978.) But even allowing this for the sake of argument, it remains undeniable that when Roger offers the moral judgment "Your actions are morally wrong!" the *kind* of practical authority that this claim purports to carry is of a quite different sort than "Your actions cause me pain!" If Roger were to try to support his moral judgment in sober debate, he would not set out to prove the presence of his hurt feelings. If there is any harm to be mentioned as evidence, it is most likely that suffered by the fox.

6. Strictly speaking, an imperative must have imperatival grammar: "Shut the window," "Don't kill," etc. But it does no harm if we follow the customary softening on this point, and allow that "You ought to shut the window" and "You ought not kill people" count (respectively) as hypothetical and categorical "imperatives," despite their indicative grammar.

7. To inescapability and authority Brink adds a third: practical *supremacy*. Prescriptions have supremacy if and only if they will always override other types of prescription. At first glance (without getting embroiled in the intricacies of Kant's text) it seems none of these three normative attributes entails any of the others. Supremacy plays no role in my arguments here. I might also mention that in other publications I have not followed Brink's terminology, but have used the words "moral authority" and "moral inescapability" in a much broader and more intuitive sense.

8. For example, it might be thought that the prohibition against eating beef is a self-regarding moral rule amongst Hindus. This assumption is undermined, however, by the observation that Hindus believe the cow to be a sacred animal whose welfare must be respected.

9. This example and the experiment that supports it are from Haidt et al. 1993.

Chapter 3

1. In this book, with apologies to those who would insist on more precision, I use the term "chimpanzee" to refer to both common chimpanzees (*Pan troglodytes*) and bonobos (*Pan paniscus*). As far as I can see, my claims are sufficiently broad that the distinction need not be drawn.

2. The ancient Greeks were fond of discussing "heap" puzzles, where you get a dupe to assent to "One grain of sand is not a heap of sand" and "If you have some sand that's not a heap, you cannot make it into a heap by adding one more grain," and then point out to her that these entail something that she doesn't believe: that a billion grains of sand do not make a heap.

3. In the same passage he writes: "When I say to my terrier, in an eager voice (and I have made the trial many times), 'Hi, hi, where is it?' she at once takes it as a sign that something is to be hunted, and generally looks quickly all around, and then rushes to the nearest thicket, to scent for any game, but finding nothing, she looks up into any neighboring tree for a squirrel. Now do not these actions clearly shew that she had in her mind a general idea or concept that some animal is to be discovered and hunted?"

4. What is thought to be distinctive about thick terms is that they have both a descriptive and an evaluative element, and in this they are supposed to contrast with so-called thin terms like "good" and "wrong." I myself am skeptical of the whole thick/thin distinction as it is usually drawn—since I hold that "good" and "wrong" (etc.) also have a descriptive element (though I grant they may have a much broader domain of application). In any case, I introduce the terminology only for the sake of those readers who are familiar with it. Nothing in my argument depends on the thick/thin distinction being robust or important.

5. In fact, to complicate things, Enid had earlier said of Seymour "He's such a clueless dork, he's almost cool." I must confess to having had the questions "Is *dork* a concept? Is dorkishness a property?" scrawled in my notebook for a few weeks after seeing this movie.

6. It may be complained that I am running together the question of what it takes to have the concept *X*, and what it takes to be ascribed intentional states (e.g., beliefs) whose content can be legitimately described using the term "X." But in this context I am perfectly willing to run these together, emboldened, perhaps, by the disarray of the present philosophical literature regarding concept possession. It is, in any case, difficult to imagine on what grounds one might concede that animals lack the concept *moral wrongness* while nevertheless allowing that they have beliefs of the form "X is morally wrong" or, more generally, that they make moral judgments about moral wrongness.

7. My citing of Daniel Dennett as an instrumentalist reflects the fact that he is widely interpreted this way, and on very many occasions he has sounded very much like one. I am, however, mindful of the fact that he has eschewed the label and has adopted a rather more nuanced position. Therefore not everything that I claim here about "the instrumentalist" should be unquestioningly associated with Dennett.

8. For the sake of simplicity I make the background assumption that the first language was vocal, but in fact there is a plausible alternative hypothesis that the first language consisted of gestures, with speech gaining autonomy from gesture (in so far as it has) much later (Corballis 1999). Even under this alternative hypothesis the argument of section 3.2 still holds, bearing in mind that well-known gestures may by convention "express attitudes" as clearly as vocalized words.

9. The general hypothesis was presented speculatively by the pioneer of ethology Desmond Morris in his bestseller *The Naked Ape* (1967)—a book so controversial that the issue of whether school children should have access to it was debated before the U.S. Supreme Court.

10. I owe this reference Donald Brown (2000).

11. At present there is much better evidence that the capacity to recognize the expression of different emotions in others can be selectively impaired. See Gray et al. 1997; Sprengelmeyer et al. 1999.

12. The latter hypothesis gains support over the former when one considers that in fictional encounters people enjoy and seek out emotions that they otherwise generally avoid (fear, sadness, etc.). The evolutionary hypothesis holds that the capacity to engage with fiction and make-believe is a kind of "safe training" for real-life risks and opportunities. Natural selection has made the accompanying emotions enjoyable in order to motivate the activity (for the same reason as it makes eating and sex enjoyable). See Steen and Owen 2001.

Chapter 4

1. One might wonder why I don't just call it a "*sincere* speech act." But sincerity is a somewhat more complex notion, as I have discussed elsewhere (Joyce, forthcoming a).

2. For a sensitive philosophical discussion of how "must" and "ought" can affect practical deliberation, see Williams 1981.

3. "I really don't like X" can be *an element of* a justification: "I really don't like X, and in these circumstances it is acceptable for my actions to be guided by my strong preferences." Clearly, though, the latter part of the justification introduces a normative principle. Often the latter part will be tacit: "I like coffee" can seem like a perfectly good justification alone for drinking coffee, but that there is an unspoken premise here (to the effect that one is in circumstances where preferences may legitimately guide action) is obvious if we compare "I like torturing children."

4. "Man as a hunter, forager, or toolmaker can hardly be too clever and versatile; he will always benefit from more foresight and a greater arsenal of selfish schemes. But man as a social companion can be too astute even in his own interest" (Kummer 1978: 43).

5. In this Frank builds on Darwin's arguments in *The Expression of the Emotions in Man and Animals* (1872).

6. I add this parenthetical comment in order to bring under the same heading the personal commitments that were discussed in section 4.2. Psychologists emphasize personal commitments, whereas game theorists emphasize how a commitment may affect others' choices. (See Nesse 2001: 14–15.) For our purposes these notions are profitably brought together.

7. Damasio remarks: "We can infer at least that he lacked the feeling of embarrassment, given his use of foul language and his parading of self-misery" (1994: 51). The last remark refers to Gage's willing appearance in a touring "freak show."

8. In the ultimatum game there are two players, A and B. A is given a fixed amount of money and must make an offer to B regarding how the money shall be divided between them. If B accepts the offer, the money is distributed as A proposed, and that's the end of things; if B rejects the offer, then neither of them get anything. One might expect that B should accept any non-zero amount offered, and that A, predicting this, will offer B the minimal non-zero amount. But interestingly this is not what happens when humans play the game (Güth and Tietz 1990; Roth 1995). If A's offer drops too far below what is perceived as a "fair" division, then a tendency appears for B to reject it. A-players, seemingly knowing this, tend to offer B-players a substantial amount. Though different societies apparently have different standards of "fairness" in this game, the traits of *not* offering and of not accepting the minimal non-zero amount are robustly cross-cultural (Henrich et al. 2001).

9. For further discussion of these non-implications, see Joyce forthcoming b.

10. It must be added that he goes on to say the following: "Of course, we lack evidence to advance this hypothesis with beaming confidence" (Nichols 2004: 176).

11. Haidt's use of brackets is intended to indicate "target words." In this experiment, some subjects got the vignette containing "tries to take"; others got it with "often picks."

12. What I am calling "paradigmatic moral judgments" here are not the same as what I called "canonical moral judgments" in section 4.2. There I claimed that public moral judgments typically *express* a conative state, and now I have also claimed that certain moral judgments involve the *projection of* a conative state. But these two respective conative states are distinct. The former is something like *subscription to a normative framework*; the latter is an emotion such as anger or disgust. I have not claimed that public moral judgments *function to express* the emotions that are being projected; on the contrary, speakers and audience alike are generally unaware that their moral judgments are products of anger or disgust, though they are perfectly aware that in publicly morally praising something they are endorsing a certain normative outlook.

13. Male white-crowned sparrows need to hear the typical "white-crowned sparrow song" if they are ever to sing it: Individuals raised in audial isolation never sing the normal song, whereas those played the song, even briefly when a mere hatchling, will when mature sing the typical full, complex sparrow song. The interesting result is that a hatchling that is played *two* different songs—one from a white-crowned adult male and one from some other songbird—will sing only the former. The young sparrow needs environmental stimuli in order to learn to sing, but its neural mechanisms are seeking and are sensitive to a particular kind of input, a particular kind of song. See Marler and Tamura 1964; Marler 1991.

14. Sugiyama and his colleagues take their results to support a more specific hypothesis: that there is a discrete "cheater-detection subroutine" in the human mind. They may be correct (and indeed this may be the right interpretation of the data collected by Cummins and by Harris and Núñez, too), but here I am highlighting the more general and less controversial result: that there is a human-typical dissociation in processing skills of indicative and deontic conditionals. One problem with the "cheater-detection" explanation of this phenomenon is that one can observe the dissociation effect using an abstract deontic conditional that involves no cheating, such as "If one is to take action A, one must first satisfy precondition P" (Cheng and Holyoak 1989). Still, it appears that subjects perform better with an "adaptive" deontic conditional than with an abstract one (Fiddick 2003).

15. Other empirical results cast doubt on deontic reasoning being a unitary phenomenon. See Cosmides and Tooby 1997; Fiddick 2003, 2004; Nucci 2001; Smetana 1993.

16. Rousseau is far from oblivious of this problem, admitting a couple of sentences later that "the idea of property depends on many prior ideas, which could only be acquired successively, and cannot have been formed all at once in the human mind." Indeed, a major goal of his essay is to explain how this gradual emergence of the idea of property came about. Unfortunately, his speculative explanation—though a valiant effort by eighteenth-century standards—casts little light on the matter.

17. Even the speculations I offered in section 4.2 about how moralized thinking bolsters motivation in the social realm did not imply that reciprocity must be the explanatory process. Although at one point I mentioned how moralized thinking might enable a person to engage more effectively in reciprocal relationships, this was just one illustration of moralized thinking reinforcing helping behavior. It was not my intention to suggest that whenever helping involves the foregoing of a short-term gain for greater future dividends it must always satisfy the cost-benefit structure of a reciprocal relationship. These greater future dividends, for example, may not be benefits given by another individual, or group of individuals, at all, but may instead accrue as the consequence of some collective group effort (i.e., mutualism may be the explanatory process).

18. This perhaps should be put down to a sloppy choice of wording, for elsewhere in *Descent* Darwin argues staunchly against psychological egoism.

Chapter 5

1. In his 1994 paper (and in chapter 11 of his 1985 book) Kitcher expressed skepticism that descriptive evolutionary ethics could have any metaethical implications. He has since revised this view. (See Kitcher 1998, 2005.) His position is discussed further at the end of the present chapter.

2. What Dennett says is literally true: Deriving an "ought" from an "is" *is often called* "the naturalistic fallacy." But he goes on to accept this terminology himself, and in doing so he promulgates a widespread misreading of Moore.

3. Parenthetical page references here are to this book.

4. I confess to having given up trying to make sense of on what principle Moore applies or withholds quotation marks. Here I merely quote his punctuation. I also cannot forgo pointing out the perversity of Moore's example—oranges are orange, not yellow!

5. Recall my misgivings about "defining good."

6. See Place 1956 and Smart 1959. In a later work, Smart quite correctly describes Moore's philosophy of language as "hopelessly confused" (1984: 22). In the posthumously published revised edition of *Principia Ethica*, Moore admits that in 1903 he had been confused about certain matters pertaining directly to the naturalistic fallacy and OQA. Serious back-pedaling is apparent—see Casebeer 2003: 21.

7. I am assuming here that ". . . ought not . . ." is a two-place predicate. Never mind if it is more than two—the example can be changed to fit. (For arguments that ". . . morally ought . . ." is, despite appearances, a four-place predicate, see Harman 1975.)

8. Perhaps there are non-Tarskian accounts of validity according to which the argument *may* count as valid, on the grounds that the premise needed to make it obviously valid—"Water is H$_2$O"—is a necessary truth, and thus there is no possible world at which P1 and P2 are true and the conclusion false. It would accomplish little here to attempt to argue for one version of validity over another. The main point is that deduction is not the issue for the moral naturalist.

9. There is some evidence that religious belief might be an adaptation (Boyer 2001; D. S. Wilson 2002).

10. In fact, it is doubtful that Campbell's non-cognitivism is stable even in the terms in which he describes it, for he places *guilt* at the heart of morality, seemingly willing to treat it as simply a non-cognitive feeling. But we know that this is incorrect; guilt involves considerable cognitive sophistication. (See sections 3.6 and 3.7.)

11. Williams 1985: 101.

12. In other words, for Aristotle the adjective "good" should always be used attributively rather than predicatively. Plato disagreed, holding that sometimes when we call something "good" we mean *good, period*, not *is a good so-and-so*. The difference between attributive and predicative adjectives can be brought out as follows. The adjective "square" is predicative because when we say that X is a square book we mean that X is a book *and* that X is square; thus, if X is also something else (say, a possession of mine) we can conclude that it is a square possession of mine. Not so with attributive adjectives, such as "big." If Y is a big mouse, we cannot break this down to "Y is big" and "Y is a mouse," for if Y is also something else (say, a pet of mine) it does not follow that it is a big pet of mine; it may be my smallest pet.

13. The kithara is an ancient Greek instrument of the lyre family. Its name is probably an etymological ancestor of "guitar." A kitharode is a kithara player.

14. The quotations here are from Aristotle, *Nicomachean Ethics* I.7 (1992: 13–14).

15. According to Empedocles, first of all limbs and organs were produced spontaneously in the earth. These then ambled around independently for a while ("eyes wandered alone, begging for foreheads"—Simplicius, *Commentary on the Heavens* 586.6), eventually coming together randomly to form all manner of weird hybrids. (Ox-faced men and man-faced oxen are singled out for mention.) "Wherever then all the parts came about just what they would have been if they had come be for an end, such things survived, being organized spontaneously in a fitting way; whereas those which grew otherwise perished and continue to perish" (Aristotle, *Physics* II.8 (1941: 249)). Disappointingly, Empedocles has no mechanism for ongoing cumulative evolution.

16. That Casebeer thinks that self-harm is the basis of moral evaluation seems clear when he provides his grounds for criticizing someone who ignores the plight of others who are suffering: ". . . human beings who are insensitive to the needs of those around them will be dysfunctional in myriad respects: they will not enter into productive social relationships that sustain the acquisition of base-level needs, and they will not partake of a rich and varied diet of social interactions" (63–64).

17. This is the substance of the counterargument I would give to Kitcher's attempt to provide an evolutionary vindication of morality at the end of his "Biology and ethics" (2005). The point is discussed further in section 6.4 below. Here I have run the argument as concerning competing imperatives ("ought" claims), but it would be just as effective if couched in terms of clashing values. I should also add that the background assumption of the argument is not that it is a criterion of adequacy for any moral theory that moral norms must turn out to be overriding (this is something on which I don't state an opinion in this book); the argument can rest on a vaguer but much less contentious platitude: that moral norms must not be able to be overridden *easily*.

18. See Joyce 2000b, 2001a, 2001b, 2003, 2004.

Chapter 6

1. The case is, nevertheless, sufficient to refute the principle that one often hears touted as "the genetic fallacy": that knowing the origin of a belief can never show the belief to be false.

2. It has been pointed out to me that this fanciful example may not even be a conceptual possibility. How could a pill (one might ask) result in a belief that is *about* Napoleon? It depends on what one thinks determines belief content. I admit the possibility of incoherence, but I suggest that on occasion even impossible thought experiments may serve a useful pedagogic or intuition-priming role.

3. The claim that you lose all *positive* Napoleon beliefs indicates that you remain able to form such beliefs as "I used to believe that Napoleon lost Waterloo" and "I wonder whether this guy Napoleon really existed"—beliefs that do not imply or presuppose the existence of Napoleon.

4. Two slightly pedantic clarifications: First, there is a distinction between the view that knowledge of the genealogy can *render* our beliefs unjustified (i.e., our beliefs were justified prior to gaining this knowledge), as opposed to the view that this knowledge reveals that the beliefs were unjustified all along. Which to prefer depends on one's epistemological theory. For the reliabilist (who will be discussed later in the chapter) it is the latter; for various kinds of internalist epistemological theory it is the former. Since I am not taking sides, my conclusion is ambiguous in this way, but I tend to express things in the former way. Second, there is a distinction between a person being justified in holding a belief and that belief being justified in some more

general sense (or, perhaps better, the proposition that is the object of that belief being justified). In some contexts this distinction matters, though I am inclined to think that here it doesn't. For the record, I intend throughout to be referring to the former phenomenon, though I see nothing wrong with paraphrasing this with an expression like "X's belief that *p* is unjustified"; and if *everyone* is in the same boat as X, it seems reasonable just to say "The belief that *p* is unjustified."

5. Some philosophers doubt that mathematical propositions are true, and there is, of course, a juicy philosophical question about how they possibly could be true (i.e., what kind of facts obtain that make them true). But the dialectic within which I am working here assumes that if an argument that moral beliefs are unjustified or false would by the same logic show that believing that $1 + 1 = 2$ is unjustified or false, this would count as a reductio ad absurdum.

6. In his 1986 paper, Harman downgrades the example to someone hitting a cat with a stick.

7. Karen Bennett (forthcoming), when discussing the place of *mental* properties in the natural world, usefully distinguishes between physical properties narrowly construed and broadly construed. The narrowly construed are the kind invoked in the laws and generalizations of the natural sciences (e.g., *being an electron*); the broadly construed are formed from narrowly natural ones in a manner that can be clearly articulated (e.g., *being the fourth step I take on the way to the kitchen*). A non-reductive naturalist denies that moral properties (or mental properties, in Bennett's case) are identical to natural properties *narrowly* construed, but does not deny that they are identical to physical properties *broadly* construed. Either kind of identity, I take it, would suffice to defeat Harman's challenge, and thus on this occasion (but certainly not on every other occasion) it seems acceptable to lump them together as "ontological reductions."

8. This section and the next draw on chapters 2–5 of Joyce 2001a.

9. Here I quote John Mackie (1977: 35) on the status of "objective prescriptivity."

10. Harman (1986: 65) also looks favorably upon "impartial spectator" theories. I cannot see that such theories have much hope of guaranteeing the practical authority of the moral, and in this respect they are less promising than practical reasoning theories. Why do the opinions of an impartial spectator provide me with reasons, any more than do the opinions of a drunken spectator or a zealously patriotic one? Although there are certainly attempts to answer this question out there, I think it is fair to say that none but the antecedently sympathetic have been persuaded. Some such attempts fall under the heading of "self-conceptions strategies," which are criticized below.

11. Yet more precisely: We are after an account of what a correctly reasoning version of a person would advise the actual (possibly incorrectly reasoning) person to do. See Smith 1994.

12. Copp associates these views with Immanuel Kant, Christine Korsgaard, Thomas Nagel, and Stephen Darwall, respectively.

13. For a more detailed criticism of Korsgaard's views, see pp. 123–133 of Joyce 2001a.

14. Bob Dylan, "Highway 61 Revisited."

15. The naturalist will have to say the same about the argument I offered in section 4.3, because a non-authoritative morality is not going to serve so effectively as an interpersonal commitment device. Who is going to be chosen as a partner in cooperative ventures: (A) a person who wants to cooperate because of the prudential benefits doing so will bring him, (B) a person who (in addition to having prudential reasons in favor of cooperation) wants to cooperate because he thinks cooperation is morally required, but is also aware that modifying his desires will cause his reason to be moral to evaporate or (C) a person who (in addition to having prudential reasons in favor of cooperation) wants to cooperate because he thinks cooperation is morally required, and thinks that he will retain good reason to be moral regardless of how his desires may change? I think it is pretty clear that C wins this competition. Thus, if being chosen for such ventures is adaptive, then, ceteris paribus, C-type individuals will have a higher fitness than the others. This suggests that if it is true that natural selection favored moral judgment as an interpersonal commitment device, it would have preferred the trait of supposing moral prescriptions to be authoritative (in some firm but perhaps inchoate way), and not subject to the usual standards of deliberative reasoning. This is not necessarily to say that people *do* always have reason to act as morality prescribes, but it is to suggest that they are disposed to think that they do. This in itself speaks against the likelihood that moral naturalism without clout is an adequate satisfier of our moral platitudes.

16. One might be tempted to think that this redundancy problem will haunt *any* version of moral naturalism, including the kind that attempts to accommodate practical clout. If this is correct, it's no skin off my nose. But the problem actually seems less acute for the naturalist attempting to accommodate clout, for he is not committed to the view that moral discourse could be replaced by a language simply of wants and needs. The natural properties with which he seeks to identify moral properties are (supposedly) ones with desire-transcendent practical authority—natural properties the reference to which could, one assumes, still play the desirable calculation-silencing, conversation-stopping role both personally and interpersonally.

17. On other occasions I have argued for the stronger position that we should actually *disbelieve* moral propositions (as opposed to remaining agnostic). I have not changed my mind; I am simply bracketing off those arguments here.

18. Carruthers is a reliabilist who thinks that justification is unnecessary for knowledge. Thus his argument is not, in fact, an attempt to show that innate beliefs are justified, but rather that they constitute knowledge. However, it is obvious that his

argument can be modified to the conclusion that innate beliefs are justified—which is what I am doing here.

19. This is not to be confused with the coherentist *method* of belief revision ("reflective equilibrium"), associated most prominently with the work of John Rawls.

20. ". . . if someone really thinks, *in advance*, that it is open to question whether such an action as procuring the judicial execution of the innocent should be quite excluded from consideration—I do not want to argue with him; he shows a corrupt mind" (Anscombe 1958: 16–17).

Conclusion

1. Were one to insist that agnosticism is the view that we lack knowledge of God's existence, this would create the possibilities of theistic agnosticism (believing in God but admitting not to know) and atheistic agnosticism (disbelieving in God but admitting not to know), thereby giving rise to the need for further labels (types of "gnosticism") for those who have these beliefs and also claim to know. Such a taxonomy would not necessarily be objectionable. My point is just that this is not how people usually conceive of the relation between these positions, and it is not how I am conceiving of it here.

2. Hallvard Lillehammer has argued that a moral error theory cannot be derived directly from a genealogy of morals, but he restricts his use of the term "error theory" to the atheistic version (Lillehammer 2003).

3. I am banking on the assumption that no great tennis players are likely to read this book.

4. Support for this hypothesis comes from consideration of the prototypical elicitors of disgust. Vegetable matter often contains toxins but is much less likely than meat to harbor pathogens or parasites. Since infected meat often does not have any giveaway odor or taste, consumers need to be hypersensitive to its qualities. Sure enough, evidence strongly suggests that disgust is far more likely to be elicited by animal products than by plant products (Fallon and Rozin 1983). Cross-cultural studies also reveal that the food product women are most likely to be disgusted by in the early stages of pregnancy is meat—a finding that dovetails with the fact that during pregnancy a woman's immune system is suppressed (so as to lower the chances of rejection of the "alien" form within her body), making her more susceptible to infection and disease. Natural selection's solution to the problem of individuals made vulnerable to infection by suppressed immunes systems appears to be a mechanism that temporarily lowers the disgust threshold while focusing its target (Fessler 2002).

5. A.k.a. "globophobia"—but this latter term seems to be in the process of shifting to mean *fear of globalization* (arguably a perfectly rational condition).

6. That philosopher is Colin Radford (1995). For arguments against Radford, see Joyce 2000a.

7. In his discussion of the evolution of the moral sense, Darwin saw fit to quote Marcus Aurelius: "Such as are thy habitual thoughts, such also will be the character of thy mind; for the soul is dyed by the thoughts" (*Meditations*, book V, quoted in Darwin (1879) 2004: 148).

8. A Pyrrhonian (named after Pyrrho of Elea) is a global skeptic who gives assent to nothing.

9. My hunch is that the kind of moral foundations espoused by Peter Singer would be looked upon very sympathetically by Darwin. Criticism of the adequacy of such a view is implicit in my chapter 6.

Bibliography

Adolphs, R., Tranel, D., and Damasio, A. R. 2003. "Dissociable neural systems for recognizing emotions." *Brain and Cognition* 52: 61–69.

Aiello, L. C., and Dunbar, R. I. M. 1993. "Neocortex size, group size, and the evolution of language." *Current Anthropology* 34: 184–193.

Aiello, L. C., and Wheeler, P. 1995. "The expensive-tissue hypothesis." *Current Anthropology* 36: 199–221.

Ainslie, G. 1992. *Picoeconomics: The Strategic Interaction of Successive Motivational States within the Person.* Cambridge University Press.

Alexander, R. 1987. *The Biology of Moral Systems.* Aldine de Gruyter.

Allen, C. 1999. "Animal concepts revisited: The use of self-monitoring as an empirical approach." *Erkenntnis* 51: 33–40.

Allen, C., and Hauser, M. 1991. "Concept attribution in non-human animals: Theoretical and methodological problems in ascribing complex mental processes." *Philosophy of Science* 58: 221–240.

Allen, C., Bekoff, M., and Lauder, G., eds. 1998. *Nature's Purposes: Analyses of Function and Design in Biology.* MIT Press.

Allman, J. 2000. *Evolving Brains.* Scientific American Library.

Anderson, S. R., Bechara, A., Damasio, H., Tranel, D., and Damasio, A. R. 1999. "Impairment of social and moral behavior related to early damage in human prefrontal cortex." *Nature Neuroscience* 2: 1032–1037.

Anscombe, G. E. M. 1958. "Modern moral philosophy." *Philosophy* 33: 1–19.

Aristotle. 1941. *The Basic Works of Aristotle.* Random House.

Aristotle. 1992. *Nicomachean Ethics.* Oxford University Press.

Augustine. c. 426. "The care to be taken for the dead." In *The Fathers of the Church,* volume 27. Catholic University of America, 1968.

Austin, J. L. 1971. "Performative-constative." In *The Philosophy of Language*, ed. J. Searle. Oxford University Press.

Austin, J. L. 1970. "Performative utterances." In *The Philosophy of Language*, ed. A. Martinich. Oxford University Press, 1990.

Axelrod, R. 1984. *The Evolution of Cooperation*. Basic Books.

Ayer, A. J. 1936. *Language, Truth and Logic*. Penguin, 1971.

Bandura, A. 1999. "Moral disengagement in the perpetration of inhumanities." *Personality and Social Psychology Review* 3: 193–209.

Bandura, A., Barbaranelli, C., Caprara, G. V., and Pastorelli, C. 1996. "Mechanisms of moral disengagement in the exercise of moral agency." *Journal of Personality and Social Psychology* 71: 364–374.

Bargh, J. A. 1992. "Does subliminality matter to social psychology? Awareness of the stimulus versus awareness of its influence." In *Perception without Awarenes*, ed. R. Bornstein and T. Pittman. Guilford.

Barkow, J. H. 1992. "Beneath new culture is old psychology: Gossip and social stratification." In *The Adapted Mind*, ed. J. Barkow et al. Oxford University Press.

Barrett, K. C. 1995. "A functionalist approach to shame and guilt." In *Self-Conscious Emotions*, ed. J. Tangney and K. Fischer. Guilford.

Barrett, L., Dunbar, R., and Lycett, J. 2002. *Human Evolutionary Psychology*. Palgrave.

Bateson, P. P. 1966. "The characteristics and context of imprinting." *Biological Reviews* 41: 177–220.

Bateson, P. 1991. "Are there principles of behavioural development?" In *The Development and Integration of Behaviour*, ed. P. Bateson. Cambridge University Press.

Batson, C. D. 1991. *The Altruism Question: Toward a Social-Psychological Answer*. Erlbaum.

Batson, C. D. 2001. "Unto Others: A service . . . and a disservice." In *Evolutionary Origins of Morality*, ed. L. Katz. Imprint Academic.

Baumeister, R. F., Stillwell, A. M., and Heatherton, T. F. 1994. "Guilt: An interpersonal approach." *Psychological Bulletin* 115: 243–267.

Beer, J. S., Heerey, E. A., Keltner, D., Scabini, D., and Knight R. T. 2003. "The regulatory function of self-conscious emotion: Insights from patients with orbitofrontal damage." *Journal of Personality and Social Psychology* 85: 594–604.

Benedict, R. 1946. *The Chrysanthemum and the Sword*. Houghton Mifflin.

Bennett, K. Forthcoming. "Exclusion again."

Bingham, P. M. 2000. "Human evolution and human history: A complete theory." *Evolutionary Anthropology* 9: 248–257.

Blackburn, S. 1981. "Reply: Rule-following and moral realism." In *Wittgenstein: To Follow a Rule*, ed. S. Holtzman and C. Leich. Routledge and Kegan Paul.

Blair, R. J. R. 1995. "A cognitive developmental approach to morality: Investigating the psychopath." *Cognition*: 57: 1–29.

Blair, R. J. R., Jones, L., Clark, F., and Smith, M. 1997. "The psychopathic individual: A lack of responsiveness to distress cues?" *Psychophysiology* 34: 192–198.

Boghossian, P. A., and Velleman, J. D. 1989. "Colour as a secondary quality." *Mind* 98: 81–103.

Boyd, R., and Richerson, P. J. 1985. *Culture and the Evolutionary Process*. University of Chicago Press.

Boyd, R., and Richerson, P. J. 1988. "The evolution of reciprocity in sizable groups." *Journal of Theoretical Biology* 132: 337–356.

Boyd, R., and Richerson, P. J. 1989. "The evolution of indirect reciprocity." *Social Networks* 11: 213–236.

Boyd, R., and Richerson, P. J. 1992. "Punishment allows the evolution of cooperation (or anything else) in sizable groups." *Ethology and Sociobiology* 13: 171–195.

Boyd, R., and Richerson, P. J. 2000. "Memes: Universal acid or a better mouse trap?" In *Darwinizing Culture*, ed. R. Aunger. Oxford University Press.

Boyer, P. 2001. *Religion Explained: The Evolutionary Origins of Religious Thought*. Basic Books.

Brink, D. 1989. *Moral Realism and the Foundations of Ethics*. Cambridge University Press.

Brink, D. 1997. "Kantian rationalism: Inescapability, authority, and supremacy." In *Ethics and Practical Reason*, ed. G. Cullity and B. Gaut. Oxford University Press.

Brown, D. E. 1991. *Human Universals*. Temple University Press.

Brown, D. E. 2000. "Human universals and their implications." In *Being Human: Anthropological Universality and Particularity in Transdisciplinary Perspectives*, ed. N. Roughley. Walter de Gruyter.

Bruening, W. H. 1971. "G. E. Moore and 'is-ought'." *Ethics* 81: 143–149.

Butterworth, B. 1999. *What Counts: How Every Brain Is Hardwired for Math*. Free Press.

Cacioppo, J. T., Priester, J. R., and Bernston, G. G. 1993. "Rudimentary determination of attitudes, II: Arm flexion and extension have differential effects on attitudes." *Journal of Personality and Social Psychology* 65: 5–17.

Calder, A. J., Keane, J., Manes, F., Antoun, N., and Young, A. W. 2000. "Impaired recognition and experience of disgust following brain injury." *Nature Neuroscience* 3: 1077–1078.

Campbell, R. 1996. "Can biology make ethics objective?" *Biology and Philosophy* 11: 21–31.

Carpenter, J., Matthews, P., and Ong'Ong'a, O. 2004. "Why punish? Social reciprocity and the enforcement of prosocial norms." *Journal of Evolutionary Economics* 14: 407–429.

Carroll, L. 1895. "What the Tortoise said to Achilles." *Mind* 4: 278–280.

Carruthers, P. 1992. *Human Knowledge and Human Nature*. Oxford University Press.

Casebeer, W. D. 2003. *Natural Ethical Facts: Evolution, Connectionism, and Moral Cognition*. MIT Press.

Chagnon, N. A., and Bugos, P. E., Jr. 1979. "Kin selection and conflict: An analysis of a Yanomamö ax fight." In *Evolutionary Biology and Human Social Behavior*, ed. N. Chagnon and W. Irons. Duxbury.

Cheney, D. L., and Seyfarth, R. M. 1990. "The representation of social relations by monkeys." *Cognition* 37: 167–196.

Cheng, P. W. and Holyoak, K. J. 1989. "On the natural selection of reasoning theories." *Cognition* 33: 285–313.

Cicero. 45 B.C. *On Moral Ends*. Cambridge University Press, 2001.

Cobbe, F. P. 1872. *Darwinism in Morals and Other Essays*. Williams and Norgate.

Conee, E., and Feldman, R. 1998. "The generality problem for reliabilism." *Philosophical Studies* 89: 1–29.

Connor, R. C. 1995. "Altruism among non-relatives: Alternatives to the Prisoner's Dilemma." *Trends in Ecology and Evolution* 10: 84–86.

Copp, D. 2001. "Realist-Expressivism: A neglected option for moral realism." *Social Philosophy and Policy* 18: 1–43.

Copp, D. 2004. "Moral naturalism and three grades of normativity." In *Normativity and Naturalism*, ed. P. Schaber. Ontos-Verlag.

Corballis, M. C. 1999. "The gestural origins of language." *American Scientist* 87: 138–145.

Cosmides, L., and Tooby, J. 1989. "Evolutionary psychology and the generation of culture, part II: Case study: A computational theory of social exchange." *Ethology and Sociobiology* 10: 51–97.

Cosmides, L., and Tooby, J. 1997. "Dissecting the computational architecture of social inference mechanisms." In *Characterizing Human Psychological Adaptations*, ed. G. Bock and G. Cardew. Wiley.

Covert, M. V., Tangney, J. P., Maddux, J. E., and Heleno, N. M. 2003. "Shame-proneness, guilt-proneness, and interpersonal problem solving: A social cognitive analysis." *Journal of Social and Clinical Psychology* 22: 1–12.

Cummins, D. D. 1996a. "Evidence of deontic reasoning in 3- and 4-year-old children." *Memory and Cognition* 24: 823–829.

Cummins, D. D. 1996b. "Evidence for the innateness of deontic reasoning." *Mind and Language* 11: 160–190.

Daly, M., and Wilson, M. I. 1988. *Homicide*. Aldine de Gruyter.

Damasio, A. R. 1994. *Descartes' Error: Emotion, Reason and the Human Brain*. Quill.

Damon, W. 1988. *The Moral Child*. Free Press.

Darwin, C. 1859. *The Origin of Species*. Modern Library, 1998.

Darwin, C. 1872. *The Expression of the Emotions in Man and Animals*. HarperCollins, 1999.

Darwin, C. 1879. *The Descent of Man, and Selection in Relation to Sex*. Penguin, 2004.

Darwin, F., ed. 1887. *The Life and Letters of Charles Darwin*, volume 2. John Murray.

Dasser, V. 1988. "A social concept in Java monkeys." *Animal Behaviour* 36: 225–230.

Dawkins, R. 1981. *The Selfish Gene*. Granada.

Dennett, D. C. 1987. *The Intentional Stance*. MIT Press.

Dennett, D. C. 1995. *Darwin's Dangerous Idea*. Simon and Schuster.

de Waal, F. B. M. 1992. "The chimpanzee's sense of social regularity and its relation to the human sense of justice." In *The Sense of Justice*, ed. R. Masters and M. Gruter. Sage.

de Waal, F. B. M. 1996. *Good Natured: The Origins of Right and Wrong in Primates and Other Animals*. Harvard University Press.

de Waal, F. B. M., and Luttrell, L. 1988. "Mechanisms of social reciprocity in three primate species: Symmetrical relationship characteristics or cognition." *Ethology and Sociobiology* 9: 101–118.

Dugatkin, L. A. 1999. *Cheating Monkeys and Citizen Bees*. Harvard University Press.

Dugatkin, L. A., and Reeve, H. K. 1994. "Behavioral ecology and levels of selection:—Dissolving the group selection controversy." *Advances in the Study of Behavior* 23: 101–133.

Dunbar, R. I. M. 1993. "Coevolution of neocortical size, group size and language in humans." *Behavioral and Brain Sciences* 16: 681–735.

Dunbar, R. I. M. 1996. *Grooming, Gossip, and the Evolution of Language.* Harvard University Press.

Durham, W. H. 1991. *Coevolution: Genes, Culture and Human Diversity.* Stanford University Press.

Dwyer, S. 1999. "Moral competence." In *Philosophy and Linguistics,* ed. K. Murasugi. Westview.

Ehrlich, P. R. 2000. *Human Natures: Genes, Cultures, and the Human Prospect.* Penguin.

Elster, J. 1984. *Ulysses and the Sirens.* Cambridge University Press.

Emde, R. N. 1980. "Levels of meaning for infant emotions: A biosocial view." In *Development of Cognition, Affect, and Social Relations,* ed. W. Collins. Erlbaum.

Emler, N. 1990. "A social psychology of reputations." *European Journal of Social Psychology* 1: 171–193.

Emler, N. 1992. "The truth about gossip." *Social Psychology Newsletter* 27: 23–37.

Enquist, M., and Leimar, O. 1993. "The evolution of cooperation in mobile organisms." *Animal Behaviour* 45: 747–757.

Essock-Vitale, S. M., and McGuire, M. T. 1980. "Predictions derived from the theories of kin selection and reciprocation assessed by anthropological data." *Ethology and Sociobiology* 1: 233–243.

Fallon, A. E., and Rozin, P. 1983. "The psychological bases of food rejections by humans." *Ecology of Food and Nutrition* 13: 15–26.

Fanaei, A. 2003. The Methods of Moral Inquiry: An Inquiry into the Problem of Justification in Moral Epistemology. Doctoral dissertation, University of Sheffield.

Fehr, E., and Fischbacher, U. 2004. "Third party punishment and social norms." *Evolution and Human Behavior* 25: 63–87.

Feldman, R. 1985. "Reliability and justification." *Monist* 68: 159–174.

Ferguson, T. J., Stegge, H., Miller, E. R., and Olsen, M. E. 1999. "Guilt, shame, and symptoms in children." *Developmental Psychology* 35: 347–357.

Fessler, D. M. T. 2002. "Reproductive immunosuppression and diet: An evolutionary perspective on pregnancy sickness and meat consumption." *Current Anthropology* 43: 19–39, 48–61.

Fessler, D. M. T., and Haley, K. J. 2003. "The strategy of affect: Emotions in human cooperation." In *The Genetic and Cultural Evolution of Cooperation,* ed. P. Hammerstein. MIT Press.

Fiddick, L. 2003. "Is there a faculty of deontic reasoning? A critical re-evaluation of abstract deontic versions of the Wason selection task." In *Evolution and the Psychology of Thinking*, ed. D. Over. Psychology Press.

Fiddick, L. 2004. "Domains of deontic reasoning: Resolving the discrepancy between the cognitive and moral reasoning literatures." *Quarterly Journal of Experimental Psychology* 57A: 447–474.

Finck, H. T. 1887. *Romantic Love and Personal Beauty*. Macmillan.

Fisher, R. A. 1930. *The Genetical Theory of Natural Selection*. Oxford University Press, 1999.

Fiske, A. P. 1991. *Structures of Social Life*. Free Press.

Flack, J. C., and de Waal, F. B. M. 2001. "'Any animal whatever': Darwinian building blocks of morality in monkeys and apes." In *Evolutionary Origins of Morality*, ed. L. Katz. Imprint Academic.

Fodor, J. A. 1975. *The Language of Thought*. Harvard University Press.

Fodor, J. A. 1994. *The Elm and the Expert: Mentalese and Its Semantics*. MIT Press.

Foot, P. 1958. "Moral arguments." *Mind* 67: 502–513. Reprinted in Foot, *Virtues and Vices* (Blackwell, 1978).

Foot, P. 1972. "Morality as a system of hypothetical imperatives." *Philosophical Review* 81: 305–316.

Frank, R. H. 1988. *Passions within Reason: The Strategic Role of the Emotions*. Norton.

Frankena, W. 1939. "The naturalistic fallacy." *Mind* 48: 464–477.

Frazer, J. G. 1890. *The Golden Bough: A Study in Magic and Religion*, abridged edition. MacMillan, 1925.

Frege, G. 1897. "Logic." In *The Frege Reader*, ed. M. Beaney. Blackwell, 1997.

Freud, S. 1929. *Civilization and Its Discontents*. Hogarth Press and Institute of Psycho-Analysis, 1975.

Garner, R. T. 1990. "On the genuine queerness of moral properties and facts." *Australasian Journal of Philosophy* 68: 137–146.

Garner, R. T. 1994. *Beyond Morality*. Temple University Press.

Ghiselin, M. T. 1974. *The Economy of Nature and the Evolution of Sex*. University of California Press.

Gibbard, A. 1990. *Wise Choices, Apt Feelings*. Harvard University Press.

Gimpl, G., and Fahrenholz, F. 2001. "The oxytocin receptor system: Structure, function, and regulation." *Physiological Reviews* 81: 629–683.

Godfrey-Smith, P. 1996. *Complexity and the Function of Mind in Nature.* Cambridge University Press.

Godfrey-Smith, P. 2004. "On folk psychology and mental representation." In *Representation in Mind: New Approaches to Mental Representation,* ed. H. Clapin et al. Elsevier.

Gould, S. J. 1977. "The nonscience of human nature." In Gould, *Ever Since Darwin.* Norton.

Gould, S. J. 1978. "Sociobiology: The art of storytelling." *New Scientist* 80: 530–533.

Gould, S. J., and Lewontin, R. C. 1979. "The spandrels of San Marco and the Panglossion paradigm: A critique of the adaptationist programme." *Proceedings of the Royal Society: Biological Sciences* 205: 581–598.

Gray, J. M., Young, A. W., Barker, W. A., Curtis, A., and Gibson, D. 1997. "Impaired recognition of disgust in Huntington's disease gene carriers." *Brain* 120: 2029–2038.

Green, O. H. 1992. *The Emotions: A Philosophical Theory.* Kluwer.

Greene, J. D. 2002. The Terrible, Horrible, No Good, Very Bad Truth about Morality and What to Do About It. Doctoral dissertation, Princeton University.

Greene, J. D., and Haidt, J. 2002. "How (and where) does moral judgment work?" *Trends in Cognitive Sciences* 6: 517–523.

Greene, J. D., Sommerville, R. B., Nystrom, L. E., Darley, J. M., and Cohen, J. D. 2001. "An fMRI investigation of emotional engagement in moral judgment." *Science* 293: 2105–2108.

Griffiths, P. E. 1997. *What Emotions Really Are: The Problem of Psychological Categories.* University of Chicago Press.

Griffiths, P. E. 2002. "What is innateness?" *Monist* 85: 70–85.

Grinde, B. 2002. *Darwinian Happiness: Evolution as a Guide for Living and Understanding Human Behavior.* Darwin Press.

Gruen, L. 2002. "The morals of animal minds." In *The Cognitive Animal,* ed. M. Bekoff et al. MIT Press.

Güth, W., and Tietz, R. 1990. "Ultimatum bargaining behavior: A survey and comparison of experimental results." *Journal of Economic Psychology* 11: 417–449.

Haidt, J. 2001. "The emotional dog and its rational tail: A social intuitionist approach to moral judgment." *Psychological Review* 108: 814–834.

Haidt, J. 2003a. "The moral emotions." In *Handbook of Affective Sciences,* ed. R. Davidson et al. Oxford University Press.

Haidt, J. 2003b. "The emotional dog does learn new tricks: A reply to Pizarro and Bloom (2003)." *Psychological Review* 110: 197–198.

Haidt, J., and Joseph, C. 2004. "Intuitive ethics: How innately prepared intuitions generate culturally variable virtues." *Daedalus* 133: 55–66.

Haidt, J., Koller, S. H., and Dias, M. G. 1993. "Affect, culture, and morality, or is it wrong to eat your dog?" *Journal of Personality and Social Psychology* 65: 613–628.

Hamilton, W. 1964. "The genetical evolution of social behavior" I and II. *Journal of Theoretical Biology* 7: 1–52.

Hare, R. M. 1952. *The Language of Morals*. Oxford University Press.

Hare, R. M. 1963. *Freedom and Reason*. Oxford University Press.

Harman, G. 1975. "Moral relativism defended." *Philosophical Review* 84: 3–22.

Harman, G. 1977. *The Nature of Morality: An Introduction to Ethics*. Oxford University Press.

Harman, G. 1985. "Is there a single true morality?" In *Morality, Reason and Truth*, ed. D. Copp and D. Zimmerman. Rowman and Allanheld.

Harman, G. 1986. "Moral explanations of natural facts: Can moral claims be tested against moral reality?" In *Spindel Conference: Moral Realism* (*Southern Journal of Philosophy* suppl. 24), ed. N. Gillespie.

Harnden-Warwick, D. 1997. "Psychological realism, morality, and chimpanzees." *Zygon* 32: 29–40.

Harris, P. L., and Núñez, M. 1996. "Understanding of permission rules by preschool children." *Child Development* 67: 1572–1591.

Hauser, M. 2000. *Wild Minds: What Animals Really Think*. Henry Holt.

Heinsohn, R. G., and Packer, C. 1995. "Complex cooperative strategies in group-territorial lions." *Science* 269: 1260–1262.

Hejmadi, A., Rozin, P., and Siegal, M. 2004. "Once in contact, always in contact: Contagious essence and conceptions of purification in American and Hindu Indian children." *Developmental Psychology* 40: 467–476.

Henrich, J., and Boyd, R. 1998. "The evolution of conformist transmission and the emergence of between-group differences." *Evolution and Human Behavior* 19: 215–242.

Henrich, J., and Boyd, R. 2001. "Why people punish defectors: Weak conformist transmission can stabilize costly enforcement of norms in cooperative dilemmas." *Journal of Theoretical Biology* 208: 79–89.

Henrich, J., Boyd, R., Bowles, S., Camerer, C., Fehr, E., Gintis, H., and McElreath, R. 2001. "Cooperation, reciprocity and punishment in fifteen small-scale societies." *American Economic Review* 91: 73–78.

Hinckfuss, I. 1987. The moral society: Its structure and effects. Discussion Paper in Environmental Philosophy 16, Philosophy Program (RSSS), Australian National University.

Hirshleifer, J., and Martinez Coll, J. C. 1988. "What strategies can support the evolutionary emergence of cooperation?" *Journal of Conflict Resolution* 32: 367–398.

Hoffman, M. 1982. "Affect and moral development." In *New Directions for Child Development*, ed. D. Cicchetti and P. Hesse. Jossey-Bass.

Hollos, M., Leis, P. E., and Turiel, E. 1986. "Social reasoning in Ijo children and adolescents in Nigerian communities." *Journal of Cross Cultural Psychology* 17: 352–374.

Hughes, A. L. 1988. *Evolution and Human Kinship*. Oxford University Press.

Hume, D. 1740. *A Treatise of Human Nature*. Clarendon, 1978.

Hume, D. 1742. "The sceptic." In *Essays, Moral, Political, and Literary*, revised edition, ed. E. Miller. Liberty Classics, 1987.

Hume, D. 1751. *An Enquiry Concerning the Principles of Morals*. Hackett, 1983.

Hume, D. 1762. "A new letter to Hugh Blair from July 1762." *Mind* 95 (1986): 411–416.

Huxley, T. H. 1894. "Evolution and ethics." In T. H. Huxley and J. Huxley, *Evolution and Ethics 1893–1943*. Pilot, 1947.

Isen, A. M., and Levin, P. F. 1972. "Effect of feeling good on helping: Cookies and kindness." *Journal of Personality and Social Psychology* 21: 384–388.

Jankowiak, W. R., ed. 1995. *Romantic Passion: A Universal Experience?* Columbia University Press.

Jankowiak, W. R., and Fisher, E. F. 1992. "A cross-cultural perspective on romantic love." *Ethnology* 31: 149–155.

Johnson-Laird, P. N., and Oatley, K. 2000. "Cognitive and social construction in emotions." In *Handbook of Emotions*, second edition, ed. M. Lewis and J. Haviland-Jones. Guilford.

Johnston, V. S. 1999. *Why We Feel: The Science of Human Emotions*. Perseus Books.

Joyce, R. 1999. "Apologizing." *Public Affairs Quarterly* 13: 159–173.

Joyce, R. 2000a. "Rational fear of monsters." *British Journal of Aesthetics* 40: 209–224.

Joyce, R. 2000b. "Darwinian Ethics and Error." *Biology and Philosophy* 15: 713–732.

Joyce, R. 2001a. *The Myth of Morality*. Cambridge University Press.

Joyce, R. 2001b. "Moral realism and teleosemantics." *Biology and Philosophy* 16: 723–731.

Joyce, R. 2002. "Expressivism and motivation internalism." *Analysis* 62: 336–344.

Joyce, R. 2003. "Paul Bloomfield: *Moral Reality*." *Mind* 112: 94–99.

Joyce, R. 2004. "Why humans judge things to be good—Robert A. Hinde's *Why Good Is Good*." *Biology and Philosophy* 19: 809–817.

Joyce, R. 2005. "Moral fictionalism." In *Fictionalism in Metaphysics*, ed. M. Kalderon. Oxford University Press.

Joyce, R. Forthcoming a. "Expressivism, motivation internalism, and Hume." In *Reason, Motivation, and Virtue*, ed. C. Pigden. University of Rochester Press.

Joyce, R. Forthcoming b. "What neuroscience can (and cannot) contribute to metaethics." In *Moral Psychology: Morals in the Brain*, ed. W. Sinnott-Armstrong.

Joyce, R. Forthcoming c. "Is morality innate?" In *The Innate Mind: Culture and Cognition*, ed. P. Carruthers et al.

Kagan, J. 1984. *The Nature of the Child*. Basic Books.

Kahneman, D., and Tversky, A. 1979. "Prospect theory: An analysis of decision under risk." *Econometrica* 47: 263–292.

Kalderon, M. E. 2005. *Moral Fictionalism*. Oxford University Press.

Kalish, C. W. 1999. "What young children know about contamination and contagion and what that tells us about their concepts of illness." In *Children's Understanding of Biology and Health*, ed. M. Siegal and C. Peterson. Cambridge University Press.

Kant, I. 1783. *Groundwork for the Metaphysic of Morals*. Oxford University Press, 2002.

Keddy-Hector, A., Allen, C., and Friend, T. H. Forthcoming. "Cognition in domestic pigs: Relational concepts and error recognition."

Keltner, D. 2003. "Expression and the course of life: Studies of emotion, personality, and psychopathology from a social-functional perspective." In *Emotions Inside Out* (*Annals of the New York Academy of Sciences* 1000), ed. P. Ekman et al.

Keltner, D., and Buswell B. N. 1996. "Evidence for the distinctness of embarrassment, shame, and guilt: A study of recalled antecedents and facial expressions of emotion." *Cognition and Emotion* 10: 155–172.

Keltner, D., Moffitt, T. E., and Stouthamer-Loeber, M. 1995. "Facial expressions of emotion and psychopathology in adolescent boys." *Journal of Abnormal Psychology* 104: 644–652.

Ketelaar, T., and Au, W. T. 2003. "The effects of feelings of guilt on the behavior of uncooperative individuals in repeated social bargaining games: An affect-as-information interpretation of the role of emotion in social interaction." *Cognition and Emotion* 17: 429–453.

Kiehl, K. A., Smith, A. M., Hare, R. D., Mendrek, A., Forster, B. B., Brink, J., and Liddle, P. F. 2001. "Limbic abnormalities in affective processing by criminal psychopaths as revealed by functional magnetic resonance imaging." *Biological Psychiatry* 50: 676–684.

Kitcher, P. 1985. *Vaulting Ambition*. MIT Press.

Kitcher, P. 1994. "Four ways of 'biologizing' ethics." In *Conceptual Issues in Evolutionary Ethics*, second edition, ed. E. Sober. MIT Press.

Kitcher, P. 1998. "Psychological altruism, evolutionary origins, and moral rules." *Philosophical Studies* 89: 283–316.

Kitcher, P. 2005. "Biology and ethics." In *The Oxford Handbook of Ethics*, ed. D. Copp. Oxford University Press.

Knutson, B. 2004. "Sweet revenge?" *Science* 305: 1246–1247.

Korsgaard, C. 1996. *The Sources of Normativity*. Cambridge University Press.

Kort, L. F. 1975. "What is an apology?" *Philosophy Research Archives* 1: 80–87.

Kummer, H. 1978. "Analogs of morality among nonhuman primates." In *Morality as a Biological Phenomenon*, ed. G. Stent. University of California Press.

Laakso, M. P., Vaurio, O., Koivisto, E., Savolainen, L., Eronen, M., Aronen, H. J., Hakola, P., Repo, E., Soininen, H., and Tiihonen, J. 2001. "Psychopathy and the posterior hippocampus." *Behavioural Brain Research* 118: 186–193.

Lahti, D. C. 2003. "Parting with illusions in evolutionary ethics." *Biology and Philosophy* 18: 639–651.

Lamarque, P. 1981. "How can we fear and pity fictions?" *British Journal of Aesthetics* 21: 291–304.

Lamarque, P. 1991. "Essay review of *Mimesis and Make-Believe*." *Journal of Aesthetics and Art Criticism* 49: 161–166.

Lerner, M. J. 1980. *The Belief in a Just World: A Fundamental Delusion*. Plenum.

Levins, R., and Lewontin, R. C. 1985. *The Dialectical Biologist*. Harvard University Press.

Levy, R. I. 1973. *Tahitians*. University of Chicago Press.

Lewis, D. K. 1970. "How to define theoretical terms." *Journal of Philosophy* 67: 426–446.

Lewis, D. K. 1989. "Dispositional theories of value." In Lewis, *Papers in Ethics and Social Philosophy*. Cambridge University Press, 2000.

Lewis, M. 1992. "Self-conscious emotions and the development of self." In *Affect: Psychoanalytic Perspectives*, ed. T. Shapiro and R. Emde. International Universities Press.

Lewontin, R. C. 1970. "The units of selection." *Annual Review of Ecology and Systematics* 1: 1–18.

Lewontin, R. C., Rose, S., and Kamin, L. J. 1984. *Not in Our Genes*. Pantheon.

Lieberman, D., Tooby, J., and Cosmides, L. 2003. "Does morality have a biological basis? An empirical test of the factors governing moral sentiments relating to incest." *Proceedings of the Royal Society: Biological Sciences* 270: 819–826.

Lillehammer, H. 2003. "Debunking morality: Evolutionary naturalism and moral error theory." *Biology and Philosophy* 18: 566–581.

Locke, J. 1693. *Some Thoughts Concerning Education*. Clarendon, 1989.

Lorenz, K. 1937. "The companion in the bird's world." *Auk* 54: 245–273.

Lycan, W. G. 1987. *Consciousness*. MIT Press.

Mackie, J. L. 1977. *Ethics: Inventing Right and Wrong*. Penguin.

Mackie, J. L. 1982. *The Miracle of Theism*. Clarendon.

Marler, P. 1991. "The instinct for vocal learning: Songbirds." In *Plasticity of Development*, ed. S. Brauth et al. MIT Press.

Marler, P., and Tamura, M. 1964. "Culturally transmitted patterns of vocal behavior in sparrows." *Science* 146: 1483–1486.

Mathews, K. E., and Canon, L. K. 1975. "Environmental noise level as a determinant of helping behavior." *Journal of Personality and Social Psychology* 32: 571–577.

Maynard Smith, J. 1998. "The origin of altruism." *Nature* 393: 639–640.

McAdams, R. H. 1997. "The origin, development, and regulation of norms." *Michigan Law Review* 96: 338–443.

McBrearty, S., and Brooks, A. S. 2000. "The revolution that wasn't: A new interpretation of the origin of modern human behavior." *Journal of Human Evolution* 39: 453–563.

Mellars, P. 1995. *The Neanderthal Legacy: An Archaeological Perspective from Western Europe*. Princeton University Press.

Mithen, S. 1996. *The Prehistory of the Mind*. Thames and Hudson.

Moll, J., de Oliveira-Souza, R., Eslinger, P. J., Bramati, I. E., Mourão-Miranda, J., Andreiuolo, P. A., and Pessoa, L. 2002. "The neural correlates of moral sensitivity: A functional magnetic resonance imaging investigation of basic moral emotions." *Journal of Neuroscience* 22: 2730–2736.

Moll, J., de Oliveira-Souza, R., and Eslinger, P. J. 2003. "Morals and the human brain: A working model." *NeuroReport* 14: 299–305.

Moore, G. E. 1903. *Principia Ethica*. Cambridge University Press, 1948.

Murdock, G. P. 1980. *Theories of Illness: A World Survey*. University of Pittsburgh Press.

Nagel, T. 1978. *The Possibility of Altruism*. Princeton University Press.

Neill, A. 1995. "Emotional responses to fiction: Reply to Radford." *Journal of Aesthetics and Art Criticism* 53: 75–78.

Nesse, R. M. 2001. "Natural selection and the capacity for subjective commitment." In *Evolution and the Capacity for Commitment*, ed. R. Nesse. Russell Sage Press.

Nichols, S., and Folds-Bennett, T. 2003. "Are children moral objectivists? Children's judgments about moral and response-dependent properties." *Cognition* 90: 23–32.

Nichols, S. 2004. *Sentimental Rules: On the Natural Foundations of Moral Judgment*. Oxford University Press.

Niedenthal, P. M., Tangney, J. P., and Gavanski, I. 1994. "'If only I weren't' versus 'if only I hadn't': Distinguishing shame and guilt in counterfactual thinking." *Journal of Personality and Social Psychology* 67: 585–595.

Nolan, D., Restall, G., and West, C. 2005. "Moral fictionalism versus the rest." *Australasian Journal of Philosophy*: 83: 307–329.

Nowak, M., and Sigmund, K. 1993. "A strategy of win-stay, lose-shift that outperforms tit-for-tat in the prisoner's dilemma game." *Nature* 364: 56–58.

Nowak, M., and Sigmund, K. 1998. "Evolution of indirect reciprocity by image scoring." *Nature* 393: 573–577.

Nucci, L. P. 1986. "Children's conceptions of morality, societal convention, and religious prescription." In *Moral Dilemmas*, ed. C. Harding. Precedent.

Nucci, L. P. 2001. *Education in the Moral Domain*. Cambridge University Press.

Nucci, L. P., Turiel, E., and Encarnacion-Gawrych, G. E. 1983. "Social interactions and social concepts: Analysis of morality and convention in the Virgin Islands." *Journal of Cross Cultural Psychology* 14: 469–487.

Nunner-Winkler, G., and Sodian, B. 1988. "Children's understanding of moral emotions." *Child Development* 59: 1323–1338.

O'Connell, S. M. 1995. "Empathy in chimpanzees: Evidence for theory of mind?" *Primates* 36: 396–410.

Öhman, A., Flykt, A., and Esteves, F. 2001. "Emotion drives attention: Detecting the snake in the grass." *Journal of Experimental Psychology: General* 130: 466–478.

Öhman, A., and Mineka, S. 2001. "Fears, phobias, and preparedness: Toward an evolved module of fear and fear learning." *Psychological Review* 108: 483–522.

Paine, R. 1967. "What is gossip about? An alternative hypothesis." *Man* 2: 278–285.

Panchanathan, K., and Boyd, R. 2003. "A tale of two defectors: The importance of standing for the evolution of reciprocity." *Journal of Theoretical Biology* 224: 115–126.

Panchanathan, K., and Boyd, R. 2004. "Indirect reciprocity can stabilize cooperation without the second-order free rider problem." *Nature* 432: 499–502.

Pigden, C. 1989. "Logic and the autonomy of ethics." *Australasian Journal of Philosophy* 67: 126–151.

Pilliavin, J. A., and Charng, H. W. 1990. "Altruism: A review of recent theory and research." *American Sociological Review* 16: 26–65.

Pillutla, M. M., and Murnighan, J. K. 1996. "Unfairness, anger, and spite: Emotional rejections of ultimatum offers." *Organizational Behavior and Human Decision Processes* 68: 208–224.

Pinker, S. 1994. *The Language Instinct: How the Mind Creates Language*. William Morrow.

Place, U. T. 1956. "Is consciousness a brain process?" *British Journal of Psychology* 47: 44–50.

Plutchik, R. 1980. *Emotion: A Psychoevolutionary Synthesis*. Harper and Row.

Pollock, G. B., and Dugatkin, L. A. 1992. "Reciprocity and the evolution of reputation." *Journal of Theoretical Biology* 159: 25–37.

Premack, D. 1983. "The codes of man and beasts." *Behavioral and Brain Sciences* 6: 125–167.

Premack, D. 1984. "Pedagogy and aesthetics as sources of culture." In *Handbook of Cognitive Neuroscience*, ed. M. Gazzaniga. Plenum.

Premack, D., and Woodruff, G. 1978. "Does the chimpanzee have a theory of mind?" *Behavioral and Brain Sciences* 4: 515–526.

Prior, A. N. 1960. "The autonomy of ethics." *Australasian Journal of Philosophy* 38: 199–206.

Quine, W. V. 1960. *Word and Object*. Wiley.

Radford, C. 1995. "Fiction, pity, fear, and jealousy." *Journal of Aesthetics and Art Criticism* 53: 71–75.

Railton, P. 1986. "Moral realism." *Philosophical Review* 95: 163–207.

Railton, P. 2000. "Darwinian building blocks." In *Evolutionary Origins of Morality*, ed. L. Katz. Imprint Academic.

Ray, L. 1998. "Why we give: Testing economic and social psychological accounts of altruism." *Polity* 30: 383–415.

Richards, R. J. 1986. "A defense of evolutionary ethics." *Biology and Philosophy* 1: 265–293.

Ridgeway, D., Waters, E., and Kuczaj, S. A. 1985. "Acquisition of emotion-descriptive language: Receptive and productive vocabulary norms for ages 18 months to 6 years." *Developmental Psychology* 21: 901–908.

Roberts, S. 1979. *Order and Dispute: An Introduction to Legal Anthropology.* St. Martin's Press.

Robinson, R. 1950. *Definition.* Clarendon.

Rosenberg, A., and Sommers, T. 2003. "Darwin's nihilistic idea: Evolution and the meaninglessness of life." *Biology and Philosophy* 18: 653–668.

Roth, A. E. 1995. "Bargaining experiments." In *The Handbook of Experimental Economics*, ed. J. Kagel and A. Roth. Princeton University Press.

Rousseau, J.-J. 1758. "Discourse on the origin and foundations of inequality among men." In Rousseau, *The Discourses and Other Early Political Writings.* Cambridge University Press, 1997.

Rozin, P., and Fallon, A. E. 1987. "A perspective on disgust." *Psychological Review* 94: 23–41.

Rozin, P., Fallon, A. E., and Augustoni-Ziskind, M. 1985. "The child's conception of food: The development of contamination sensitivity to 'disgusting' substances." *Developmental Psychology* 21: 1075–1079.

Rozin, P., Haidt, J., Imada, S., and Lowery, L. 1999a. "The CAD triad hypothesis: A mapping between three moral emotions (contempt, anger, disgust) and three moral codes (community, autonomy, divinity)." *Journal of Personality and Social Psychology* 76: 574–586.

Rozin, P., Haidt, J., McCauley, C. R., Dunlop, L., and Ashmore, M. 1999b. "Individual differences in disgust sensitivity: Comparisons and evaluations of paper-and-pencil versus behavioral measures." *Journal of Research in Personality* 33: 330–351.

Rozin, P., Haidt, J., and McCauley, C. R. 2000. "Disgust." In *Handbook of Emotions*, second edition, ed. M. Lewis and J. Haviland-Jones. Guilford.

Rozin, P., Markwith, M., and McCauley, C. R. 1994. "The nature of aversion to indirect contact with other persons: AIDS aversion as a composite of aversion to strangers, infection, moral taint and misfortune." *Journal of Abnormal Psychology* 103: 495–504.

Rozin, P., and Nemeroff, C. J. 1990. "The laws of sympathetic magic: A psychological analysis of similarity and contagion." In *Cultural Psychology*, ed. J. Stigler et al. Cambridge University Press.

Ruse, M. 1986. *Taking Darwin Seriously*. Blackwell.

Ruse, M., and Wilson, E. O. 1986. "Moral philosophy as applied science." *Philosophy* 61: 173–192.

Sachs, J. L., Mueller, U. G., Wilcox, T. P., and Bull, J. J. 2004. "The evolution of cooperation." *Quarterly Review of Biology* 79: 135–160.

Sahlins, M. D. 1965. "On the sociology of primitive exchange." In *The Relevance of Models for Social Anthropology*, ed. M. Banton. Tavistock.

Sanfey, A. G., Rilling, J. K., Aronson, J. A., Nystrom, L. E., and Cohen, J. D. 2003. "The neural basis of economic decision making in the Ultimatum Game." *Science* 300: 1755–1757.

Sapontzis, S. F. 1987. *Morals, Reason, and Animals*. Temple University Press.

Saver, J. L., and Damasio, A. R. 1991. "Preserved access and processing of social knowledge in a patient with acquired sociopathy due to ventromedial frontal damage." *Neuropsychologia* 29: 1241–1249.

Sayre-McCord, G. Forthcoming. "Rational agency and normative concepts."

Schelling, T. C. 1980. "The intimate contest for self-command." *Public Interest* 60: 94–118.

Schilpp, P. A., ed. 1942. *The Philosophy of G. E. Moore*. Northwestern University Press.

Segal, N. L., and Hershberger, S. L. 1999. "Cooperation and competition between twins: Findings from a prisoner's dilemma game." *Evolution and Human Behavior* 20: 29–51.

Segerstråle, U. 2000. *Defenders of the Truth: The Sociobiology Debate*. Oxford University Press.

Seligman, M. E. P. 1970. "On the generality of the laws of learning." *Psychological Review* 77: 406–418.

Seligman, M. E. P. 1971. "Phobias and preparedness." *Behavior Therapy* 2: 306–320.

Shaffer, J. 1983. "An assessment of emotion." *American Philosophical Quarterly* 20: 161–173.

Shepher, J. 1971. "Mate selection among second generation kibbutz adolescents and adults: Incest avoidance and negative imprinting." *Archives of Sexual Behavior* 1: 293–307.

Shepher, J. 1983. *Incest: The Biosocial View.* Academic Press.

Shweder, R. A, Mahapatra, M., and Miller, J. G. 1987. "Culture and moral development." In *The Emergence of Morality in Young Children,* ed. J. Kagan and S. Lamb. University of Chicago Press.

Simpson, E. H. 1951. "The interpretation of interaction in contingency tables." *Journal of the Royal Statistical Society B* 13: 238–241.

Sinnott-Armstrong, W. 2005. "Moral intuitionism meets empirical psychology." In *Metaethics after Moore,* ed. T. Horgan and M. Timmons. Oxford University Press.

Smart, J. J. C. 1959. "Sensations and brain processes." *Philosophical Review* 48: 141–156.

Smart, J. J. C. 1984. *Ethics, Persuasion and Truth.* Routledge and Kegan Paul.

Smetana, J. G. 1981. "Preschool children's conceptions of moral and social rules." *Child Development* 52: 1333–1336.

Smetana, J. G. 1993. "Understanding of social rules." In *The Development of Social Cognition,* ed. M. Bennett. Guilford.

Smetana, J. G., and Braeges, J. L. 1990. "The development of toddlers' moral and conventional judgments." *Merrill-Palmer Quarterly* 36: 329–346.

Smetana, J. G., Kelly, M., and Twentyman, C. T. 1984. "Abused, neglected and non-maltreated children's conceptions of moral and social-conventional transgressions." *Child Development* 55: 276–287.

Smith, M. 1994. *The Moral Problem.* Oxford University Press.

Sober, E. 1988. "What is evolutionary altruism?" In *New Essays on Philosophy and Biology (Canadian Journal of Philosophy* suppl. 14), ed. M. Matthen and B. Linsky.

Sober, E., and Wilson, D. S. 1998. *Unto Others: The Evolution and Psychology of Unselfish Behavior.* Harvard University Press.

Song, M. J., Smetana, J. G., and Kim, S. Y. 1987. "Korean children's conceptions of moral and conventional transgressions." *Developmental Psychology* 23: 576–582.

Sprengelmeyer, R., Young, A. W., Schroeder, U., Grossenbacher, P. G., Federlein, J., Büttner, T., and Przuntek, H. 1999. "Knowing no fear." *Proceedings of the Royal Society: Biological Sciences* 266: 2451–2456.

Sripada, C. S. 2005. "Punishment and the strategic structure of moral systems." *Biology and Philosophy* 20.

Sripada, C. S., and Stich, S. Forthcoming. "A framework for the psychology of moral norms." In *The Innate Mind: Culture and Cognition*, ed. P. Carruthers et al.

Starnecker, G., and Hazel, W. N. 1999. "Convergent evolution of neuroendocrine control of phenotypic plasticity in pupal colour in butterflies." *Proceedings of the Royal Society: Biological Sciences* 266: 2409–2412.

Steen, F. F., and Owen, S. A. 2001. "Evolution's pedagogy: An adaptationist model of pretense and entertainment." *Journal of Cognition and Culture* 1: 289–321.

Sterelny, K. 1996. "The return of the group." *Philosophy of Science* 63: 562–584.

Sterelny, K., and Fitness, J., eds. 2003. *From Mating to Mentality: Evaluating Evolutionary Psychology*. Psychology Press.

Sterelny, K., and Griffiths, P. 1999. *Sex and Death: An Introduction to Philosophy of Biology*. University of Chicago Press.

Stevenson, C. L. 1937. "The emotive meaning of ethical terms." *Mind* 46: 14–31.

Strack, F., Martin, L. L., and Stepper, S. 1988. "Inhibiting and facilitating conditions of the human smile: A nonobtrusive test of the facial feedback hypothesis." *Journal of Personality and Social Psychology* 54: 768–777.

Sturgeon, N. L. 1985. "Moral explanations." In *Morality, Reason and Truth*, ed. D. Copp and D. Zimmerman. Rowman and Allanheld.

Sturgeon, N. L. 1986. "Harman on moral explanations of natural facts." In *Spindel Conference: Moral Realism* (*Southern Journal of Philosophy* suppl. 24), ed. N. Gillespie.

Sugden, R. 1986. *The Economics of Rights, Co-operation and Welfare*. Blackwell.

Sugiyama, L. S. 1996. In Search of the Adapted Mind: A Study of Human Cognitive Adaptations among the Shiwiar of Ecuador and the Yora of Peru. Doctoral dissertation, University of California, Santa Barbara.

Sugiyama, L. S., Tooby, J., and Cosmides, L. 2002. "Cross-cultural evidence of cognitive adaptations for social exchange among the Shiwiar of Ecuadorian Amazonia." *Proceedings of the National Academy of Sciences* 99: 11536–11542.

Tangney, J. P. 1992. "Situational determinants of shame and guilt in young adulthood." *Personality and Social Psychology Bulletin* 18: 199–206.

Tangney, J. P. 2001. "Constructive and destructive aspects of shame and guilt." In *Constructive and Destructive Behavior*, ed. A. Bohart and D. Stipek. American Psychological Association.

Tangney, J. P., and Fischer, K. W., eds. 1995. *Self-Conscious Emotions: The Psychology of Shame, Guilt, Embarrassment, and Pride.* Guilford.

Thalberg, I. 1978. "Could affects be effects?" *Australasian Journal of Philosophy* 56: 143–154.

Tinbergen, N. 1963. "On the aims and methods of ethology." *Zeitschrift für Tierpsychologie* 20: 410–433.

Tisak, M. S., and Turiel, E. 1984. "Children's conceptions of moral and prudential rules." *Child Development* 55: 1030–1039.

Trivers, R. L. 1971. "The evolution of reciprocal altruism." *Quarterly Review of Biology* 46: 35–57.

Trivers, R. L. 1985. *Social Evolution.* Benjamin Cummings.

Turiel, E. 1983. *The Development of Social Knowledge: Morality and Convention.* Cambridge University Press.

Turiel, E. 1998. "The development of morality." In *Handbook of Child Psychology,* fifth edition, volume 3, ed. W. Damon. Wiley.

Turiel, E., Killen, M., and Helwig, C. C. 1987. "Morality: Its structure, functions, and vagaries." In *The Emergence of Morality in Young Children,* ed. J. Kagan and S. Lamb. University of Chicago Press.

Uvnäs-Moberg, K. 2003. *The Oxytocin Factor.* Da Capo.

Vidmar, N., and Miller, D. T. 1980. "Social psychological processes underlying attitudes toward legal punishment." *Law and Society Review* 14: 401–438.

Waller, B. N. 1997. "What rationality adds to animal morality." *Biology and Philosophy* 12: 341–356.

Wang, L., and Fischer, K. W. 1994. The Organization of Shame in Chinese. Cognitive Development Laboratory, Harvard University.

Wheatley, T., and Haidt, J. 2005. "Hypnotically induced disgust makes moral judgments more severe." *Psychological Science* 16.

Williams, B. 1981. "*Ought* and moral obligation." In Williams, *Moral Luck.* Cambridge University Press.

Williams, G. C. 1966. *Adaptation and Natural Selection: A Critique of Some Current Evolutionary Thought.* Princeton University Press.

Williams, G. C. 1993. "Mother Nature is a wicked old witch!" In *Evolutionary Ethics,* ed. M. Nitecki and D. Nitecki. State University of New York Press.

Williams, P. A. 1993. "Can beings whose ethics evolved be ethical beings?" In *Evolutionary Ethics,* ed. M. Nitecki and D. Nitecki. State University of New York Press.

Wilson, D. S. 2002. *Darwin's Cathedral: Evolution, Religion, and the Nature of Society*. University of Chicago Press.

Wilson, J. 2002. "The accidental altruist: Biological analogues for intention." *Biology and Philosophy* 17: 71–91.

Wilson, J. Q. 1993. *The Moral Sense*. Free Press.

Wootten, J. M., Frick, P. J., Shelton, K. K., and Silverthorn, P. 1997. "Ineffective parenting and childhood conduct problems: The moderating role of callous-unemotional traits." *Journal of Consulting and Clinical Psychology* 65: 301–308.

Wright, R. 1994. *The Moral Animal*. Vintage Books.

Yamakazi, K., Beauchamp, G. K., Curran, M., Bard, J., and Boyse, E. A. 2000. "Parent-progeny recognition as function of MHC odortype identity." *Proceedings of the National Academy of Sciences* 97: 10500–10502.

Yau, J., and Smetana, J. G. 2003. "Conceptions of moral, social-conventional, and personal events among Chinese preschoolers in Hong Kong." *Child Development* 74: 646–658.

Yu, P., and Fuller, G. 1986. "A critique of Dennett." *Synthese* 66: 453–476.

Zahavi, A., and Zahavi, A. 1997. *The Handicap Principle: A Missing Piece of Darwin's Puzzle*. Oxford University Press.

Zahn-Waxler C., and Kochanska, G. 1989. "The origins of guilt." In *Socioemotional Development*, ed. R. Thompson. University of Nebraska Press.

Index

Aiello, Leslie, 89
Alexander, Richard, 16, 17, 31, 32, 89, 90
Allen, Colin, 84
Altham, J. E. J., 57
Altruism, 13–19, 26, 47–51, 142, 222.
  See also Egoism; Selfishness
Aristotle, 33, 168–170
Augustine, Saint, 227
Austin, J. L., 54, 55
Authority, moral, 62–64, 111, 131, 174,
  190–199, 208, 217. *See also* Clout
Ayer, A. J., 53–56

Benedict, Ruth, 103
Boyd, Robert, 26, 42
Brink, David, 62
Bugos, Paul, 47

Campbell, Richmond, 160–165, 173,
  175
Carroll, Lewis, 156, 157
Carruthers, Peter, 212–215
Casebeer, William, 168–176, 191, 198
Categorical imperatives, 60–63, 68
Chagnon, Napoleon, 47
Cicero, 46
Clout, moral, 57–64, 92, 111, 136, 167,
  191–209
Cobbe, Frances, 229, 230
Coherentism, epistemic, 216, 217
Conservatism, epistemic, 216

Conventional/moral distinction. *See*
  Moral/conventional distinction
Copp, David, 197
Cosmides, Leda, 90, 91
Cultural evolution, 26, 40–43, 141

Daly, Martin, 46, 47
Darwin, Charles, 19, 20, 31, 32, 41, 81,
  84, 96, 101, 102, 133, 142, 228, 229
Dawkins, Richard, 17, 19, 37
Dennett, Daniel, 111, 112, 134, 137,
  146, 163–168, 173, 175
Desert, 66–70, 80, 92, 93, 132, 181
De Waal, Frans, 77–80, 93
Disgust, 51, 94–97, 105, 116, 123, 130,
  141, 225, 226
Dugatkin, Lee, 40
Dunbar, Robin, 89, 91

Egoism, psychological, 14, 17, 47–49.
  See also Selfishness
Ehrlich, Paul 146
Emler, Nicholas, 90
Emotion, 7, 47–51, 70, 72, 76, 81, 93,
  94, 100, 105, 113, 116–123, 135, 175,
  176, 216, 218, 225–228. *See also*
  Disgust; Guilt
  and beliefs, 97–101
  evolution of, 94–97
  and fiction, 98–100
  projection of, 108, 123–133

Essock-Vitale, Susan, 46
Etiquette, 61, 62, 192–194, 202–204
Evolutionary ethics
  descriptive, 143–145
  prescriptive, 143–146, 149, 152, 155,
  156, 160, 176, 190, 222
Evolutionary psychology, 5–12, 17, 18,
  114
Externalism
  epistemological, 212
  motivational, 109, 212

Fictionalism, 167, 168
Foot, Philippa, 61–64, 193,
Foundationalism, epistemic, 217–219
Frank, Robert, 119–122
Freud, Sigmund, 103

Generality problem, 212–214
Genetic determinism, 8, 9
Ghiselin, Michael, 17
Gould, Stephen Jay, 8, 9, 133, 134
Group selection, 16, 33–43, 49, 90, 108,
  141
Guilt, 67–70, 75, 76, 80, 97, 99,
  101–105, 112–123, 142

Haidt, Jonathan, 116, 130, 135
Hamilton's Rule, 20, 21, 48
Hamilton, William, 19, 20
Harman, Gilbert, 184–190, 193–198,
  209, 210
Hauser, Marc, 81
Henrich, Joe, 42
Hume, David, 23, 45, 46, 125–128, 228,
  229
Huxley, Thomas, 221–223
Hypothetical imperatives, 60, 78, 79,
  170–172

Inescapability, moral, 61–63, 70, 131,
  190–199, 208, 217. See also Clout
Instrumentalism, 85–88

Internalism, motivational, 109. See also
  Externalism

Justification, instrumental vs. epistemic,
  162–166, 175, 176

Kamin, Leon, 10
Kant, Immanuel, 50, 60–62, 78, 113
Kin selection, 19–26, 39, 40, 44–49, 70
Kitcher, Philip, 144, 175, 183, 184, 219
Korsgaard, Christine, 197, 198

Lahti, David, 114, 117, 123
Levins, Richard, 11
Lewis, David, 200
Lewontin, Richard, 10, 11
Lillehammer, Hallvard, 144
Locke, John, 7

Mackie, John, 173–175, 182, 192, 200,
  221, 223
Maynard Smith, John, 39
McGuire, Michael, 46
Mill, John Stuart, 219
Moore, G. E., 55, 146–155, 190
Moore's paradox, 55, 56, 85
Moral/conventional distinction, 63, 70,
  125, 136–139
Mutualism, 22, 23, 39, 40, 49

Naturalism
  definitional, 149, 151
  evolutionary moral, 145, 146, 151,
  154, 155, 158, 176, 177, 190, 191,
  198
  global, 145, 146, 189, 200, 209, 217
  metaphysical, 149, 151
  moral, 145, 146, 149–156, 160, 165,
  168, 174, 185, 190–211
Naturalistic fallacy, 145–155
Nichols, Shaun, 129
Non-cognitivism, 52–58, 109, 125, 126,
  163, 175, 176, 209

Non-naturalism, moral, 209–211
Nucci, Larry, 129, 130

Open Question Argument, 147–152
"Ought," deriving from "is," 143–160
Oxytocin, 22, 49

PAVLOV, 30, 31
Pigden, Charles, 153, 154
Prisoner's Dilemma, 27–31, 47
Projectivism. *See* Emotions

Quine, W. V., 83

Railton, Peter, 183
Realism, 85–88
Reciprocal altruism. *See* Reciprocity
Reciprocity, 23, 39–43, 46, 65, 112, 113,
    140–142, 180
  calculated, 25
  direct, 24–31, 33, 37, 39, 40
  indirect, 31–33, 40, 44
  language and, 88–92
Reliabilism, 211–215
Richards, Robert, 154–160, 175, 176
Richerson, Peter, 26
Rose, Steven, 10
Rousseau, Jean-Jacques, 138
Rozin, Paul, 96, 97
Ruse, Michael, 2, 188

Sahlins, Marshall, 46
Sayre-McCord, Geoffrey, 81, 82
Selfishness, 13–18, 26, 47–49, 142. *See
    also* Altruism; Egoism
Sexual selection, 32, 33
Shepher, Joseph, 21
Sinnott-Armstrong, Walter, 216–218
Skepticism, moral, 2, 163, 173, 181,
    182, 188, 223–230
Smith, Michael, 149
Sober, Elliott, 34, 38, 39, 41
Sociobiology, 4, 5, 8–11, 144

Sociopathy, acquired 124, 125
Socrates, 52, 147
Sterelny, Kim, 39
Stevenson, Charles, L., 189, 190
Sturgeon, Nicholas, 187
Supernaturalism, moral, 209–211

Tit for tat, 27–30
Tooby, John, 90, 91
Trivers, Robert, 24–29, 80
Turiel, Elliot, 136–139

Williams, George, 142, 221
Williams, Patricia, 9
Wilson, David Sloan, 34, 38, 39, 41
Wilson, James Q., 112
Wilson, Margo, 46, 47
Wright, Robert, 146

Zahavi, Amotz, 32